'I love this woman's outlook and her attitude. She's formidable and indomitable, but in a totally sunny and loveable way.'

TURIA PITT

'Emma Carey is a powerhouse. This book will change a lot of perceptions about what you think it's like to live with disability.'

DYLAN ALCOTT

'The accident honestly is the least interesting thing about Em Carey. The real story is the remarkable lens through which she views the world. I truly believe that the moment that changed her life could also change yours.'

SAM MAC

'Emma Carey has proven that, no matter what life throws her way, nothing can dim her fire.'

Michelle & Zara, SHAMELESS

Emma Carey is an artist, speaker and aspiring writer from Canberra. After following her love for travel and adventure around the world, she found herself in Switzerland where an unexpected near-death experience completely altered her life. Following the turbulence and transformation of her accident, she has been on a mission to share her unique story to inspire and enhance the lives of those around her.

Writing has been a huge passion for Emma since she was young, and writing a book, whether it be fiction or non-fiction, has been a lifelong goal. After her accident, she started writing diary entries to document what she was experiencing and began sharing some snippets of those thoughts and musings on her Instagram page (@em_carey), where she now has loyal followers from around the world.

Emma now resides on the Gold Coast, where she moved to create a fresh life for herself, and she spends her days drawing, writing, swimming, spending time with her people and soaking up her second chance at life.

THE GIRL WHO FELL FROM THE SKY

An extraordinary true story of resilience, courage, hope and finding lightness after the heaviest of landings

EMMA CAREY

ALLEN&UNWIN
SYDNEY • MELBOURNE • AUCKLAND • LONDON

First published in 2022

Allen & Unwin
Cammeraygal Country
83 Alexander Street
Crows Nest NSW 2065
Australia
Phone: (61 2) 8425 0100
Email: info@allenandunwin.com
Web: www.allenandunwin.com

Allen & Unwin acknowledges the Traditional Owners of the Country on which we live and work. We pay our respects to all Aboriginal and Torres Strait Islander Elders, past and present.

A catalogue record for this book is available from the National Library of Australia

ISBN 978 1 76106 578 1

Internal design by Julian Mole, Post Pre-press Group
Set in 12.5/17.5 pt Adobe Garamond Pro by Post Pre-press Group, Australia
Printed and bound in Australia by Pegasus Media & Logistics

10 9 8 7 6 5 4 3 2

The paper in this book is FSC® certified. FSC® promotes environmentally responsible, socially beneficial and economically viable management of the world's forests.

For anyone who has ever fallen from the sky of their life,
these words are for you.

For the girl who was lying on the ground, hoping for it all to end,
look at how good it got.

Contents

THE GIRL WHO FELL FROM THE SKY

1

THE FALL

It started like this.

The deafening beats of the propellers matched the thundering of my heart. I felt electric as the ground shrank beneath us, snow-capped mountains disappearing into the landscape—a patchwork of green, brown and white as the grey sky yawned open around me, large and endless. The town below looked like a dollhouse, and then an oil painting, as we rose.

Just as I thought we must almost be at the right altitude to jump, my instructor told me we hadn't even reached halfway. I startled at my own insignificance as the helicopter continued dizzyingly upwards—a similar feeling to when you look into the night sky and realise that you're looking into the past.

An anxiety that I hadn't been expecting caught in my throat, and the memory of my signature over a dotted line flashed back to me—suddenly the danger laid out in a black-and-white liability form felt somewhat plausible.

My hand entwined with Jemma's, I turned to my instructor. Eager for reassurance, I asked how many times he had jumped. The number was absolutely staggering, and I imagined that he had spent more time in midair than he had with his feet on the ground. This reassured me, along with his honest answer when I asked if anyone had ever been injured diving with him. He told me about a jumper who had broken their ankle on landing a couple of years ago, and his candour and warmth in the telling comforted me.

And then before I knew it, it was time. Fourteen thousand feet in the air, the door of the helicopter opened. As the wind rushed in, it felt as if all my senses were coming alive. This sensation was what I'd been craving, this is what my life in all its daily monotony had been missing.

Jemma and I looked at each other, her fear obvious through the tears welling in her eyes. I felt a pang in my heart knowing that my love of adrenaline was the only reason she was here, but I gave her one last squeeze and let go of her hand. Strapped to my instructor, I turned towards the door and a new version of myself. For a moment we sat on the edge of the helicopter, legs dangling in the space between who I was and who I was about to become.

And then I was falling.

The instructor had launched us from the edge, throwing us into wide open nothingness. I remembered the instructions we'd been given on the ground and moved my body into the correct position—and just like that, the world stopped. The sound of the helicopter, the sound of the air whooshing by, the sound of my screaming voice—it all became silent. I was flying.

I was enraptured by the picturesque ground below: the snowy alps, the winding rivers, the endless green farmlands. Again, that feeling of insignificance overwhelmed me and all the troubles I'd left on the ground no longer mattered. This was where I was meant to be. Everything seemed so clear; an undeniable sense of peace in the chaos. It was like a nudge from the future whispering, 'Remember this feeling, this is what happiness feels like.'

A tap on my shoulder pulled me from my epiphany. We'd been told the tap meant the parachute was about to be pulled. I crossed my arms over my chest and prepared myself for the jolt of the parachute slowing us down.

When it came, it felt like my hair was being ripped from my head and I was surprised at the pain—no one had warned me that it would hurt. I expected my instructor to say something, to give me a high-five like I'd seen in videos online, but he didn't move, and as we continued to plummet a sudden terror ripped through me.

Why weren't we slowing down? It had been hard to tell at first, because when you're that high up you barely notice the shift in the landscape as you fall towards it, but as you get closer suddenly you notice the drop of every foot—details on the ground below start blooming into clarity.

Then I saw it, the parachute. Red like a warning, it whipped before me in a tangled mess. It hadn't opened. I screamed at the instructor, desperate as an indescribable wave of panic consumed me. He didn't answer and I wondered if he was even attached to me anymore. I couldn't turn my head against the velocity of the wind, I could only watch as the earth seemed to come forwards to meet me. I knew we were about to crash, I knew there'd been some kind of mistake, I knew we were only seconds away from impact, but I hadn't yet thought about what that meant. The gravity of the situation dawned on me as quickly as it was pulling me down—I was about to die.

My desire to live pounded through my veins with increasing urgency and I felt fear beyond anything I had ever experienced before. 'Fear'. What a dull word for what it is. I imagined the sandwich I'd made earlier that morning waiting for me on the ground. The clothes in the washing machine that would never get a chance to dry. My half-packed bag sitting on my bed, belongings thrown carelessly around the room in the implicit belief that I would return safely to pack them away. How was this happening? I wasn't ready for this yet.

I wanted to live. The longing was palpable—for my future, my old age, my sandwich. I wanted all of these things but mostly I wanted to scream at myself for only realising I wanted them once it was too late.

The ground was so close now, and the beautiful rolling fields I'd been admiring moments ago now looked hard and unforgiving. I wondered what being dead would feel like; I wondered if I would know that I had died. And then I realised that the fear coursing through my body was the last thing I would ever feel.

People say that your whole life flashes before your eyes when you die, but as I counted the seconds to impact I only saw one face. I wondered if Ben knew how much I loved him.

My death was so close I could almost touch it.

3, 2, 1.

2

LANDING IN A NEW LIFE

I hit the ground and the force was strong enough to alter an entire universe.

I wasn't dead. Well, at least I was pretty sure I wasn't. I could hear myself panting and I could taste the blood filling my mouth. I was face down in an expanding pool of dirt, blood and shock. I didn't understand. How could I not be dead? I wasn't even unconscious. I had somehow remained completely awake for the moment of impact. I wondered how rare that was, to be so acutely present at the precise moment your world changes.

There was a split second of relief, followed by total disbelief and confusion. I couldn't accept that I had just been in a skydiving accident. Things like that don't happen in real life. Not in my world. I was supposed to be running over to my best friend, arms outstretched, with a smile so wide at the sheer rush of being alive. It wasn't supposed to be like this.

I had landed on my stomach with my instructor strapped to my back, so his weight was pinning me to the ground. He wasn't moving or making any noise, so despite my state of shock, I assumed he was dead. I went cold at the abrupt awareness of our impermanence. My ears had been the last to hear his words.

Even though the fall had seemed infinite, it had all happened so fast. Just a minute or two earlier I had been in the helicopter looking down at this very field, and now I was embedded into it. It didn't make any sense, and it took a few seconds for my brain to catch up. All I could see were the Alps that surrounded us and a waterfall in the distance. There was not a single person or building in sight.

Out of nowhere, a feeling came over me that I had never experienced before in my twenty years on this earth. Pain. Real, gut-wrenching, unbearable, straight-to-your-core pain. It enveloped me and with every second it grew worse. I didn't know where it was coming from, all I knew was that it was pure hell. Maybe I really had died and this was the afterlife that was chosen for me. The pain swallowed me to the point where it was all I was. There was no room left for thoughts or movements or words. I wondered if it was possible to die from pain alone; I wasn't sure how much more I could endure. All I could do was scream.

Through the blur came a solitary coherent thought. I was hit with the sudden and panicked realisation that help wasn't coming. We hadn't landed where we were supposed to land, there was nobody around to see it happen, the instructor was dead, and we were in the middle of the Swiss Alps. I had thought after surviving the fall my life was guaranteed, but it dawned on me that until I got help, I was still living on borrowed time. I had no idea how I was going to get out of there, but I knew it was up to me to go and search for help. I didn't know if it was humanly possible to move through the pain, but it was my only chance to be saved.

I inhaled a shaky breath, gathered all my remaining strength, gritted my teeth together and prepared to do what I knew I had to. I began to roll over to get the instructor off me and, just like that, the earth stopped turning. In a single moment, the life I knew, my heart, my spirit, every plan I had ever made and every ounce of who I was, were shattered.

My legs wouldn't move.

My soul dropped. Time froze.

I felt my life instantaneously tear into a distinct Before and After. I could hear my heartbeat pulsing in my ears with the sudden and disorienting awareness that nothing would ever be the same. Surely there must be some mistake. I must have hit my head harder than I thought because nothing was making sense.

I couldn't move. I was trying as hard as I could but it wasn't the pain that was stopping me now. In fact, the pain that just a moment ago had been the most unbearable thing I'd ever faced now seemed like the easiest thing in the universe. I tried to roll over again but even the muscles in my stomach wouldn't work. I tried a different approach. I attempted to bend my knees underneath me so I could stand up with my legs, but they wouldn't respond. I tried to wriggle my toes. Nothing happened.

A lump formed in my throat the size of the earth. I needed to get up off the ground. Why couldn't I just stand up? I tried to recall how I'd told my legs to move for the past twenty years, but I couldn't. It was like trying to remember a person I'd never even met. That's how utterly impossible it felt. One word kept circling in my head. *Undo.* I just wanted to rewind. I wanted to go back in time two unthinkable minutes. I wanted to reverse the irreversible.

I had only landed seconds ago, but time didn't seem to flow like it used to. In fact, it didn't seem to exist at all. Everything was happening so fast that I barely had time to comprehend my reality, yet on the other hand it was passing so slowly that I had multiple streams of thought at once.

I still couldn't believe any of it was real. I couldn't fathom why half of my body would suddenly stop working. Then it hit me. I must have broken my back. The realisation was so obvious yet utterly shattering. I didn't know how I was only just figuring this out. I'd seen this scene play out in so many movies—when someone loses feeling in their legs, they're always told not to move. I had been throwing myself around trying to get up from under the instructor. I thought for sure that I must have brought this injury on myself, that my back hadn't broken until I started moving.

My chest was hurting even more than my back now. It was so heavy I could barely breathe. I didn't know where the pain was coming from at first but then suddenly I understood. It was heartbreak. It was worse than all the physical pain. The loss felt worse than death. My body was ruined. My one body. I had to live in this body for the rest of my life and I had destroyed it. I felt claustrophobic in my own skin. I wanted to get out. How could I not control my own body? How could I not move? I didn't understand what was happening, but I knew I couldn't live like this. I wouldn't.

While I was falling to the ground, I had been so petrified of dying that it never crossed my mind there could be something even worse. My biggest fear was that my life was going to be too short, but now I feared that it was going to be far, far too long. I had thought I only had ten seconds left to live and now it seemed I had a lifetime, but I didn't want it. I tried to reason with myself. It was fine. When someone finally found me, I would tell them to let me die. I wasn't doing this. This ground was where my story would end.

I had always thought the saying 'you don't know what you've got 'till it's gone' was a clichéd lie. I can now tell you from the bottom of my heart that it's not. In that moment, I could feel the weight of its truth pushing down on me with so much force that it was impossible to ignore. That morning I'd woken up in the bunk of our cabin feeling melancholic and unappreciative. Now there was only one thought in my mind. Distinct, definite and soul-destroying: *My life was perfect two minutes ago and I didn't even know.*

3

THE WAITING

I was only alone on the ground for a few minutes, but it felt like an eternity.

I was still screaming out. To anyone and everyone, yet seemingly no one. I had so many questions. I yelled, 'Why did you do this?' I don't know if my question was aimed at the universe or the instructor, but to my surprise, a groggy voice answered me. The instructor was alive! He was okay! I wasn't alone anymore. He mumbled, 'Both of my legs are shattered,' unclipped himself, rolled off me sideways so that he was on his back and passed out again.

I still couldn't move from my stomach down, but I could now turn my head. Out of the corner of my eye I caught a flicker of movement. Jemma's parachute was floating down to the ground a few metres away. The relief of being found was simultaneously euphoric and laced with dread. I didn't want to stay in this moment, but I also didn't want to face the reality of whatever came next. Jemma was smiling and her instructor was still filming her. I could tell from her face that she had no idea what had happened to me.

There was more movement in the distance and I could see a couple walking by. They were laughing and talking to each other like nothing was wrong. *What the hell?* How was everyone still going on like the world hadn't just ended? I wanted to scream: *'Can't you all feel this?'*

It's a very disconcerting and jarring feeling to watch the world go on when yours has completely stopped. To know that in that very same moment people were sipping coffees in cafes, walking dogs through parks and laughing at jokes while my world was frozen in time. How could a feeling so large only be inside of me? How could a moment so horrendously pivotal in the story of my life be a moment others didn't even realise was passing by?

I screamed out to Jemma as loud as I could. I told her I couldn't move my legs. As she ran towards me, I could see her train of thought unfolding on her face. She wanted to believe I was joking. I could see her brain doing what mine had already had time to do. It was trying to catch up with a reality that seemed so unimaginable just moments ago. Her survival instincts kicked in and she ran over to the couple walking by and asked to use their phone. She gave it to her instructor to call for help. Then when he'd finished she called my mum.

I don't really remember what my mum said to me or what I said to her, but I remember feeling so far away. When you're overseas, life often doesn't feel real. It can feel like you're in a make-believe world and what happens while you're away doesn't impact your real life back home. Hearing my mum's voice coming through the phone, picturing her standing there in our kitchen on the other side of the world, made this all too true. The real world was merging with the inconsequential overseas world and I didn't like it. I wanted to believe there was another version out there, a version where I would fly home and this would all be one long forgotten memory.

While we were waiting for the paramedics to arrive, I still had a tiny sliver of hope that my body was just in shock. For a few more minutes I could hold onto the idea that there was a magic cure the doctors could give me to get my legs moving again.

The first people to arrive on the scene were policemen. They couldn't speak a word of English and I couldn't speak a word of Swiss German. One of the policemen began questioning Jemma's instructor, while the other one sat down on the ground beside me and Jemma and held my hand. I squeezed his fingers like I was pulling every ounce of courage from him and absorbing it into myself. I didn't let go for as long as I lay there. I don't know this man's name and I wouldn't recognise him if he knocked on my front door tomorrow, but I will remember him and his warmth for the rest of my life.

I was still face down in the dirt because no one would move me. I was begging to be rolled onto my back because I thought maybe it would hurt less if I was in a different position. The pain was intolerable. When the ambulance finally arrived, I thought the moment was coming where they would tell me it was all going to be okay, that this was just a natural response from the body after so much trauma. The paramedics took one look at us splayed out across the ground and called for an emergency helicopter to come immediately. A woman examined me and I could see the urgency in her eyes. She was speaking rapidly to the other paramedic, but I couldn't understand any of it. It didn't matter though, I didn't need to know everything that was happening. I only needed the answer to one question. I kept asking, but no one would answer. I thought maybe they couldn't understand me, but their eyes told me they could. I started screaming for the answer. I needed to know if my legs would be okay. It was all I cared about. I begged the paramedic to tell me if I would ever be able to walk again and when she looked at me, I knew. Even though we spoke different languages, I could understand 'no' in any.

My chest began to hurt again. That moment had confirmed what I already knew. This was my real life. There was no going back. This was something I could never erase.

After the most excruciating hour of my life, the emergency helicopter arrived. I was transferred onto a spinal board and my neck was braced. Whatever liquid was flowing through the drip and into my veins must have been working because everything stopped hurting so much. I could hear the propellers starting to turn and it was impossible not to compare this helicopter ride to the one we'd had just an hour earlier. The first one had been filled with anticipation, this one was filled with the consequences.

We were flying above the Alps on our way to a place I'd never heard of, more scared than I'd ever been, when Jemma and I looked at each other. At the same time, we both pulled a face that we'd been making since we were little kids. The one where you tuck your upper lip under itself and give a creepy smile. We did it simultaneously, without saying a word, and we both laughed. It was the tiniest moment, so small I don't think anyone else on that helicopter would have even noticed, but it was the first time in my life I learned that it was possible to feel more than one thing at once. You can laugh when your world is ending. You can feel hope when there is none. You can be grieving the loss of your body but realise you have something far more valuable. A true friend.

Even through my pain I realised there was something good to be found here, buried beneath the blood and dirt of my ground zero. A mother's voice, a friend's solidarity, the squeeze of a stranger's hand—it was small, but it wasn't nothing. There on that helicopter, somewhere over Switzerland on a Sunday in June, came the first tiny whisper. A voice that came from a place so deep inside of myself that I hadn't even known it existed. One that would carry me for years to come. *I'm going to be okay. There's still joy here.*

4

A NEW WORLD

My memories from the moment I entered the hospital have been reduced to flashes. Between the drugs that were being pumped into my arm, the trauma my body had just experienced and the speed with which my mind was trying to process information that was so far-fetched and unfathomable just hours earlier, it was hard to stay aware of everything that was going on around me.

~

As soon as I was pushed through the doors, countless doctors ran over to my body. There were no hellos, no 'I'm your doctor and I will be treating you today,' and no one who looked me in the eye. It was clear that this wasn't a time for pleasantries. Their urgency reminded me for the first time since I was found that my life was still hanging in the balance. I wasn't in the clear yet, and time was the only thing standing between me dying on this hospital stretcher and living out the rest of my life.

I was in the middle of the emergency room, lying flat on my back when they began cutting my clothes off with scissors. Right there in the middle of the room, with other patients and visitors all watching on in horror. I couldn't see Jemma in the crowd, I couldn't see the nurse from the helicopter, I couldn't see the policemen whose hand I had been holding. I was surrounded by people, but I was entirely alone.

~

I opened my eyes to what looked like the inside of a tunnel. It was loud and bright—an MRI machine, I quickly realised—but rather than anxiety and fear, I felt a mild sense of calm. The enclosed space created a sense of safety and comfort, and the noises were loud enough to drown out my terror. Lying there in the protection of the hospital, I felt a sudden wave of hope. *Okay Emma, you're all good. This scan will show that nothing major is actually wrong and that your body is just in shock. Your legs will start moving again, you'll get out of here, and you'll be off to Rome tomorrow. Okay fine, maybe the bus will leave without you and you'll be a day late, but you'll be back with everyone soon.*

~

I woke up later in a dark room. A nurse came to my side and told me in very broken English that I had just come out of surgery and the drowsiness I was feeling was from the anaesthetic.

Surgery? How long had it been? It felt like weeks since I'd been carried into that helicopter—surely it wasn't still the same day? Surely Ben and my family were here by now?

I probably should have asked what the surgery was for, or how it went, or what day it was, but at that point I didn't care. I just wanted to see a familiar face, to hear a voice I could understand. I begged the nurse to help me find a phone. Thankfully she understood and brought me a mobile. I typed in the only number that I could remember—my boyfriend's. I wondered if Ben knew what had happened yet. Surely my mum would have called him straight after she got off the phone to me earlier? He was probably worried sick and on a plane right now, racing over to make sure I was okay.

Eagerly, I pressed the call button, but all I heard was an automated voice coming through the speaker in another language. *Oh!* I thought. *Of course I can't just call his mobile from another country. How on earth do I call Australia? What time is it in Australia? What time is it here? Where even is here?* I frantically asked the nurse to help me, but she had no idea how to call back home either. I asked her if she knew where Jemma was, but she didn't know who I was talking about. She took the phone and left my room. I was crying and screaming and begging for someone to help me, but nobody came.

~

Suddenly, I was in a different room. I didn't think I was in the emergency department or recovery anymore; it looked like a place where you stay for a while. I could see light trying to break in through the curtains and I wanted to open them to see where I was. In that obscure state between sleep and wakefulness, for a blissful moment I forgot the finer details of my reality. I remembered going up in the helicopter, the accident, the ambulances, waking up from surgery, not being able to find Jemma . . . Shit. I almost fell from the bed on my way to open the curtains. The one thing I didn't remember was that I couldn't fucking walk.

~

When the surgeon finally came to see me, I wasn't ready to hear what he had to say.

'Okay, so the surgery was a success. You have broken your sacrum, your sternum and your L1 vertebrae. Your spinal cord has been crushed, so information is unable to get from your brain to below your waist, which is why you can't move your legs. This is permanent. You have also broken your pelvis, so we had to stabilise it with a metal . . .'

That's all I heard before my ears stopped absorbing sound. Before I knew it, the doctor had casually closed the door behind him to move on to the next patient. Was he about to deliver another world-changing blow to the room next door? Or was he going to tell them their breakfast was ready? I imagined his tone would be the same either way. I was certain someone was pulling a prank on me—that's how casual, informal and apathetic he had been when he delivered the news.

I had always imagined that the moment you're told something as significant as the fact that you'll never walk again would be a monumental, carefully worded and gently delivered event. That's what it looks like in the movies. Everyone sits around your bed, holds your hand, assures you that it's going to be okay, tells you that you're brave and eventually lets you cry into their arms. It turns out, much like when I was told my parents were getting divorced, or that Santa wasn't real, it's less like a dramatic and poignant scene from a scripted film and more like a passing sentence. It wasn't crushing or defining or unforgettable to anyone else, it was just an ordinary Monday morning.

This is permanent. The words played over and over in my mind. I tried to think of other permanent things, but I couldn't. Aren't we taught that nothing lasts forever? From the moment I'd felt the pain ricochet through my body, I had known this was going to be major but I hadn't thought it would be *permanent.* Permanent. As in forever. Perpetual. The brutal finality of it was too much to comprehend. I had been clinging to a glimmer of hope that this was just a glitch in my holiday, not in my *life*. I'd completely underestimated the severity of the situation, and I couldn't imagine ever accepting it. I lay there alone and in shock.

I couldn't shake the sense that my future had swerved drastically away from the script. That life had taken a catastrophic wrong turn and led me into some outlandish alternate world, one that seemed completely plausible to leave. Elsewhere, in a parallel universe holding the intended version of me, I was hiking to the waterfall I'd spotted the day before, complaining that my legs were tired, completely oblivious to the fact that there was nowhere and no one else I would rather be.

5

FIVE WORDS

The moment I entered the hospital, I stumbled upon a whole new world that I hadn't known existed and, in doing so, discovered a plethora of ways to suffer that I hadn't properly acknowledged before. I realised how very sheltered and privileged my existence had been before I fell. It was like I had been living in a world where suffering existed as broken families, boyfriend problems and university stress, then all of a sudden I turned a corner, was thrust into a new realm and uncovered an entirely new reality. I found there was a world not too far from the one I had always known where grief existed, problems could be permanent and entire identities could be shattered in the time it takes for someone on the outside to reheat leftovers.

Days blurred into each other without the timestamp of routine. There was no getting out of bed, no getting dressed for the day, no going outside and nothing to fill the hours between morning and night. There was only lying in bed and staring at the four walls surrounding me.

I had always imagined that spending an extended amount of time in hospital (if there was no threat of dying) would be relaxing to an extent. I liked to envision it as a hotel stay with endless movies, food delivered to your bed, as much sleep as you desired and someone there to tend to your every need while the only thing expected of you was that you rest and heal. Unsurprisingly, I couldn't have been more wrong. Life in hospital did have all of these things, but it was impossible to revel in them when being there meant losing everything I loved about myself.

Instead, I found hospital to be a mixture of physical pain, unbelievable boredom, intrusive tests and agonising thoughts like, 'Is this what the rest of my life is going to feel like?'

A few days and another surgery later, I had collected so many IV drips in both of my hands that I needed to wear gloves just to keep them all attached to me. The concoction of painkillers and whatever else I was being fed through my veins was so strong that my mind was no longer my own; it was a hazy place filled with fear, confusion and, unexpectedly, rage.

I'd come to the completely uninformed (yet in my mind obvious) conclusion that a life without my legs was one I didn't want any part in. I was certain that it wasn't possible for a human to experience genuine happiness again after such severe trauma and the mere thought of that scared me more than anything else I was facing. To me a life without happiness was a far more terrifying concept than a life without walking—it seemed insurmountable. I tried to picture my future without the fundamental element of joy intertwined in it and immediately decided I wasn't strong enough to stick around to find out how it would feel. Instead, I tried my best to rip the tubes out of my hands and lungs, I attempted to throw myself off the bed onto the floor, I yelled and screamed and was rude to anyone who tried to help me because to put it simply: I didn't want their help, I wanted them to let me die.

~

I missed my legs, I missed Ben and I missed life being something I recognised. Jemma slept on the floor next to my bed each night, but, even with her right beside me, I couldn't seem to sleep. Partly because of the pain, but mainly because I didn't know how to switch off my ever-racing thoughts. I would inevitably wake up multiple times throughout the night, and each time I would see a nurse sitting at the end of my bed, regardless of the time. Few of the nurses could speak English, so I didn't think there was much use in questioning why she was always there, but on one particularly bad night, in the midst of my pity-party, I decided I might as well attempt to strike up a conversation. I asked her why she sat in my room 24/7 instead of checking on the other patients in the ward. Up until that night, I had just assumed that the severity of my injury meant I wasn't allowed to be left alone (in my grief-stricken mind, there wasn't a single injury on planet earth that was more catastrophic and debilitating than mine), but when she answered me with the truth, I was stunned.

Much to my discomfort, she wasn't the type of nurse to beat

around the bush. She told me, without even the slightest hint of empathy, that there were countless other people in this very same hospital at this very same moment, who were far worse off than I was and that my injury was not at all the reason she was here at midnight. She told me that so many others had lost far more than just the use of their legs and needed far more care and attention than I did. She even went so far as to inform me that the older lady I had been sharing my room with, who had gone in for surgery that morning and not yet returned, had died on the operating table.

For the very first time since my accident, I was humbled. This hospital room was torturous, yes, but I was still in it. I needed that harsh truth; I needed something to shake me out of my inability to see past the four walls of my situation. It's not very often that people will give you brutal honesty when you're hurting and vulnerable. Your loved ones want to tread carefully, and nurses typically ease you very gently into the truth—and only when they think you're ready to hear it (unlike the doctors, it seems). It dawned on me that without anyone openly acknowledging it, you became cushioned from the realities of the outside world when your own was crumbling.

It still didn't make sense though. Why would she be here every night if other patients needed her more? I reassured her that I would be fine so she could go elsewhere. She rolled her eyes, looked at me with what could only be described as annoyance and told me matter-of-factly that I was on suicide watch, so she wasn't legally allowed to leave. Someone had to be by my side at all times. I was floored. Suicide watch? Surely that couldn't be right? Surely I had been alone since I got here? The more I thought about it, the more I realised there had been someone with me for every moment since I was found face down in that field. Ever since the first paramedics arrived at the scene and I told them not to save me and begged them to just let me die. Every day since, I had been monitored. I had Jemma and nurses or doctors stopping me each time I would try to pull out all the cords plugged into me, in the hopes that one of them was the only thing keeping me alive. Every time I tried to throw myself off the bed, someone had been there to forcibly strap me down or sedate me.

She was right. I was a risk. I guess I just hadn't really viewed it as 'suicide' in these circumstances. Death seemed like a right that was mine for the taking if I so decided. In fact, it felt less like a choice and more like a necessity. It struck me suddenly that everyone must feel this way before they choose to end their life. The prospect of it felt less like giving up and more like a valid choice you should be able to make when the reality of life was too cruel to bear. It scared me to realise how detached from myself I had become to be thinking this way.

Did I really want to die? Was my life worth living if I wasn't even in control of my own body? Would I be able to find peace with so much pain and loss inside me? The answer was sad but true: I sincerely didn't want to be here anymore. Not just here in this hospital, but here on earth. I wasn't one of those people who could handle hardship, who could take it in their stride and grow from its soil. I could barely even handle the mundane. Life had always felt like something others just *got* and I, for reasons

I couldn't understand, just didn't. I wasn't innately positive, or resilient, or capable—I was despondent. I couldn't foresee any possible outcome in my new future where I would ever be okay.

~

Along with all my other dark thoughts, the day of the accident played on a constant loop in my brain. I would reminisce on all the tiny but necessary details that led me to that particular helicopter at that precise time. I remembered how I'd been so adamant to skydive in Switzerland, even though a few days later we were heading to Austria where it would have been far cheaper. The way I'd volunteered to jump first, because the rest of the group was hesitant and nervous while I was nothing but excited. The way I'd chosen that specific instructor because he said he could do flips out of the helicopter and I thought it sounded fun.

None of those things really bothered me, though. There was only one memory from that day that haunted me, and I replayed it over and over in my mind, focusing on this one detail every time.

The night before the skydive, I had promised myself that I was going to wake up and go for a run along a picturesque walking trail to explore the town we had just arrived in. Switzerland was breathtaking and I desperately wanted to see more of it. Running was my happy place; it made me feel free and wild and powerful, and it was something I had trained myself to be good at. When I woke up the morning of the skydive, I talked myself out of going because I was feeling lazy and couldn't be bothered. I put it off for another day, a tomorrow that I naively and blindly trusted would arrive, just as it always had.

There I was in Lauterbrunnen, a town famous for being the most beautiful place on earth, with the option to explore it on my own two feet, yet I had been too *lazy*. I'd had the opportunity to do the very thing I loved most, the thing that made me feel most alive, yet I *couldn't be bothered*. The words lingered in my brain. Like an embarrassing sentence I'd blurted out at a party and desperately wished I could take back, they sat there shameful and unchanging, taunting me with their irony.

Sure, I could have justified it with the fact that I was on holidays and there was absolutely no need for me to go running on that particular day, but the truth is that I *had* wanted to, I'd just counted on there being another time.

How naive was I to assume my body was forever going to be available to me in the same way it always had been? How had I never stopped to marvel at all it allowed me to do and to realise that one day, even if not due to an accident but simply due to old age, it would no longer work in the same youthful, carefree way it did at twenty? I had never felt regret before, but as I was lying in my hospital bed with every inch of me sore and exhausted, it suddenly pierced through me with an excruciating ferocity. I couldn't be bothered doing the thing I loved most in the entire world while I had the chance, and now it seemed I never would again. And not only would I never be able to run again, I couldn't even walk. I couldn't even sit up. The realisation was so sharp, so painful and so unthinkable, it tore me apart.

I couldn't explain why but even at the time I knew I needed to remember that feeling of utter despair. It was the strongest emotion I had ever experienced and, despite how agonising it was, I knew a part of me needed to hold on to it so I couldn't ever forget its power. I opened the notes app in my phone and tried to type out something that would remind my future self of this moment. I didn't know how to put everything I was feeling into a sentence, so instead I wrote down five words: *if you can, you must.*

What I meant was: if by some miracle there comes a day when I can ever run again, I must—for this version of me that can't. I wanted to make sure I never forgot the excruciating urgency and longing I felt when I was unable to do something that I deeply ached for. I was so angry at myself for not grabbing an opportunity while it was right in front of me and I wanted to make sure I would never make that mistake again.

I couldn't imagine how, but I hoped that someday, when everything wasn't quite so dark, the words could help me if I ever needed them. I closed the notes app, put my phone away and sobbed.

6
REUNITED

Jemma hadn't left my side from the moment she found me again after my first surgery. It was bizarre to think that only a week earlier we had touched down in London and spent the day wandering around the city with a camera and travel card in hand, feeling so grown up and worldly. Now, it felt like we were little kids thrust into the true reality of adulthood. It wasn't anything like what I had imagined it would be.

We had been best friends for more than fifteen years by this point so I was certain it wasn't possible for us to be any closer than we already were. We had shared everything: clothes, childhoods, core memories, tears—but what we were experiencing now was unlike all the years that came before. I had the sense that even if we were strangers when we jumped out of that helicopter together, we would be bound in a way that couldn't be explained with words. Living through the same trauma was like being handed the key to a box only we could see inside of. Like being let in on a secret that was impossible to explain to anyone who wasn't there. We had been close before, but now we were fused.

I didn't yet have the awareness to properly register how traumatic this time would have been for Jemma. Likely far more than it was for me. Not only had her entire world been spun off its axis in a matter of days, she was witnessing her best friend lose her desire to live. But instead of being able to express her sadness and fear like I was, she was forced to go into survival mode and take care of us both. As well as feeling heartbroken for her friend, I now realise she would have been experiencing her own inner turmoil when she looked at me in that bed. I can imagine the awful combination of gratitude and guilt that must have been swirling in her mind, alongside the words that remained unspoken between us—*that could have been me.* To this day, I am eternally thankful it wasn't.

Despite everything Jemma was going through, she was amazing at speaking up for me with the doctors, forgiving me when I was cruel and organising everything back home with my family. My mum didn't have a passport at the time and inconveniently my accident happened at 11pm on a long weekend in Australia, so she had no idea how to get one. Somehow, with the help of our family and friends, they found a way to make it happen and Mum got a passport in only a matter of hours. She was then on the first available flight to Switzerland, along with my older sister, Tara.

I awoke from a nap one afternoon to see my mum and sister

standing in the doorway to my room. Seeing them was an immediate relief—a sense of security washed over me at the sight of something familiar and safe. Yet at the same time, seeing them here in this alternate world, one we had never planned for, was a reminder of the stark shift in our reality.

They stood in the doorway waving at me, trying to hold back their shock and tears at seeing me dishevelled and hurt in my hospital bed, and I couldn't help but compare the moment to one we'd shared only two weeks earlier. There they were standing in another doorway on the other side of the world—the doorway of our home—waving goodbye to me as I walked out the door and headed off on my trip. Back when my hands were free of cannulas and the only thing pumping through my veins was giddy excitement and trust in the whole damn universe.

~

As I was eating breakfast one morning, a panicked and urgent thought hit me. I couldn't remember the last time I had been to the bathroom. I racked my delirious brain for a memory and realised it was at the skydive shop just before we got in the helicopter. That was days ago.

I quickly buzzed a nurse and asked her to help me out of bed so I could go to the toilet. I definitely didn't feel like I needed to go and reasoned it was because I hadn't been eating or drinking anywhere near as much as I normally would—but surely it was dangerous for me to not even try.

When the nurse arrived, she looked as confused as I felt. I opened my mouth to empathise with her bewilderment, but then she took a deep breath and gently explained that when I arrived in hospital the doctors had inserted a catheter into my urethra and it had been draining my bladder all this time. She lifted the blankets so I could see the tube coming out of me and pointed at a large bag beside the bed, which to my surprise did indeed look to be filled with my urine. Who knew?

I was shocked by how disconnected I was from my body, but to make light of the situation said I was thankful not to have to get out of bed and go to the bathroom because I wasn't sure how I would get there. I watched the nurse's face transform into what looked like confusion once again, before settling into what could only be described as pity. She'd assumed somebody else would have told me this by now. She took my hand and explained to me that my paralysed legs and inability to get to the toilet weren't the only reason for the catheter. In fact, they weren't even the main one. She said that people with spinal cord injuries typically lose the capacity to control their bladder entirely, so they will usually need to use a catheter for the rest of their life.

I didn't understand. How could I not use my bladder anymore? It wasn't something that required a lot of muscle or effort, like walking; it was the simplest thing in the world. I tried not to absorb her words because it was far too overwhelming to even think about. I shut the idea out and convinced myself that it wouldn't be the case for me. I was going to be the exception to the rule. Surely I would be able to do it just as soon as I was strong enough to get out of bed and try. Quietly though, I wondered what else I didn't know about my body and how many years it would take for me to feel like it was my own again.

~

I assumed it must be a similar situation for my bowels as well. Much to my horror, I learned that this wasn't the case. It turns out number twos aren't anywhere near as simple or inconspicuous to handle while you're paralysed in a hospital bed. There was no drainage bag attached to me—everything had to be 'evacuated' manually by the nurses. To make matters worse, I wasn't able to sit on a toilet because, along with my legs, my abs were also paralysed, which meant that anytime I tried to sit up, my blood pressure would plummet and I would pass out or vomit. Instead, I had to lie in bed, while my undies were removed and I was rolled onto my side, allowing a nurse to lay a waterproof sheet under my hips and insert an enema into me. From that point, the process took hours. The nurse had to massage my belly to try and move things along and then put gloves on and physically pull everything out of me.

I would lie there squeezing my eyes shut, trying to forget where I was and how uncomfortable I felt about a stranger staring at my naked bum, their fingers inside me, my poo reeking on the bed between us, while they tried to make awkward small talk in a language neither of us could really understand. I tried to imagine where my tour group was and what they must be doing at that very moment, and I was once again hit with the impossible truth that one decision was the difference between me being here instead of there.

I hoped that the alternate version of me—the one that was currently sipping an Aperol Spritz, eating pasta and wandering the cobblestone streets of Venice—knew how lucky she was. I don't think she could have though. It seems to me that it's only when we lose something that we stop to think about how very lucky we were to have once had it at all.

7

THE TURNING POINT

I opened my eyes to the familiar sight of a white hospital blanket and the Switzerland summer sun streaming in through the window. I could hear the usual sounds of beeping and shuffling happening outside my door in the hallway. I could smell the antiseptic that filled the room and clung to my skin. Everything seemed to be the same as it had been for the past week, but I could sense that something had changed. My legs were still paralysed, the catheter bag was still attached to me, the nurses still had to give me my enema in bed later that day, but there was something distinctly different. I couldn't pinpoint why or what caused it, but I noticed with a surprised yet welcome *huh*, that suddenly I wasn't so sad. I had become so accustomed to feeling down that I just expected it. I assumed it would always be this way.

It was like someone had pricked the tiniest of holes in a black-out curtain and, for the first time in what felt like an age,

I could see a small, single beam of light trying to break through. It wasn't enough for me to see clearly in the dark, but the knowledge that the light was there, hiding behind the thick curtain of what I had to go through, and that I was still capable of seeing it, was enough to change everything.

I could feel myself moving tangibly past the denial stage of grief and into whatever came next. Suddenly, without any effort on my part, I understood with a newfound clarity that what had happened, happened. There was no rhyme or reason to it and there was no explaining it or wishing it away. It had happened and it couldn't be undone. Instead of this information feeling jarring, it felt freeing. The accident was something I didn't ask for, but it was also something I couldn't ever reverse. If there was nothing I could do about it, there really wasn't much use in spending all of my energy willing the clock to spin backwards. I knew there was still an enormous winding road ahead of me, one so vast I couldn't even begin to see its entirety from where I was sitting in week two of my New Life, but I could sense that I was at a crossroads and that whatever I did next would be important. That my next decision could ultimately determine how the rest of my life turned out. I considered my options and stared down the only two paths I could see in front of me; I could be paralysed and miserable, or I could be paralysed and try to live a fulfilling life regardless. Either way the injury remained, so I figured I might as well try to trek blindly down the second route and see where it led me. After all, the only thing I had to lose was my misery, and I was more than willing to let that go.

~

I still hadn't showered since I had arrived in hospital so I wasn't feeling overly fresh. The nurses had given me a sponge bath in bed each day but, because I couldn't sit upright, I wasn't able to sit on a shower chair and experience the full rejuvenation of a proper shower. By this stage my hair was a greasy, matted and itchy mess resembling a bird's nest on top of my head. I was fairly certain it still had dirt and blood in it from when I landed in the field. I had the overwhelming feeling that if I could simply wash my hair, life itself would be infinitely better. But I had been told days ago that it wouldn't be possible while I was in bed and that even if it were, the nurses didn't have enough time between tending to all their other patients and tasks. To be fair, I couldn't imagine the logistics of getting my hair wet and soapy while lying down either, so I accepted that the sponge baths would have to do until I could sit up.

Suddenly, I heard an enthusiastic voice yell 'surprise' as the door to my room opened. I looked over expecting to see a person, but instead saw a yellow wheelie bin (exactly like the one you put out on the street on garbage day) being pushed towards me. Equal parts confused and curious, I looked up to see the face behind the bin and instantly knew this was going to be something good. It was my favourite nurse, Nadia, and she was smiling at me like she always did and looking eager to tell me something. Over the past week I had grown to adore this woman; she was warm, funny and sweet, and I always looked forward to her shifts. She made me feel important and genuinely cared for at a time when I otherwise felt like a problem that needed to be dealt with.

I had no idea what the bin was for but the timing felt

serendipitous, as though my newfound optimistic thoughts from the morning had been played out loud over the hospital speaker and Nadia had been sent here to catch my shift in perspective before it passed. I realised I was feeling something I'd almost forgotten: anticipation. I was looking forward to seeing what the next moment brought and I wondered if maybe, just maybe, that meant one day I could also look forward to seeing what the rest of my life had in store.

Nadia skipped towards me, with a smile wider than I'd ever seen on her, and proclaimed she was going to wash my hair using the wheelie bin. I felt excitement soar through me; I couldn't wait to feel fresh again after so long, but my elation stemmed from a place far deeper than mere hygiene. Someone (a near stranger at that) cared enough about me to remember something I had mentioned in passing and they'd found a way to make it happen. Someone was doing something well beyond their job description with the pure goal of making me smile. And perhaps most astonishingly of all, someone was validating that my desires, despite being incredibly trivial in the grand scheme of things, still mattered. I felt a tug in my chest at the simplicity and sincerity of it all.

With my mum's help, my bed was pulled out from the wall and Nadia placed the wheelie bin and a chair behind it. She then shuffled me backwards so that my hair could hang off the back of the bed and filled up a tub of warm water. What was already a beautiful and kind gesture became even more powerful when she sat down on the chair, gently poured water over my hair and into the bin and told me to close my eyes and savour the next thirty minutes. Instead of simply washing my hair and being done with it, she took her time and gave me a head massage, then combed and braided it tightly so it would stay out of my face until the next time she could wash it. I knew she had other places to be and a whole day filled with stressful and important jobs, but she didn't let me see any of that. She didn't do it for the recognition or praise, she did it to make me happy. I didn't know much about healing yet but I was certain that this act of humanity was part of it.

After she left, I felt the transformation that comes with cleanliness and kindness. I had been right; my life was infinitely better than it had been half an hour ago. Sometimes things really are that simple.

~

I began to notice beauty in other places as well. I wondered if it was just now showing up or if it had always been there and I'd been too blinded by grief to notice. I saw it in the flowers by my bedside, sent from friends across the world; in the sounds of the birds chirping outside my window; in the ice-cream my mum bought me for dessert each night.

I started drawing patterns inside my notebook to make cards for the nurses and was surprised to find that despite not having drawn before, it felt wonderfully therapeutic and calming. I filled the pages of my book with shapes and flowers and lyrics that lifted me up.

One morning, after spending what felt like years inside my

room, the nurses arranged to wheel my bed out into the courtyard for a few minutes so I could breathe in the fresh air and feel the summer sun on my face. I looked at the blue sky above me and marvelled at just how remarkable it felt to be immersed in nature and the world.

I was receiving hundreds of messages wishing me well from people I hadn't seen or spoken to in years and realised that as humans we matter to a lot more people than we think we do.

I witnessed the epitome of patience and sacrifice as my mum, Tara and Jemma tended to my most basic needs, and I understood for perhaps the first time what it truly means to love someone.

Not only was I noticing things I hadn't *since* the accident, I was noticing things I had *never* noticed before. I was developing talents, like drawing, that I hadn't had even when my body had all of its abilities. I was so intrigued by this that I decided to try something new. Instead of focusing my thoughts solely on what I had lost, which at that point seemed to be my entire identity, I tried to shift the focus onto what I still had.

Even through my pain and exhaustion I could see that I had an awful lot. I had people who cared about me, phenomenal health care, the movement in my hands, my mind and, most importantly, I had my life, despite all odds. I tried to take it one step further and asked myself if there was anything I had possibly gained from all of this. At first it seemed ridiculous to even ponder because it sure didn't feel like it. Life post-accident had felt like loss after devastating loss. But when I let myself dive deeper, when I allowed myself to look past the obvious 'on paper' realities of my world, I realised there was a whole lot more to find.

There was plenty I had gained and it was incredibly rich and valuable. I had an immense appreciation for my body, something I'd never had before. I had developed a spirit-altering gratitude for my life that would stay with me eternally. I had the extraordinary knowledge that I'd survived something impossible, which meant I had quite literally experienced a miracle.

I knew I had survived for a reason and, even though I didn't yet know what it was, I was determined to find out.

8

WHAT HAPPENED

I was lying in my hospital room when I heard a knock on the door followed by unfamiliar voices. They were deep and accented. Two Swiss policeman entered the room and told me they were there to talk about what had happened.

The policemen asked me questions about my injuries and what I could remember from the fall and landing. 'All of it,' I told them. When they left, investigators came by for more interrogations and I repeated the same story. I felt guilty, like I was a criminal finally caught out for a crime I didn't remember committing. I asked if perhaps my hair-tie coming loose could have been the reason this all unfolded. Did I talk too much in the helicopter? Or not enough? Did I miss something crucial in the briefing that left us plummeting to the ground?

At the time of the fall, I didn't know why it was happening; all I knew was that we were dropping far too quickly and for far too long. It wasn't until the investigators returned a few days later and explained it to me that I finally understood. They had discovered there were multiple factors at play, individual pieces of a puzzle that all joined together to lead us to that infamous field and this new-found world.

The pieces went like this: the sky was cloudy so we had to jump from a different height to the usual one. The instructor forgot to wear his altimeter (a device that tells you when you've reached the correct altitude to pull the parachute). He didn't account for our new jump height, which meant he pulled the chute too late. There is an emergency parachute which deploys automatically at a certain height if you are still dropping too fast. By some unheard of twist of fate, the instructor pulled the main chute at the precise time the emergency one was coming out on its own. Everything tangled together. The cords caught on my hair and yanked it backwards. They wrapped around the instructor's neck and strangled him. The parachutes couldn't open to slow us down. The instructor was unconscious for the entire fall. I was wide awake. We hit the ground like a freight train.

The instructor had been found to be at fault for a multitude of reasons, and he himself acknowledged this. It felt strange being told someone was at fault. That someone's actions had directly led me to an entirely new reality. I hadn't expected or prepared for that outcome; up until then I had presumed it was a freak accident. I couldn't process the weight of what I was hearing, couldn't grasp what it meant. All I felt was an immense empathy and sadness at the thought of what he must be going through. I couldn't imagine the heaviness of living with a mistake that can't be undone.

Throughout the explanation of the accident, there was something the policemen mentioned in passing that caused the air to catch in my throat. I heard the words 'one second was all it took. If the parachute had been pulled one second earlier, or even one second later, you would have landed safely and all of this could have been avoided.'

I hadn't given the timing of it all much thought, but the simplicity and the cold hard truth of what happened rattled me. *One second.* Less than the time it took for him to say those words. Far less time than it's taken me to write this sentence. The time it took for me to look into his eyes to make sure I heard him correctly. That was all it took to change a life.

Suddenly life seemed so frighteningly precarious. Like each individual step had to be decided on with the caution and deliberation of a jury. One second is nothing in the scheme of a day—sometimes thousands can pass us by without any meaning or significance—but it was the difference between me living that life and this one.

If the instructor had pulled the parachute one second earlier, it would have opened normally and we would have drifted down slowly while I looked on in awe at the pattern of brown and emerald fields below us. I would have called the experience 'life-changing' without knowing that walking back to the cabin ten minutes later to eat a sandwich and check my phone didn't exactly constitute any kind of transformation. Alternatively, if he had waited one second longer, the emergency chute would have opened safely and I would have had an exhilarating story about that one time I went skydiving in Switzerland and had to use the backup parachute because my instructor made a mistake. I would have told it at parties with a little added spice, the way people can only tell dramatic stories when they weren't actually traumatic or impactful at all.

~

I didn't know anything about personal injury claims but the fact that there would be one had seemed evident from day one. As far as I could tell it was just a standard, assumed part of the process. I was beginning to realise the extreme expense of having a spinal cord injury and I knew I was only just scratching the surface of what was to come, so it seemed obvious that I would need some form of compensation to help cover the costs.

I imagined the process would be pretty straight forward: you had an accident, the cause was investigated, you provided medical documents to back up your claims, you were paid what you needed to cover the costs of your injury, and you carried on with the rest of your life. I imagined personal injury law was a system put in place to help guide people forward and raise them up in their most trying moments. I imagined it would be something that happened in the background of my life while I got on with living it.

Little did I know that what I was blindly embarking on would be the cause of some of my greatest rage, most honest tears and hardest learnings. Never in my wildest dreams could I have guessed the strength with which this case would pull me back and hold me under at a time when keeping my head above water is all I should have had to do.

9

MY NEW BODY

By the second week, life in hospital became so familiar to me that I would often forget I was ever meant to be somewhere else and this wasn't the plan all along. The nurses and staff began to feel like genuine friends and with each of them I found our personal balance of vocabulary that enabled us to communicate. I could have in-depth, fluent conversations with some of them, while with others we could understand only a few words or small phrases from each other. Some of the nurses I couldn't understand at all, but I soon learned that words aren't the only way to communicate. A lot can be said through hand gestures and as cliché and cringe as it sounds, a smile really can be felt in any language.

Jemma had been booked to go on a fashion exchange in Florence after the initial portion of our trip and although she wanted to stay with me, I didn't want her to miss the opportunity she'd been so excited for. So, after much convincing that I was safe and feeling okay again, she headed off to Italy to continue her adventure. Life moving on without me felt odd, but I'd learned that the world didn't stop spinning for anyone, no matter how badly you wanted it to pause while you caught back up.

Mum and Tara were still sleeping in my room with me each night and we always found things to laugh at and ways to have fun throughout the day. Most mornings they would regale me with tales of the spectacularly random things I would say when I was fuelled by pain meds in the middle of the night. My mum's personal favourite was when I woke up at 3am in a panic and urgently called her over to my bed, only to ask her to tell me the story of *A Bugs Life* (a kids movie I hadn't seen or even thought about in ten years). She started to tell me the story from her memory, but considering a decade-old animation wasn't at the forefront of her mind in the early hours of the morning, her rendition wasn't entirely accurate and I got outrageously upset that she'd told it wrong.

Another time I woke up startled and suddenly began begging for a bowl of goulash, which, might I add, is something I've never eaten in my entire life.

~

Every day I was learning more about what my injury meant for me and the rest of my life, and I was surprised to find that as time passed and the initial shock wore off, I was becoming more and more okay with it. I wasn't thrilled—of course I would have preferred to be skipping down the streets of Spain in a flowing summer dress, delightfully unaware that things could have ever gone any other way—but I had finally reached an encouraging level of acceptance. I had come to the strong and unfailing belief that a damaged body didn't need to mean a damaged life.

When I first arrived in hospital I'd had surgery on both my spine and pelvis. I had a long line of stitches down my back from where I was cut open, and another line on my hip where they secured a screw to hold my pelvis in place. To me, the stitches looked like strength and I knew immediately I would love the scars once they'd healed—like unchosen but equally treasured tattoos.

During my second operation, the surgeon needed to access my spine from my side rather than my back and, in order to do this, one of my lungs had to be collapsed. I now had a thick tube coming out of the skin above my ribs that was draining fluid (and what concerningly looked to be chunks of organ) from my lung. I wasn't allowed to fly on an aeroplane until my lung was strong enough to withstand the pressure, so was told I wouldn't be heading back to Australia for the next few weeks.

Until then we'd had no guide for how long I would have to stay overseas, which was the reason Ben said he hadn't flown over to be with me yet. He didn't want to fly all the way across the world only to land and find out I was leaving the next day. His absence gave me a sense of foreboding. I was young, but I wasn't stupid. We'd been together for three years so I thought I knew him—knew *us*—better than this. I had offered to pay for his flight with the money I'd saved (and no longer needed) for my trip, so I couldn't understand why he wasn't there. I desperately wanted to get home to the comfort of my partner, but I had the feeling that, even once I did, that comfort wouldn't be what it once was. The idea hurt so deeply that I didn't even have the energy to acknowledge it yet. I couldn't lose him too. I wouldn't. Now that we had confirmation I was staying in Switzerland for a while longer, I held on to the hope that he would fly over. I reminded myself of who we used to be and imagined with every ounce of my hopelessly-in-love heart that he would be on the next available flight.

In the meantime, I was learning more every day about the risks involved with not being able to move half my body. My lack of mobility didn't just affect my ability to get from A to B, as I had previously thought, it was something that could become quite dangerous and even life-threatening if I wasn't careful. I was now at risk of developing blood clots and deep vein thrombosis due to decreased blood circulation, so to prevent this the nurses had to give me a daily injection in my leg. Watching yourself get a needle when you can't feel it is quite a surreal experience; you brace for the sting of the pain but it never comes. It's like watching someone else's body entirely.

I wanted to regain as much independence as I could, so after a few days of watching the needle be injected into me, I decided I wanted to be able to do it myself. Instead of simply asking the nurses to show me how it's done (like a regular person), I began singing 'teach me how to jab me' to the tune of 'Teach Me How to Dougie'. Not my most creative work, I will admit, but it still managed to make everyone in the room laugh. Laughter had become my favourite thing. I'd found it was a portal to childlike joy, capable of transporting you to complete contentment, even if only for a moment, but it was something I'd never harnessed the power of before.

When I did eventually learn to give myself the needle, I realised it was even more surreal being on both the giving and receiving end of it. Being paralysed was still so new to me that I was shocked every time I faced another reminder of just how much I couldn't feel. It was as though part of my brain (the part that had walked for twenty years) had become convinced I was being over-dramatic and that surely I would be able to move if I just tried hard enough. But then I would get a stark reminder, like an unfelt needle in my thigh, and remember, *oh yeah this isn't all in my head, this is very, very real.*

Another danger of paralysis was the risk of pressure sores. Pressure sores are caused by constant pressure or rubbing on an area of skin, which causes it to break down and can be incredibly dangerous and take months or even years to heal. You know that feeling when you've been sitting in a chair too long and your bum starts to go numb, so you shift your weight to reposition yourself? That's your body telling you that you're losing blood flow to that area and need to move to protect your skin. We instinctively do this all day long without even noticing. In bed we roll over or reposition our bodies ever so slightly while we're sleeping, and on a long flight we move around in our seat when we get uncomfortable—it's our body's natural response to keep us safe.

The problem is, when you have a spinal cord injury you not only also lose that innate ability to *feel* discomfort but you also lose the ability to *move* easily when you need to. Because of this, I needed to be both reminded to move and also physically *be* moved. Every few hours, two men would come into my room and reposition my body for me. Even if I was sleeping, they would come in, roll me onto my side and place a pillow between my knees to stop them rubbing together, then a few hours later come back and roll me onto the other side. At first I felt incredibly uncomfortable being touched and handled in this way, especially because they couldn't speak any English to explain what they were doing, but once I understood how important it was, I was thankful for their help.

We all rely on the slightest of movements to be comfortable and safe and we don't even realise. Lying in bed all day probably sounds like a dream to a lot of people (there was a time when I would have thought the same), but when you can't do the most basic movements, lying in bed also means being uncomfortable most of the time. Whether it was something as simple as the sheet being folded over on itself and digging into my back, or my hips being placed down slightly crooked and feeling lopsided, losing that ability to reposition myself to find comfort gave me so much appreciation for bodies and just how much they do for us without us even knowing.

The human body is so fascinating and intricate and the more you know, the more you realise just how much of a miracle it really is. It makes you wonder why we aren't all rejoicing with gratitude every waking moment about the simple fact that our body loves us so much it works twenty-four hours a day just to keep us healthy and alive. Even on my hardest days and even in the moments I resented my body, my heart was still pumping blood to the places it was needed, my kidneys were still expelling toxins, my lungs (even when semi-collapsed) were allowing me to take my next breath. My body was doing all of these things unconsciously and it would continue to do them whether or not I took the time to notice. It was the best example of unconditional love that I'd ever seen and I was in awe.

~

A few weeks after I arrived in hospital, the nurses came into my room and told me it was time to test my bladder to see if it really was paralysed or if by some miracle I was still able to control it. It had been impossible to know for sure while I had the catheter bag attached to me because my bladder never had the opportunity to fill up and expand, so I had never felt the sensation or urge to go. This moment was something I'd built up in my head ever since I learned that being incontinent might become a part of my future, and I could tell from the nurses' faces that it was a big deal. Whatever the result of this simple test was, it would determine something huge about my life that I couldn't yet fathom. I was nervous.

To do the test, my catheter was clamped closed so urine couldn't flow through to the bag, which instead allowed my bladder to fill up naturally. I was told to drink lots of water and wait to see if I felt that familiar urge to go to the bathroom. Time passed and I wasn't feeling anything, which was a bizarre thing to wrap my head around because, despite coming to terms with losing sensation to my skin, I'd never really thought about my body's *internal* feelings not existing anymore. I drank more and more and after a few hours, with a whole lot of liquid in me but absolutely no urge to go, the nurses told me it was time to call it. If I was going to feel something, I would have felt it by now. They removed the clamp and let my urine drain into the bag.

Everyone in the room looked sombre and waited for my response. Even I was waiting for my response, but strangely I didn't seem to have one. I didn't feel gutted or devastated or anything at all really. I just thought, *Okay, I'll learn how to handle it.* I had become strangely at ease with the prospect of being incontinent and had almost been expecting it. My threshold for what I believed I could bear had risen without effort. Sometimes things seem so big and scary until they actually happen, and then we realise they don't hold anywhere near as much power as we thought they would. Bladder control or no bladder control, I was still me.

The past few weeks had changed my perception of my body in so many deep and fundamental ways. Before then, I had never thought about my body as something separate from myself. I had always assumed it was *who* I was and that it was what defined my essence. I placed my worth and identity entirely on its outer appearance and capabilities. Not only was I beginning to learn just how much more my body gave me apart from aesthetics, it was also becoming clear to me that my body wasn't, in fact, who I am. Because despite now only being able to control half of me, I wasn't losing any of me at all.

10

THE DARKEST NIGHT

Almost a month after I arrived, I got clearance from my doctors to travel home. Even though I had started to feel at ease in the hospital and each day became a little easier and brighter, the prospect of flying back to Australia was electrifying. I knew I wasn't flying 'home' exactly; I wasn't even flying back to my hometown. Instead I was heading to a hospital in Sydney where I would spend the next few months living in a spinal ward. But even so, I couldn't wait. Ben hadn't managed to make it over to visit me, which was a truth I still couldn't bear to face, so I was beyond eager to see him, along with the rest of my family and friends. I was also looking forward to speaking to doctors with whom I could have a fluent conversation and find out more about what my injury really meant. I was even just excited to eat my favourite foods, see a recognisable landscape and feel the comfort of all things familiar.

An ambulance was booked to pick me up from the hospital and take me to the airport. From there I would board a flight with my mum, alongside a doctor and a nurse who would accompany us to Dubai and then on to Australia. I still wasn't able to sit up, so I was told there would be three or four rows of seats removed from the plane where my bed would go and I would lay down the whole twenty-one hours home. Honestly, it sounded like a pretty great first-class experience to me.

There was only one thing tempering my excitement; I desperately wanted to see my skydiving instructor before I left. He was in the same hospital as me, but had been refusing any visitors as well as my many attempts to see him. I knew today was my last chance, so I begged the nurses to try to convince him to visit me before I went home. I don't really know why I wanted to see him so badly, but it felt important that I did. I wanted to make sure he was okay and I wanted him to know that even though I was hurt, I was okay too.

The paramedics arrived in the afternoon and when they came to collect me, my heart sank because I knew I was out of time. I couldn't imagine when I would ever get the chance to see or talk to him again. The nurses helped me get my things together and were about to transfer me onto a stretcher when we heard a quiet knock on the door. It was him.

Right in front of my eyes, sitting in a wheelchair with both of his legs in casts, was the man I'd only ever known for about thirty minutes, but would remember forever. A face I'd barely got to know but would never forget.

He wheeled himself over to my bed and held my hand.

The room was so quiet it felt as though time had stopped. I think I forgot to breathe. After what could have been an hour or twenty seconds of looking at each other without any words, he squeezed my hand and said something I didn't really understand at the time, but that I've never let go. He said, 'You have to heal your mind before you can ever heal your body.'

I nodded and he wheeled his chair back out of the room and out of my life. A connection so short in time, yet never-ending in impact.

~

I had imagined that once I landed back in Australia, suddenly everything would be okay. That regaining some semblance of normality would feel like waking up from a strange dream. I'd fallen into an illusion where the life I'd been living in Switzerland wasn't truly mine and once I was home I'd be able to quietly slip back through my front door, slide on my pjs, climb into bed and wake up in my old life. Instead, that first night was one of the darkest nights of my life.

We landed at 10pm. I was wheeled off the plane into the cold night breeze and then loaded into an ambulance that my mum wasn't allowed inside. In less than tweny-four hours, I had gone from summer to winter and, as I breathed in the icy air, Australia felt cold to me in more ways than one. When the ambulance pulled into the hospital, I was transferred onto a bed by the paramedics, and a wardsman came to take me to the spinal ward. There were so few words spoken throughout this process, the treatment of me so clinical, that it was hard to tell if I was even back in Australia. Language still felt like a barrier with everyone I encountered, and I couldn't understand why no one would talk to me. I felt so alone.

I lay on my back looking up at the ceiling as my bed began to move through the halls of the hospital. Fluorescent lights and sterile panels started passing by above me like some form of hypnotic trance. My breath caught in my throat as a familiar memory and ache came over me. I'd been here before. Not here in this hospital, but here in this uncertainty. I remembered being wheeled through the hospital doors in Switzerland and watching the ceiling move above me as I was pushed from one room to the next, from one life to another. I had come so far emotionally since then, I had gained so much acceptance and strength, but being here again—alone while looking at the lines and lights as they rushed past, with no idea where I was going or what I was heading towards—filled me with fear.

It was late, so the hospital was eerily quiet and empty. There were no nurses or visitors filling the halls, just the sounds of the bed wheels turning below me and my shaky breath. After several elevator rides, countless corners and about a million thoughts, we arrived at what seemed to be a ward. This is where I would be spending the next few months. This is where I would become whoever I was going to become. As we passed through the entrance to the spinal ward, I couldn't help but wonder if I would walk or wheel out of this same door on my way home.

I was still lying flat on the bed and couldn't sit up to see what was around me. The man who had brought my bed here left and

I didn't know if anyone else knew I was coming. I held my breath as I waited for whatever came next. Finally, a nurse appeared above me and asked if I could transfer onto a different bed. I couldn't. In Switzerland there had always been people to help me do that. With a frustrated sigh she turned around and left, I assumed to go and find help. I was so confused—I didn't realise my inability to move would be an inconvenience in a spinal ward where surely everyone was paralysed to some degree. I yearned for the nurses I had grown so fond of over the past month and I missed having people in my corner who backed me.

The nurse returned with two men who, without speaking, lifted me onto my new bed. I couldn't feel the bottom half of my body as it was placed down but when my back and head reached the bed, it felt rock hard. I pressed into it with my hands and was concerned to find that it felt like a deflated air mattress. It was like lying on concrete. I wasn't usually too fussed with bedding but after learning about the risks of pressure sores I knew how dangerous and damaging the wrong bed could be for me now. I asked the nurse if this was how it was supposed to feel and she shrugged her shoulders.

She looked at me curiously and asked what my diagnosis was. Although I thought she must surely already know, I answered her.

'I'm a paraplegic,' I said. I was shocked to hear the words in my own voice—I'd never spoken them out loud before. The sentence felt so foreign and unnatural in my mouth, yet I knew it was one that would no doubt become as instinctive and unsurprising as my own name.

I asked the nurse if my mum could come to spend the night

in my room beside me. I hadn't been alone since the accident and I wasn't sure I knew how to be. The nurse explained that it was against hospital policy but told me that she would be able to come and see me first thing in the morning. I was terrified. I didn't know a single person in this hospital and I didn't have any way to move around. What if I needed something and couldn't reach it? What if I was in pain and nobody came to help me? What if I had a nightmare and no one was there to wake me up?

Fear flooded my veins. For the first time in my life, I felt the immense weight of being truly alone. I was alone in the room but I was also alone on my journey from here. Nobody could walk this path with me, no matter how much they wanted to. Nobody, not even my mum, could take on this challenge for me—it was something I had to do on my own. There was no way for me to be anywhere other than in my body and there was no way for anyone else to be in it for me. Usually when we feel restless or uneasy, we can get up and move around to shift our energy, or talk to someone, eat some food or go for a drive, but on this night there was nowhere to escape. There was nowhere I could be besides my mind and I was forced to feel everything in its entirety.

As I lay awake in my bed, eyes wide open, hands trembling and legs numb, all the dark thoughts and fears that I thought I'd overcome in Switzerland came back to me. I checked the clock on the wall; it was only 1am. I watched it tick by. I was certain it must be broken because the second hand was moving agonisingly slowly. I checked my phone but it was the same. Seconds felt like minutes. Minutes felt infuriatingly infinite. There were six whole hours until I could have visitors and be free from the jail of my thoughts. Six hours isn't much time in the scheme of a life, but that night it was unbearable. I have never known my mind to be such a debilitating and torturous place and I was sincerely frightened by the thought of having to endure it until morning.

Thoughts were racing through my head and piercing my soul. *What if they don't know how to look after me properly in here? What did it mean that Ben wasn't waiting to see me the moment I touched down? What if there is no day beyond this night?*

I was drowning in a sorrow so deep I didn't know if I would ever be able to surface.

~

There are some moments in life you wish you could go back to. For me, this is one of them. Not to live it again, but to pass on a message to my past self that would have comforted her deeply. As I lay in that bed, all I knew was fear and terror and heartache. But with the gift of hindsight, I now know something else.

I know that just outside my room, a few steps down the corridor, someone else was wide awake at 1am. No more than a few metres away—in a different bed, in the same spinal ward—lay a twenty-two-year-old boy named Sam who'd had an accident on his motorbike two months earlier and been told he would never walk again. In the very room next door was a person who would one day become one of my dearest friends, someone as integral and irreplaceable to me as a limb—I just didn't know him yet.

When I think of that night now and recall looking at the ceiling moving past me as I was on my way to somewhere unknown, I know I was actually on my way to him. When I remember feeling so alone it physically ached, I know he was right there beside me, so close I could have called out his name.

Sometimes life leads you down a road you don't want to go down. It might be dark, it might be uncomfortable, it might be painful, and none of that can be taken away. But if you're really lucky, there might be something else down that road too. There might be something that doesn't take away the hurt, but makes you feel okay for having endured it. There might be something or someone you stumble upon that makes you look back at the formidable road, stare at it in all its unspeakable glory, take a deep inhale and whisper, 'You were so, so worth travelling down.'

I like to remind myself of this whenever I can't see any light. When I'm hurting, or sad or lonely, I remind myself that something so good might be so close, I just don't know it yet. It might be in the very room next door. Even if I can't feel it or see any proof of it, I close my eyes and imagine it's there and it gives me the faith I need to keep going. I like to believe that if the universe was kind enough to grant me a best friend in my darkest moment, it will certainly be kind to me again.

11

TOAST

I woke up to a lady bringing me a tray of breakfast. I checked the time and realised I must have only been asleep for an hour, but everything looked entirely different in the light. Throughout everything, this simple fact continued to shock me. Time and time again, life kept showing me that the sun really would continue to rise, even on the nights where I was certain it wouldn't. It kept reminding me that I was strong enough to make it through.

In the daylight, I could now properly see the ward where I'd be spending most of my time for the foreseeable future. I was in a large room with about twenty other beds circled around the nurse's station, each with their own curtain.

I wondered who was in each of the beds and how they ended up here. I also wondered if they'd heard me crying last night.

I looked at my tray of food: orange juice, scrambled eggs and a piece of bread. My lack of sleep must have made me brave because despite normally being too shy to speak up, I asked the lady if I could toast the bread.

She replied, 'Sure, the toaster is in the next room. Help yourself,' and walked away.

I could feel tears threatening to break loose again. The combination of a full day flying across the world, severe jetlag and last night's sleepless and highly emotional night had made me the most exhausted and sensitive I'd ever been. I was also experiencing the intense dehydration and puffiness that comes after a cry so large you're certain your tear ducts have reached their lifetime capacity. I couldn't care less about not having toast, but how on earth did she think I was going to get myself to the next room? I felt so small and didn't trust that the people here were going to be able to help me—to make toast or to make my life big again.

A few minutes after she left, I heard the curtain to my room slide open, followed by the sound of my grandparents' voices. I swear hearing them felt like my spirit giving a giant exhale. It was pure relief. I wasn't alone anymore, I was safe. They hovered over my bed with watery eyes, giving me the kind of genuine smiles that said, *I'm so glad we get to see you again*. And oh my goodness, so was I.

My grandparents are my favourite people in the world. Their presence has always been my safe haven, an unwavering sense of home. So seeing them standing in front of me after so long made everything instantly better. If I know my grandparents at all, getting in to see me wouldn't have been anywhere near as effortless as they made it seem. I know that the day before they would have made sure the car had plenty of petrol in it, and, when they found that it did, they would have topped it up further *just in case*. This morning they would have set their alarm for hours earlier than they needed to, and they would have arrived and waited in the hospital carpark with plenty of time to spare, all so they could walk in here the very first moment they were allowed. They are the kindest and most generous people in the world.

Seeing them and feeling safe enough in their presence to break down, I let everything out and told them in a panic that I didn't want to be here and that I wanted to go back to Switzerland. Nanny held my hand and asked me what I needed. I needed so much and I had absolutely no idea where to start, but holding her hand felt like she'd given something to me already. All I could think to say was, 'Toast, please.'

One step at a time.

~

As the day progressed, I could see that this hospital was actually exactly where I needed to be. I was greeted every hour by someone new from the medical team and as they introduced themselves, they told me what their role in my recovery was going to be. There were physiotherapists, social workers, occupational therapists, nutritionists, psychologists, nurses and, of course, my doctor. I hadn't realised just how many people and specialties went into healing a spinal cord injury and I felt so comforted and assured by everyone's warmth and knowledge. I found myself feeling genuinely excited by the task in front of me. I couldn't wait to dive into my recovery.

I noticed that each person I met said something similar to me. They each, in some way or another, mentioned how vibrant and optimistic I was. To be fair, they probably said that to all their patients, but they were definitely words I'd never been told before. I was stunned. People saw me as vibrant? Was an optimist something I could become? My heart swelled at the thought. That spark I had felt in Switzerland was coming back and I wanted to see if I could turn it into a flame.

As well as meeting all the people who would help with my body's recovery, the day was also filled with visitors, and my spirits lifted immeasurably every time a familiar face walked through the door. I finally got to see my dad and my younger sister Hayley, who hadn't been able to come to Switzerland because she was in her final year of school. My parents hadn't been in the same room or spoken a word to each other in the four years since their divorce. Seeing them seated on opposite sides of my bed was jarring—like visiting a memory I wasn't sure ever existed—and it made me realise in a way nothing else had how momentous this accident really was.

My family brought countless cards and letters from people back home, including drawings from the kids at the childcare centre where I had worked. My room was filled with bright flowers and my favourite snacks, and colourful paintings began to line the walls. It hadn't even been a whole day since I arrived, but already it felt like a completely different space to the one I entered last night; it felt more like home.

All day I kept waiting to see one face in particular. The one that had filled my mind in the final moments before I hit the ground. The one I'd adored every day since I was seventeen.

As I waited for Ben to arrive, I was a mixture of nerves and excitement at the thought of him walking into my room. I wasn't sure why he hadn't flown to Switzerland in the end—his reasons were always quite vague, and I wasn't sure I believed them—but right now that didn't matter. I knew we were about to have our movie moment, the one I'd waited nearly a month for. Nothing can describe the feeling of wanting to be reunited with the person you love after nearly dying and thinking you'd never get to see them again. Just imagining the moment had been enough to keep me going on so many of my darker days.

He texted me when he arrived at the hospital and a few minutes later I heard his voice travelling through the hospital curtain. My heart was pounding out of my chest and my cheeks hurt from smiling so wide. I couldn't believe the moment was finally here.

He opened the curtain, walked in slowly and stood at the end of my bed. As he opened his mouth to speak, I wondered if he knew how tightly I was holding onto his next words.

When he finally spoke, he said, 'Hey, how's it going?' with the nonchalance of a regular day.

What?

My heart started to race even faster. I felt like I might faint.

There was no running toward me, no embrace, no slow motion and world-stopping kiss, no tears of *holy shit, you're alive. Thank god you're alive.* There was only someone who meant the world to me looking at me like I was a near stranger and speaking to me as though we didn't have years of history. I didn't understand. It was us. Didn't he miss me like I had missed him? Hadn't he been waiting for this moment since he found out I was hurt?

Please not him too, my insides screamed.

I didn't want this to be another lesson, not him—I wanted this to be love.

I felt like I was being split in two, but I tried not to dwell on it too much: I knew he felt uncomfortable in hospitals, so I convinced myself he was probably just feeling overwhelmed by the whole situation. It didn't matter that it wasn't how I'd imagined it—I was just so glad to see him and feel his presence after thinking I would never get the chance to again. Even if seeing him broke my heart.

~

Later that afternoon, something else came through my door. Something that, oddly enough, I hadn't even anticipated. A wheelchair. In hindsight it seemed so obvious that this would be my next step, but my mind hadn't ventured ahead to a world where I wasn't lying in this bed. I was taking each individual moment as it came and after a whole month of lying down, it had become so normal to me that I couldn't imagine anything different. The prospect of getting out of my bed and out of this room was like being handed a round-the-world ticket.

The nurses pushed the chair towards me and gently assured me that it was okay to feel anxious about using it. They explained that people often hold off from sitting in it straight away because they fear that once they accept and use it they'll never get back out again.

I understood what they were saying but that thought hadn't even crossed my mind. In fact, I felt the complete opposite. The wheelchair might not have been my own two legs, but it was my way out of this bed and a chance for me to experience the world beyond a hospital curtain again. A lot of what I'd been through made me feel nervous and uneasy, but not this. That wheelchair didn't look scary to me, it looked like freedom.

And a way to make toast.

12

SPINAL WARD

As an inherently spontaneous person, routine and planning have always hindered me. I've never liked the concept of knowing exactly what each day would hold; I much prefer to create as I go and see where that leads me. But in the spinal ward I was given a daily timetable packed full of things I had to do and therapists I had to see.

To my surprise I came to enjoy the benefits of having routine and structure in my days when the rest of my life was filled with uncertainty. The idea of life outside the hospital seemed overwhelmingly out of reach and impossible to prepare for, so being told what to do hour after hour was like being handed a lantern in the dark. I began to thrive with this sense of purpose and direction. Instead of being defeated by the challenging moments, I felt driven—a feeling that had become quite foreign to me in the previous few years.

I wondered if this was the precise reason patients were given such full schedules. I liked to think that our timetables were not only about rehabilitation but were also a disguised gift of certainty amidst the chaos.

Every day on the ward was different, but each morning started out the same. I would wake up early, sometimes to a breakfast delivery, other times to a needle being pressed into my arm to draw blood, and then I'd be transferred onto a commode and wheeled to the bathroom. There, a nurse would give me an enema over the toilet and although it was still awkward, especially because I didn't have a language barrier to hide behind anymore, it was far better than the previous bed/poo situation. Sure, sometimes I would pass out on the toilet because sitting up was still new, but hey, it was progress.

I was then wheeled across to the shower where I spent an hour washing, drying and dressing myself with the help of a nurse, and once I was ready I would head to the main room with the other patients, where I would commence a full day of rehab. A typical day involved physio, followed by wheelchair lessons, occupational therapy, then more physio. Sometimes there were scans, guest speakers and dental appointments (my teeth were wobbly from landing on my face) added into the mix as well. I found myself constantly awestruck by the knowledge that not only was this comprehensive treatment available so readily, but that the cost was completely covered thanks to the hospital being public. I was grateful to be Australian and for our healthcare system in a way I'd never acknowledged before.

Wheelchair lessons were always the highlight of my day.

My teacher, Craig, was one of those people who you just can't help but love. His job was to teach me how to navigate the world in my wheelchair, despite the world not necessarily being made with wheels in mind, so that I could live as independently as possible. He made everything an adventure and would set me little challenges like doing a wheelie or being able to jump down off a gutter. The inner athlete in me always wanted to master each challenge as quickly as I could and move on to whatever trickier task he had lined up for me next. On my first day of lessons, he showed me a video of a guy going down a huge set of stairs in his wheelchair and I knew that was the level I wanted to get to as well.

Craig had worked in his job for more than twenty years so he had seen and taught countless people as they passed through the spinal ward and headed into their new lives. I marvelled at how his job granted him access to the most intense, vulnerable and axis-shifting time in a person's life; how unique it was that he stepped into someone's most significant chapter and played a lead role for a brief moment, only to likely never see them again. I wondered if it was thankless or rewarding.

He would tell me stories about past patients and all the incredible things they had gone on to do after they left the hospital, which often had absolutely nothing to do with the fact they were living in wheelchairs. His classes were transformative; he taught me how to move around in the world, but more than that—he reminded me that the world is still very much worth moving for.

As an introvert, another favourite part of my day came after dinner. It was the time when all the visitors had gone home, the patients went into their rooms and the ward was quiet. I would spend this time either hanging out with the nurses who I had become friends with, sitting in the courtyard in my wheelchair looking up at the stars or drawing.

Drawing had quickly become a place of refuge for me. When I put pen to paper it was like I could let go of all of the thoughts and fears in my mind and be fully present. I still had no idea what I was doing, and it wasn't exactly Picasso-worthy, but being surrounded by people who had lost the use of their hands made me aware of what a gift it was that I could even pick up a pen. It made me aware of a lot of things, the main one being, how had I been so oblivious?

A few days before I'd left for my trip, I'd gone shopping for clothes to take away with me. I was in a changeroom trying on shorts and I remember looking in the mirror and feeling so disheartened by my own reflection. I'd gained weight in the previous year and clothes weren't fitting me the way they usually did. I looked down at my legs and resented how muscly they had grown from all the sports I played; I wished they would shrink so I could fit into something tighter. I looked at my face, which was eternally sprinkled with freckles, and wished I had been born with one of those perfectly clear complexions I saw on TV.

For some reason I had genuinely believed that these things would make a difference to how much fun I would have on holiday. I truly believed that if I was just a little skinnier, or prettier, or a million other irrelevant things, people would like me more and therefore I would be sure to have a better time.

As though superficial beauty is what determines who likes us. As though who likes us determines how much we like ourselves.

We are taught 'everybody has imperfections, but they are all beautiful' as the baseline of self-love, but I feel like we're missing the point. We use the word 'imperfect' as though there is a preferred way to be a human and if we don't meet that standard, we need to learn to find beauty in our stretch marks, cellulite or whatever else society doesn't deem appropriate. But who created this blueprint of perfect? And why do we need to be oozing with love about the way we look anyway? Why do we need to think we're beautiful in order to love ourselves?

Living in the spinal ward ingrained in me the kind of self-confidence and body acceptance that people tell you is unattainable. Looking around at the people I'd grown so fond of and seeing all the things they longed to do, I couldn't fathom my past self-deprecating thoughts. In fact, it made me furious that I'd ever had them. How could I have been so blinded by insecurity and outward approval that I ignored all the privileges I did have? How could I have berated a body that some people spent their whole lives wishing for and in pursuit of? A body that worked exactly as it should and that could take me down any road, up any mountain and into any ocean, without question or hesitation. I'd had a body that let me walk, feel, see, hear, taste, explore and experience, yet instead of being wonderstruck by it, I had wanted a different one.

When a part of your body is paralysed and not being used, over time it will begin to atrophy. Which, simply put, means it will shrink—I had gotten my wish. Now, when I remembered those legs I had been so ashamed of in the changeroom mirror, I saw strong, durable and capable legs holding me up, ready to take me on an adventure across the world. As I sat in my wheelchair in the hospital and longed to be able to walk across the sand to reach the ocean or stand up to hug someone at eye-level, I would have done anything to have those legs back. In fact, I would have taken any pair of legs, regardless of what they looked like, if they enabled me to walk and do the things I missed so much.

I made a conscious and very deliberate decision to change the narrative any time I noticed a negative thought about my body seeping into my subconscious. I decided to flip a switch in my mind—instead of focusing on what a certain body part looked like, I would focus on what it could do for me. Instead of looking at my face and wishing the freckles away, I became enamoured by the way it enabled me to express myself, how it could change shape into something people recognised as happiness or surprise or adoration. My skin went from freckly and flawed to the thing that holds me together and protects me, the thing that allows me to feel the elements and regulate my body temperature. My ears changed from something I'd never really given much thought to into miraculous things that allow me to hear my favourite music, the comforting sounds of waves crashing against the shore and the voice of someone telling me they love me. Every inch of my body had a purpose and I was determined to embrace all of it.

No matter which table I sat at or which room I entered in the spinal ward, I was always the one who had the *most* physical abilities. Despite losing what I had thought was so much, every other person I encountered had lost far, far more. I was the one who could help feed the other patients when they couldn't lift their fork, who would open a packet of salt when their fingers wouldn't allow them to, or tie up shoelaces when they couldn't. I was constantly floored with gratitude for all my body allowed me to do, but suddenly the notion of loving my body for its functionality rather than its aesthetics (something that had seemed radical just a few weeks earlier) now seemed overwhelmingly obvious and even slightly naive. I was beginning to uncover something well beyond body positivity; a far deeper, yet simple truth—we are not our bodies at all.

Each of the patients I was living with were clever, kind and hilarious. They were humans filled to the brim with life. People overflowing with spirit. And yet, they couldn't feel or connect to a huge percentage of their body, and some had lost feeling to every inch of their skin besides their face. But losing their body in that way didn't take away even a fraction of who they were. It didn't make them any less valuable or worthy. Even though I had only lost sensation to half my body, I recognised this in myself as well. I couldn't feel my legs, but I could still feel *me*. This realisation, although logically obvious, loudly rattled something inside me, urging me to pay attention.

For a lot of us who aren't able-bodied, and those who are less able-bodied than me, focusing on our body and placing value on what it can or can't do is ultimately meaningless. Our bodies let us experience a lot, yes. I will forever be grateful and enchanted by everything my body allows me to enjoy. But on a deeper level, I know that it is not, and has never been, *who* I am. Losing a part of my physicality forced me to find and recognise more of me.

I looked for parts that can't be taken away. Parts that I don't need to be able to feel to *feel*.

I want people to know that even if your body as you know it was taken away from you, even if you could no longer move or feel, you would still be you. Let this knowledge flow through you the next time you find yourself getting caught up with your outer shell. The next time you start to compare or criticise or resent. The next time you feel like you need to 'fix' something about yourself. The skin and bones that hold us together have absolutely no correlation to the kind of person we are inside. It isn't what makes us kind or empathetic or funny or generous—it's the very least interesting thing about us.

13

PEOPLE

When I was well enough to venture out of my room and into the rest of the spinal ward, I was surprised to find it was filled with people who were so . . . ordinary. People who had only one month earlier been out walking their dogs, playing with their grandkids, procrastinating about hanging their washing out and making plans for a future they assumed would arrive in the same manner it always had.

There were people of all different ages, backgrounds, genders and identities filling the small ward, people who would most likely never have been in the same room if circumstances were different, but the one common thread that held everyone together was the fact that none of us imagined this place would ever be a part of our story. I don't know what I had expected to find, but something about the everydayness of the people I encountered startled me. Naively, I had preferred to assume that people in places like this knew they were going to be in here, or that they had been partaking in a dangerous activity and were aware and accepting of the risks and likelihood of injury. It's easier to digest that idea than admit the unbearable fact that any person on earth, with absolutely no exceptions given to people just because we love them, could one day end up in a spinal ward.

I was the youngest on the ward and to my surprise, I also had the only injury from an extreme sport. The lady in the bed next to me had had a tree land on her house while she was sleeping, the man a few rooms down the hall simply tripped on uneven ground, another man was shot in the back at random and someone else had fallen off a wobbly stool. It's comforting to believe that we can assess a risk and act accordingly rather than acknowledge the disconcerting reality that we can never truly prepare for or avoid the moments that will ultimately shape us, the things as seemingly simple and safe as walking down the street or going to bed. The fears that keep us up at night with worry are very rarely the things that ever eventuate; our real problems are more likely to be the ones we could never, in all our wildest fretting, have dreamt up—ones that shock the air out of your lungs on an unsuspecting Wednesday when you have soccer practice to go to that afternoon and plants to water when you get home.

~

After living in the spinal ward for a while, I noticed that the sterile corridors and consistent beeping sounds began to feel like home. And in turn, so did the people. The patients and staff became my greatest allies. It was like we were all living together in a warped reality that nobody on the outside could possibly understand.

I had imagined that the atmosphere in a spinal ward would be pretty grim. In a place where everyone was going through something cosmic, I thought the assumed mood would be one of sorrow. So the day I was allowed out of bed and got to leave the confines of my hospital curtain for the first time, I was surprised to see a patient laughing like their world was the right way up. My physio helped me into a wheelchair and pushed me around the ward to show me what would be my home for the next few months. There were so many new people and sights to absorb, but among the crowd, there he sat—a 22-year-old in his wheelchair, looking like there was nowhere he'd rather be. His name was Sam and, in an instant, he showed me that life didn't have to be gloomy just because it was expected it would be—it could be whatever you made it. I was too shy to speak to him on that first day, but I knew without a doubt that he would become an important part of my life.

As I moved throughout the ward and sea of people, there was another face that stood out to me like a light in the dark. He was probably in his fifties, he had kind eyes and he appeared to be completely paralysed from the neck down. Unlike most of the people I saw, he didn't have any family or friends around him keeping him company, he was just sitting by himself in his wheelchair, completely immersed in whatever was going through his mind.

I noticed him again when I went to my first physio appointment. I saw him across the room doing his exercises and again he was on his own. I watched him throughout my session and for the entire hour I was there, his one and only exercise appeared to be moving his neck ever so slightly to the left, then to the right, over and over. I marvelled at his commitment and willingness to repeat what would have once been such a simple and thoughtless task. I also felt a sharp pang of remorse, realising once again just how much we take for granted the gift of being able to move as we please.

The next day I saw him again, doing the same exercise over and over. Something about this man drew me to him, so I began to ask the staff questions and learned that he had been in the spinal ward for eight months before I arrived. I thought about how long and life-altering the two months since my accident had been for me—he had been experiencing this new life for half a year longer than me. While I was at home celebrating my twentieth birthday, while I was twirling on nightclub dancefloors, making lunches and getting dressed for work, while I was flying across Europe and eating baguettes under the Eiffel tower, completely unaware that this world existed—he was here, going to physio, tilting his head to the left and right, doing what needed to be done. I would come and go, be admitted and discharged, and have this whole metamorphic experience in what was only a tiny glimpse of his time in here.

Not once did I see him with a visitor. Perhaps they came when I wasn't looking; I liked to imagine people dropped in on him when I was away at wheelchair lessons or off getting scans done, but I had the sinking feeling that didn't happen. The spinal ward could be a scary and isolating place, even with a support circle surrounding you, so I couldn't begin to imagine how lonely it must have felt for him to be doing it completely on his own. Yet he still showed up to physio every single day without fail and did what he needed to do. He never stopped trying and he never stopped being there for himself. I found myself in constant awe of this man who was living a life I highly doubt he ever foresaw for himself, but treating it with the same grace he would have shown if it were a path he'd deliberately chosen.

To this day I always wish I had spoken to him. I guess I was too intimidated, too enthralled and too terrified of saying the wrong thing. I would love to know what motivated him, what thoughts ran through his head, what he used to do with the hands that now stayed resting on his lap, but most of all I would have loved to have been a friend to him. Even though I will never know his name and his face begins to fade in my memory over time, I will always remember his spirit and the silent lessons he taught me. He inspired me with his work ethic and instilled in me a gratitude deeper than I knew was possible. But mostly he taught me that a complete stranger can have an impact so profound it has the power to change your life.

~

Then there was Naomi. The hilarious, vibrant, loud-mouthed girl who fate placed in the bed opposite mine. The first time I heard her voice bellowing through the curtain separating our beds, I was terrified of her. She was a person who knew what she wanted and who wasn't afraid to ask for it. If someone disrespected her, she absolutely wasn't going to stand for it. Being as reserved and shy as I was, I was petrified of her, but even more than that, I wanted to *be* her. I admired and respected her confidence and longed to learn it for myself. The first time we ever spoke, I was coming back into my room after a physio session when she called me over to her bed. I didn't even know she knew my name and I was sure I must have done something to offend her. I gathered myself and warily wheeled towards her bed, running through a list in my head of anything annoying I could have done in the past twenty-four hours. I stared at her expectantly and she simply smiled and said, 'There's some money on the shelf, do you want to go to the vending machine down the corridor and grab some chocolate for us?' And that was it, one chocolate bar later we were inseparable.

Naomi was a year older than me and we were the only two young women on the ward. Most of the other women were in their sixties or older and the few other people in their twenties were all men.

I had never met someone who had been through quite so much so young, even well before her injury. She ended up in hospital in a way that struck me as both extremely random and frightening. She told me she had been completely fine one moment, at home doing her washing, when she bent down to pick something up from the floor and without warning or reason, she couldn't get back up. That was the last time she stood on her own two feet. The doctors told her she had suffered a stroke which made its way into her spinal cord. At only twenty years old. She lost movement in not only her legs but also her upper body and had only limited movement in her arms. She could no longer walk, feed or dress herself, or even sit up on her own. She lost a lot of her physical abilities, but what she didn't lose was her sense of humour or her resolve. She had more of those than anyone I knew.

There was a period when she was the closest person to me in the entire world. Everything I thought, said or felt, she knew. We did everything together. When my family visited and took me out for the day, she would come along too. When I was bored and couldn't sleep, I would go into her room and we would laugh as we played with the controls on her bed to see how high we could make it go. When my arms were tired from wheeling up a hill, I held onto the back of her electric wheelchair and hitched a ride while people in passing cars laughed and beeped their horns, unaware we were in our own untouchable bubble. It doesn't take long to get to know someone properly in a confined setting like that, and I came to learn that there's nothing quite as unique and permanent as the bond you share with someone who is living out their toughest moments at the same time as you. As bizarre as it may sound given the circumstances, while Naomi was around, the spinal ward began to feel like one long sleepover with a friend. We rarely spoke about the fact that we were in a hospital and I never once heard her complain about what was going on in her life. Her injury was severe and life-altering, but it was only a tiny fragment of the person she was.

When we went out to restaurants together, people would pull me aside to commend me for helping Naomi with her food. I couldn't stand it. From the outside it looked like I was doing a lot for her, but in reality she had helped me far more. I was her hands when she needed them and she was my life raft. I fed her breakfast and she taught me how to trust again.

~

One of the things I found most surprising and unexpected throughout the journey of my accident and everything since was the everlasting impact of the people I met along the way, especially of those who were only in my life for a brief period. I will never forget the man with the kind eyes or Naomi, even though I haven't seen either of them in years. Wherever they are and whatever they're doing, I hope they know I think of them often and that I am endlessly proud of them. They taught me a lot simply by being themselves, but in the years following they also taught me that people don't need to stay in your life forever in order for them to be important to you. Time goes on and people move away but just because something doesn't last a lifetime, doesn't mean their impact won't. We absorb a little piece of everyone we meet and because of that, a part of them will always be with us, even from opposite sides of the planet. Circumstances and situations influence us so much but, in my experience, nothing shapes us more than people.

It makes me wonder what impact I have on other people without knowing. Is it positive or negative? Am I adding a valuable lesson or a tough one? If we're all as interconnected as I imagine we are, I want to make sure I tread lightly and strive to leave people better than I found them. I want to leave an impact so great that a stranger might one day write a book about it without me even knowing. I want to be the Naomi in someone else's story.

14

ROCK BOTTOM

Almost a month after I arrived back in Australia, Ben sat in the chair beside my bed and I realised something was drastically wrong. It was only the second time he'd visited me—which hurt in a way I couldn't verbalise or continue to justify—and he seemed deeply uncomfortable. He looked at me, looked at the ground and told me he was going to Europe.

His voice sounded unnatural, not at all like the one that had been the soundtrack to the last three years of my life. In an already tumultuous time, I had imagined there wasn't a whole lot capable of surprising me anymore. But his words shocked the air out of my lungs.

He said he was leaving the next week to go on an adventure and travel the world. He animatedly showed me the list of places he was planning on visiting; it was like looking at my own itinerary that I never got to complete. I swallowed the lump in my throat.

Surely this was simply a fear-induced fantasy, a pipedream that he'd never follow through. Still, it felt a deeply unkind thing to say. But I was in love with him and felt compelled to support his emotional process, so I told him it was a great idea. I told him it sounded incredible. It did. I just didn't know why it had to be *now*. I didn't know why he wanted to leave while I was still in hospital.

The night before he was set to leave, we stayed at a hotel together. It was my first night away from the hospital and the nurses had helped me organise my medications and supplies so that I could be away for a few hours. We were only going down the street, somewhere close by so I could come back if there was some kind of emergency, but it felt liberating. Despite my reluctance to hear what I was almost certain Ben needed to say to me, I couldn't wait to have the space to talk without the constant stream of people that came along with life in a hospital. I wanted to get back to us and, until he told me otherwise, I held onto every last drop of hope that we would.

When we got to the hotel, I felt human again. For the first time in months I was out in the real world with no doctors, no nurses and no other patients—it was just me and Ben. I was finally lying in a bed made for two and he was right beside me, where he belonged. On paper everything was exactly as I'd hoped, I was in a moment I'd been waiting for, yet somehow I could sense the air was thick with unsaid words. He was really going, I realised; he truly meant what he'd said.

I felt the cruellest form of happiness—the type you know you can't hold onto—and I had the sinking feeling that this moment of peace had an expiry. I knew I was about to taste its bitterness.

I looked around at the blank walls of the hotel room, wondering what other relationships they'd witnessed before ours, and tried to speak. I wanted to ask him to stay; I wanted to ask him so many things, but I couldn't bring myself to form the words. I could never ask someone to stay when I knew they wanted to go. Instead, we lay there together, like we had hundreds of times before and all I could think was how much I loved him. He was so close that I could reach out my hand to hold his, but I didn't. My body and lips refused to move.

I pictured myself this time tomorrow, back in my tiny hospital bed and him on the other side of the earth. Me enclosed by blue hospital curtains and limitations, and him with the world wide-open in front of him. My heart was beating out of my chest and everything hurt. He was right there, but I couldn't reach.

I knew it was over. He hadn't said it, but I knew. I knew when he didn't fly to Switzerland the moment he heard what happened. I knew when I finally saw him and he didn't rush over to me with the urgency of someone who had almost lost the love of their life. Deep down I knew it when he told me he was leaving the country. But I needed him to say it out loud. There was no way I could cope with the confusion of an unspoken break-up. No way I could feel this amount of love and spend eternity wondering if it was requited.

After what felt like hours of silence and irrelevant small talk, I finally whispered, 'Say something,' into the void between us.

'I'm sorry,' was all he replied.

You'd think a moment of impact would hurt less if you knew it was coming, but that's not true. Nothing can ever prepare you for the pain of someone breaking your heart. It cut through me like a knife. Not only was he leaving me, but he didn't even have the guts to say it out loud or to tell me why. I was so angry I could feel heat bubbling up through my veins and suddenly I needed to get as far away from him as possible. I wanted to be the woman who knows her worth and who walks away with dignity. I wanted to get out of bed, close the door behind me and never look back. So that's precisely what I tried to do. I rolled over, pulled the sheet off me, threw myself out of bed and landed with a thump on the ground. *Of course.* My legs didn't work. Somehow, I never stopped forgetting this simple fact.

I thought I'd reached my lowest point a month earlier, but lying tangled on the carpet—unable to breathe from the realisation that something I had believed was for forever was, in fact, not—I knew with a split-second consultation with myself that this was undoubtedly the worst moment of my life. That hotel room floor was my rock bottom. Both my body and my heart were broken, I was a crying mess on the ground and I couldn't get up. I wondered if this was the type of emergency the nurses had in mind when they had told me to stay close by.

I wanted him to stay; I wanted him to tell me we were going to get through this together; I wanted him to tell me he wasn't going anywhere; but, if he wasn't going to do any of those things, at the very least, I wanted to be able to walk away.

Tears were streaming down my cheeks now. Ben tried to help me get up off the carpet, but I didn't want him to touch me. I was yelling and pushing him away, even though we both knew I needed his help. I'd never seen Ben cry before, but, when I dared to meet his eyes, I saw that he was. It was awful and I couldn't bear any of it. To have your heart broken by someone is one thing, but to then have to rely on that same person to physically pick you up from the floor because you can't do it yourself . . . well, that's just cruel. It was humiliating and even as it was happening I knew it would be something I would remember forever.

~

The next day we caught a bus in near silence from the hotel to the airport. When we arrived, I felt a distant sense of déjà vu. There we were, in the same place we'd been a couple of months earlier, but in totally different lives. I imagined taking a snapshot of this moment and showing it to our past selves. They would have no clue how we possibly ended up somewhere so familiar yet foreign in such a short amount of time. Ben looked down at me and I mustn't have been doing a good job at masking my pain, because he asked if I was okay.

Am I okay? Seriously? Not long ago we stood in this exact spot as I was leaving for the trip I'd wanted to do my entire life. I walked through those departure gates and now I'll never walk again. You're about to go through those same gates and disappear into a life of travel and adventure and possibility, while I go back to the hospital alone. You're the love of my life and you're leaving me when I need you the most. How could I possibly be okay?

'Yeah, I'm fine.'

He nodded, looked at me, and said, 'The next time I see you, I want you to be walking, okay?'

I think he was trying for hopeful and supportive, but the words felt like sandpaper on an open wound. Before I could respond, he turned around and walked through the gates. He didn't cry, he didn't look back and he didn't change his mind.

He just walked away.

I sat there motionless, staring at the empty gates and blinking with disbelief. I was half-expecting him to come running back around the corner, crying, begging for forgiveness, proclaiming he'd made a big mistake because he was young and scared. I'd helped him pack, I'd sat on the bus with him, I'd followed him through the airport, but a part of me still didn't think he'd *actually* go through with it. I couldn't breathe, and I couldn't believe it. People were moving all around me, saying teary farewells, taking photos and excitedly running through the gates on the way to their next adventure, and I was sitting in my wheelchair, frozen in time.

I have no idea how long I sat there, or how life went on from that moment, but all of a sudden I knew I was going to be sick. I wheeled myself to the nearest bathroom and threw up in the sink. I wiped my mouth and as I looked up into the mirror through tear-filled eyes, I couldn't believe the person I saw staring back at me. I didn't recognise her at all.

~

There's a science experiment with baby monkeys. The Wire Mother Experiment. Hours after birth, baby monkeys were taken from their mothers, put into a cage and given a metal surrogate. It wasn't warm, it didn't move, and it didn't speak. The metal monkey just sat there, inanimate and silent, with scraps of food inside it. However, the babies all began to form an attachment to this object because it was where they got their food. They didn't realise that the surrogate monkey was doing nothing for them at all. It was a cold, emotionless object, but it was the only thing they knew of love.

Then the scientists put something scary into the cage to see how the babies would react to fear. They all instinctively ran to the metal monkey for safety and protection. They didn't realise that it couldn't protect them and it never would. Yet they still ran to it like it was their saving grace.

The point of the experiment was to show that monkeys don't need a real living, breathing being to form an attachment. When they have nothing else, they can become attached to something as incapable of love as a cold inanimate object. Something that can't do anything for them. Something that can't love them back.

People can be like this too. We can love and love and love someone who is nothing but a metal monkey to us. We can love someone because they once gave us a scrap of food and we've clung to it like they saved our life. We can love someone who has done absolutely nothing to show that they love us in return. We too can be blinded by the fact that this person is all we know of love, despite them not giving us anything worth holding on to. We see this person as love because we don't know anything else yet.

~

Eventually I picked myself up from the literal and metaphorical bathroom floor and got on a bus to go back to the hospital. This small act of catching a bus alone in my wheelchair—in a city I didn't live in, while I was unbearably sad—was the bravest thing I had ever done. I had the feeling that if my life were a movie, this bus ride would be a pivotal moment.

I was looking out the window thinking about the unexpectedness of feeling both weak and courageous when Ben texted me. He said, 'Hopefully one day we will walk through that departure gate together.' That was the moment that sealed it for me. How dare he leave me like this and still let me think that it's not completely over between us. How dare he give me a sliver of hope to hold on to when there clearly was none. How dare he think he had any right to a future with me when he was walking away from me now. No. If he wasn't staying for this version of me, he wasn't going to get to experience the person it would make me become.

All this time I had missed him more than I missed my own legs. If someone could have granted me one wish, I would have chosen him over healing without a second thought. That wasn't okay. I promised myself that I would never let anyone have that kind of power over me again. Never again would I love someone more than I loved myself.

I used to think the accident was something that happened to both me and Ben. We had been so entwined in each other's lives for such a long time that I had just assumed my mess was his too. I thought this was going to be a heartbreaking-but-one-day-beautiful chapter in the story of our love. I didn't realise I was going to be left holding the pen without him. From the moment I got that text, I had a fire in me to write a new ending. I was determined to become something more than the reliant, fragile and small version of myself I had seen in the mirror that day. I was going to create a life that was worth reading about and I was going to become someone I was proud of. It was time to get out of the cage I was living in. It was time to stop loving a metal monkey. It was time to finally let someone love me back, and that someone was going to be me.

I deserved more than scraps of food.

15

COCOON

There's an inexplicable freedom at rock bottom that you can't possibly imagine while you're on your way down. As you're falling you are scrambling to grab on to any remnant of the world you used to know, becoming more and more frantic as it moves forever out of your reach. Perhaps one of life's greatest ironies is that it's only once you hit the ground that you can embrace the solidity of where you land. I imagine we would all be a whole lot more accepting of change and calamity if we knew this to be true.

With Ben gone, so was the last tether to my Life Before. I now understood what people meant when they described someone as becoming 'a shell of themselves': I felt like every single molecule that had made up who I was had disappeared. My partner, my job, my hobbies, my athleticism, my independence—everything I had built in the first twenty years of my life had suddenly been stripped away, leaving me raw and vulnerable.

It was then that I realised what I had been holding onto wasn't necessarily Ben himself but the person I thought I was. I wasn't simply mourning the loss of my relationship or legs or any other external factor, it was something far more personal and discombobulating—the loss of my identity.

I felt the tremendous burden of having absolutely no idea of who I was, and although it felt like being dropped into a wide, tumultuous ocean without a life raft or any sign of shore, something about it also felt liberating.

I had been desperately trying to glue the pieces of my life together exactly as they were before everything changed, and I'd been holding on so tightly to a version of me which no longer existed that I hadn't even stopped to ask myself if I actually wanted that version back. Through grief-tinted glasses, I had romanticised my old life to be an enchanted, dreamlike place where everything was perfect, life was easy and I was blissfully happy, when in reality that wasn't the case at all. If I was honest with myself, I wanted my past-self back purely because she was familiar, not because I loved or missed her. I was scared of losing everything I knew because it was *all* I knew, but looking around at the rubble of my life, my face still stained with the tears of a breakup that tore my heart out, I had to ask myself a hard question: is fear of the unknown ever a good enough reason to stay somewhere you're not happy?

The answer was obvious. I knew I needed change and truthfully I had been craving it long before it was forced onto me—I just hadn't felt strong or capable enough to make it happen. I didn't dare say it out loud, but a part of me almost felt relieved by all the brokenness. It was as though I could finally let out an exasperated sigh and say, 'Thank god everything was taken away because I never would have given it up myself.'

It's an uncomfortable thing to admit that you don't particularly like the person you are, but when I reflected on my pre-accident self, that's how I felt. I loved aspects of my life, like my family and friends and health, and certain parts of my personality, but I wasn't exactly proud of me.

I used to wake up in the morning and dread going to work, not because the workplace was a bad place to be but because I could physically feel my soul being slowly crushed in a job that didn't light me up. I refused to drive in peak hour traffic and had to pull over most days because I had panic attacks at the wheel and couldn't stop my hands shaking. I had always assumed this was because I had a fear of driving, but now I wondered if it was perhaps a fear of where I was headed. I avoided any social setting where I didn't know everyone in the room because I had a paralysing anxiety that stopped my mouth from forming words to speak to strangers. I'd thought I was simply shy but now wondered if it had less to do with nerves and more to do with the fact that I had nothing interesting to say because I had no idea who I was.

As I sat on the bus, returning from the airport, I remembered the most peculiar thing—something strange that had been happening in the months before my accident. It would happen when I pulled into the carpark at work each morning and turned off the engine. Every day like clockwork, as I prepared to get out of the car, my mind gently whispered the words: *not mine*. It was so bizarre and unexplainable that I had no choice but to ignore it, pick up my lunch and walk inside. I soon started to hear that inner voice at other times too. *This job is not mine. These people are not mine. This life is not mine.* The voice didn't quieten over time as I'd predicted and hoped. Instead, it grew louder. And more insistent. It seemed that everything I did and everywhere I went, my insides were screaming, *Don't you get it? Not! Mine!*

I was alive and getting through the days with a socially acceptable amount of enthusiasm, but was that enough? If we have no explanation for why we were put on a floating rock that by some miracle happens to be perfectly positioned in the solar system to allow for our very existence, is 'getting through' really the best we can do?

An epiphany so exhilarating it energised me came to my attention just as I neared my stop outside the hospital: there was absolutely no obligation for me to mould myself back into the person I used to be. I had assumed it was necessary, I had assumed that we are who we are and our characters are concrete, but in reality, I was at the wheel and I owed it to no one to recreate my old life. I did, however, owe it to myself to do whatever the heck I wanted with my second chance. I had an opportunity for metamorphosis and instead of this period of my life being a sob story, it was going to be my cocoon. I was going to go digging in the rubble of my life, sifting through all its elements and intricacies, then get rid of the dirt and keep the gold.

There's a poem I love by Blythe Baird that I always come back to when life doesn't go the way I had hoped. It's called 'Theories About the Universe':

I am trying to see things in perspective.

My dog wants a bite of my peanut butter
chocolate chip bagel. I know she cannot have this,
because chocolate makes dogs very sick.
My dog does not understand this.
She pouts and wraps herself around my leg
like a scarf, trying to convince me to give her
just a tiny bit. When I do not give in,
she eventually gives up and lies in the corner
under the piano, drooping and sad.
I hope the universe has my best interest in mind
like I have my dog's. When I want something
with my whole being, and the universe withholds it
from me, I hope the universe thinks to herself:

Silly girl. She thinks this is what she wants,
but she does not understand how it will hurt.

As I tucked myself into my hospital bed on the first night of my New Life Without Ben, a small smile crept across my face as I let myself wonder . . . What if my future isn't just better than before? What if it's better than I can possibly imagine?

16

NOW WHAT?

One quiet night on the ward, I was drawing by myself when I heard wheels coming around the corner. All the patients had been in bed for a few hours by this stage, so I looked up to see who it was. To my surprise, I saw a guy I had never seen before—he looked like he was my age or maybe a few years older. I watched as he wheeled himself over to the nurses station and began chatting to them. I could instantly recognise from his confidence and demeanour that this was not someone who was new to life in a wheelchair. The way he glided around the corner with ease, the way he barely had to push his wheels to make them move, the way he didn't have that flicker of fear in his eyes from a fresh trauma—I could tell he'd been doing this for a long time. I didn't know why he was here so late but I didn't often see new faces in the ward, especially ones my age, so I was excited when I saw him coming towards me.

We chatted for a while and I discovered I was right, he had been injured a couple of years beforehand and was staying in the hospital for a few nights to treat an infection. He asked if I wanted to go to the pub nextdoor for a drink and I almost laughed at the absurdity. Hospital life and real life seemed so distinctly separate that I almost forgot going to the pub with a guy your own age was a perfectly reasonable thing for people to do. I'd been there for dinner a few times with my family and Naomi, I'd even been with my wheelchair teacher, but I found myself feeling so excited at the prospect of going with this guy I'd just met. For a moment I felt less like a patient and more like a regular twenty-year-old.

We wheeled across the road together, ordered a beer (I tried to act casual about this, like alcohol was a frequent part of my hospital experience) and started talking. While we were chatting, he said something to me that I've never forgotten. We were talking about tattoos, and I told him I was thinking of getting one with the date of my accident. He asked why and I explained that it would be a nice reminder of how every day I was alive after that date was essentially extra time I got to live. A reminder not to take it for granted. I asked if he ever planned on getting any himself and he told me he would get the date he learned to walk again, if that ever happened. I asked him why and he said because it would be the day he found happiness. He told me he wouldn't be happy unless he could walk.

Those words stood out to me like a truth I hadn't yet wanted to acknowledge. Subconsciously, I guess I had felt the same. In hospital it seemed that walking was the aim of the game; it was what we were all striving towards. But hearing the words laid out so simply like that—'I won't be happy unless I can walk'—rattled me deeply. I realised how big of a gamble it was. We were placing our entire future joy on one specific and statistically unlikely thing. That was risky. It was in that moment, sitting in a pub with a stranger, holding a beer I barely took a sip from, that I realised it wasn't a risk I was willing to take. I vowed to myself then and there that I would always put my energy into healing emotionally and mentally, not just physically.

Even though I desperately wanted to walk again, I didn't want that to become the sole purpose of my life. I wanted to learn to be okay even without something I had always seen as fundamental. Even if I spent the rest of my life in a wheelchair, I didn't want that to stop me from being happy if that's how I truly felt. I knew I had to reframe walking from my number-one goal to something that would be an added bonus if it ever happened. It was something I wanted with all my heart, but was it something I needed? I didn't think so. I thought back to the state of pure contentment I had felt while freefalling, before it went wrong. I remembered how at peace I'd felt, even in the midst of falling to the ground. I'd met so many people through the spinal ward and I'd done enough research to know that there were people out there living completely fulfilling lives sitting down. If that's what my life path was going to look like, then I would learn to wheel myself down it with a smile.

That night in the pub also made me ask myself a hard question. One that it seemed absurd and ungrateful to think there could be multiple answers to. What would happen if I woke up tomorrow and was magically healed? What would happen if I suddenly got everything I wanted? The answer was clear. I would be thankful beyond words and I would make the most of my body every day. I would run a marathon, I would climb Everest, I would let scientists study my body to try and find a cure so everyone else could experience it too. But then, after all of that, I imagined there would come a day when I would stop, look around, realise the thrill had worn off and ask 'Now what?'

I still had the rest of my life to live, whether or not I was on my feet.

~

When you're so focused on one specific target, it's easy to forget that there are other areas in life that matter too, other things that still need your attention, emotion and time, irrespective of the result of your main goal. Even if I could walk, it didn't mean every other hurdle or life experience suddenly couldn't affect me anymore. I would still need to find work that fulfilled and supported me, I would still need to create meaningful relationships, I would still need to learn inner peace and confidence and individuality. Walking wasn't the magical ticket to solve everything in my life for the rest of my life, it was simply a way to get from A to B.

This wasn't the first time I'd placed the burden of my happiness on something outside of myself. I realised it's something we do all the time. We tell ourselves, I'll be happy when I learn to walk again, when I get a boyfriend, when I finish school, when

I get that job, when I get to the weekend, when I buy my dream house, when I get married, when I have kids, when I lose weight, when I make enough money to retire. I started to wonder, when does it stop? Does it ever? Is there ever an endpoint where this elusive happiness is waiting for us or do we just believe there is? Is it only once we are lying in a nursing home waiting to die that we realise our entire lives have slipped by and the feeling we were longing for never arrived? Is there ever a moment where we pause, look around, and say, 'Ah yes, everything is perfect. I can finally be happy now'?

I doubted it. If walking was the thing I was working towards in order for my life to be perfect, if it was the only key to my happiness, then why hadn't I been happy when I'd had it? I had walked before, I had experienced twenty years of walking. There was a time when I had everything I now wished for: working legs, a competent bladder and bowel, a boyfriend, no pain—and yet I wasn't happy when I'd had them. Perhaps healing my body wasn't the only thing sitting between me and the future I wanted. Perhaps happiness isn't actually dependent on these ever-changing external circumstances at all. I realised that as long as I was reaching for something outside of myself, I would continue to feel like I wasn't quite there yet, like I was always *almost* at the moment where I got to finally sit back and enjoy it all.

~

I read a quote once that said 'be where your feet are', and it resonated with me deeply. I craved that sense of being sincerely present, and I now strive to embody the words daily and be exactly where I am while I'm there. Instead of looking back and wishing things were different and instead of looking forward and hoping for things to change, I want to look around. I want to ask myself, 'What magic is hiding in the corners of my world that I can't see right now? Where do I need to squint a little harder and focus a little more strongly? What beauty is right in front of me, in this exact moment in my life, as this exact version of myself?' Because what we find there is what can fill us up. It isn't something we might one day have, it's something we really do have. It isn't placing our happiness on something in the future, it's putting it in the here and now. And that's something that can't be taken away.

I feel like we can get caught up thinking that our real life is always about to begin. When we're in an in-between phase like our twenties or moving house or healing from a breakup, it can feel like we're waiting for reality to start again. The thing is, life doesn't begin only once everything is aligned perfectly in the precise way we always envisioned it, it's happening right now. The time in between what you have and what you want isn't just a filler chapter, it's your real story. It's your life. Don't push your current happiness aside in pursuit of a future one. Don't live your life waiting for a feeling that won't fulfil or complete you. Don't let yourself spend your days constantly climbing and searching, only to get to the top of your mountain, look around and ask, 'Now what?'

17

EYES WIDE OPEN

The first day I could sit in a wheelchair for more than ten minutes without needing to faint, I felt like I was the luckiest person in the world. I'd never thought to look forward to this moment and I wouldn't even have considered it special a few months earlier, but it was now an achievement that meant everything to me. A nurse came into my room shortly afterwards and when she saw how well I was sitting she asked, 'Would you like to go to the bathroom and brush your teeth?'

You might think she was hinting that my breath smelt, but she must have been in her job long enough to know exactly how much those words would mean to me. Up until then I had been brushing my teeth in bed every day, rinsing and spitting the toothpaste into a little bowl someone put on the table in front of me. I had been doing it this way for months, so I had just accepted that this was how it would always be from now on.

The thought of brushing my teeth at a sink and being able to use my hands to scoop up the water running from the tap, then rinsing as many times as I wanted, sounded like heaven to me.

My eyes widened with excitement, and all I could stutter out was, 'Really? Can I really do that?' The nurse nodded enthusiastically and showed me where the bathroom was, and I wheeled my chair up to the sink to get ready for a moment I never thought I'd experience again. I squeezed some toothpaste onto my brush and cleaned my teeth with a smile so big you'd think I'd won the lotto. In my world, I had.

There really aren't enough words that do justice to how much a moment can mean to you. It's an appreciation that is so overpowering, it becomes a full body experience. I experienced moments like this almost every day when I was in the spinal ward but the funny thing was, it was usually over things I'd done countless times before in my life. I'd just never understood the importance and privilege of them until they'd been taken away.

It was only a few months ago that I had shivered at the thought of my life being long, and now I deeply hoped it would be. For twenty whole years I had been the cynical realist who gagged at the thought of flowers being delivered, who assumed cheerfulness was performative and fake, who thought melancholy was what made her interesting. It took a lot for me to feel the kind of genuine happiness that reaches your eyes and becomes visible to other people, but now I felt it hourly.

I remember looking at women who shone so brightly for the world and wondering what on earth they knew that I didn't. I assumed they had always been this way and that it was luck.

I had thought it was naivety that kept them light, and that they obviously hadn't experienced hardship, but I was learning that it was actually the opposite. It wasn't chance or mere luck when someone radiated brightness, it was a very deliberate and conscious act. Staying soft when the world could have made you hard, and keeping your heart open when it wants to close, are some of the bravest things humans can do.

Over the months in hospital my legs had remained unfeeling, but much to everyone's surprise they started to regain some movement. I tried not to get too excited by this. Of course, I still did to some degree (I'm not Buddha, and I was experiencing a miracle), but I was always sure to balance it out by checking in on my mental health and making sure I was finding happiness in other places too. And I was. An indescribable amount. It was as though I had been looking out at the world through a dust-covered screen my whole life and suddenly it had been removed, finally allowing me to see the world for what it really was: utterly magnificent.

The doctors would often come into my room and laugh at all the seemingly bizarre, but in my mind perfectly reasonable, things I would speak about. They were perplexed that, in the midst of my heaviest challenge, I could find so much lightness just by gazing out my window. But it was impossible not to—I was suddenly seeing life and nature in the awe-filled way it was intended. One day I was very passionately explaining to an intern how toast is far better when eaten upside down, because that way the side with the flavour directly touches your taste buds and makes the experience even more delicious and intense.

As he took a bite of my toast, his eyes lit up and he exclaimed, 'You're right!' In hindsight, he was probably just saying that to appease the super weird girl in Bed 11, but at the time it felt important. Like I'd finally managed to share a little bit of this incredible perspective I'd uncovered with someone else.

Had the world always been this way? Surely not. Surely I hadn't spent years moping around with my eyes closed while this was right here all along. I wondered if anyone else could see it too, and I soon found myself being magnetically drawn to other people who noticed all of the light and beauty as well. It felt like we were in an exclusive club and had been let in on life's biggest secret—that the world is a breathtaking miracle—while everyone else was rushing about with their eyes on the ground. I wanted to stop and shake people who passed by it all without pausing. I wanted to tilt their heads upward to the sky, point and say, 'Look, right there, can't you see this? How lucky are we to see this!'

Mostly though, I just wanted to shake my past-self. I wanted to show her all the good that surrounded her and all the things she had turned a blind eye to while waiting for something better. She'd had it all, her life was overflowing with miracles, but she had no idea. Now I knew the truth—that magic isn't only in the big moments, it's in the mundane, casual, monotonous ones like brushing your teeth at a sink.

All you have to do is open your eyes to see it.

18

ONE STEP AT A TIME

If someone asks me when I first learned to walk again, I tell them I don't know exactly. Getting back on my feet and learning to walk was one of those things that happened so gradually, with so many points in between, that I didn't even notice I had reached the final stage when I took my first unassisted steps. It wasn't as though one day I was paralysed and the next I was suddenly healed; between wheeling and walking, there was a plethora of phases to get through and master, all which felt equally monumental. There was never a specific Best Day of Your Life, one-foot-in-front-of-the-other moment where everyone in the room looks on in awe and you know you've conquered something huge.

That's the diluted, programmed response I tend to give whenever anyone asks, and although it's entirely true, it's also kind of a lie. There *is* a specific moment that comes to mind when I think of my first steps. It was the moment I truly realised that walking on my own two feet was going to be a part of my future after all. It wasn't when I first stood up or even when I first used crutches, in fact it was none of the typical stages of recovery. It happened in secret and was something my doctors never even heard about. Before that though, I had to get out of my chair and onto the physiotherapy bed.

Physio was less about learning to walk and more about maximising the muscles and movements that were available to me so I could use them to my advantage. When my legs were paralysed, it was about strengthening my abdominal muscles so I could sit up on my own and use a wheelchair and commode. Then it was about conditioning my arms and shoulders for pushing my chair and transferring myself in and out of a car or bed. The goal was always about becoming as independent as possible with whatever abilities I had.

As I began to regain some movement in my legs, we moved on to strengthening each new improvement my body was giving me. The rehab wasn't what was making my paralysed muscles work again—that was pure chance—but it was helping to make the most of the ones that were working. After weeks of gruelling and strenuous exercises lying down, eventually my legs got to a place where the physios wanted to see how I would go standing upright. The prospect of seeing the world from my old height again was exhilarating. It had only been a few months, but I knew I'd be looking out through entirely new eyes.

The first stage was learning to walk with a walking frame. The frame was strong enough to hold my entire body weight, so I held myself up using my upper body and dragged my legs below me without them actually taking any of the load.

Much like when I first learned to sit up, as soon as I stood, my blood pressure would drop rapidly and I could only manage a few seconds before my vision went white and I had to lie down.

After a few weeks of adapting to this, we moved on to the parallel bars. Here I could use my arms to balance and hold the majority of my weight while practising standing. It was exhausting beyond words. I gasped for air as I stood between the bars and realised I'd never felt the true weight of gravity before now. The strength it took to rise up against its pull was remarkable; how had I never noticed before? Within a few seconds I would feel sweaty and faint, the same way I used to after running ten kilometres, even though now I was barely moving. It was excruciating but I pushed through the pain because what the heck, I was standing!

Unfortunately, being upright meant gravity was working its magic in other ways as well, and as a result bowel accidents became a lot more frequent. I was well beyond the stage of being embarrassed by this (it only takes a few before you realise the nurses and physios don't bat an eyelid) but it was frustrating because it meant going back to my room to shower and missing out on the rest of my session which I desperately wanted to make the most of.

Once my blood pressure became more stable when I was upright, the next stage was using a treadmill. It wasn't a typical treadmill—this one had a hoist above it to hold my weight, and the physio would kneel beside me and physically move my legs for me, guiding them in the right direction. The harness of the hoist felt awfully similar to a skydiving harness and although there was nowhere to fall besides the treadmill directly below my feet, I felt like I was so high up.

It was almost like healing this much was too risky, because what if I lost it all again? And even more than that, what if all my new friends didn't even get to the walking-frame stage? Standing up in a room full of people who are watching on while they remain sitting down . . . it's soul shattering in a way that can't be explained. Everyone expects you to be overjoyed beyond measure, and you are, but how can you fully embrace it when you're breaking other people's hearts in the process? Outwardly my friends were happy for me and as they cheered me on I know they truly meant it, but the look in their eye showed me their fear as well. It said *Why am I not getting better too?* Survivor's guilt and gratitude stabbed at my chest like a double-edged sword. It felt like we'd all lived through this shared experience and related to each other in every way possible, but now due to nothing more than sheer dumb luck, I was leaving them behind.

At every new stage I reached, the physios would gently warn me not to get too excited. When I could stand, they told me I'd still always need my wheelchair to get around. When I could walk in the bars, they explained that didn't necessarily mean I'd be able to walk in the outside world. In the kindest way possible, they let me know that even though I was showing improvement, it probably wouldn't be enough for me to ever realistically live without my wheelchair.

Eventually my legs grew strong enough that I could try to

walk using only crutches to hold me up. I couldn't do it very well or for very long, but when I took my first steps like this, I was so happy that I physically couldn't contain it. It felt as though the joy inside me was so full to the brim that unless I did something to move the energy, it would burst right out of me. I don't know if I'd ever known happiness to be something so physical and all-encompassing before. In the same way I'd felt my heart tangibly break a month earlier, I now felt so tremendously full of elation that it actually hurt to be still. I felt the urge to run around or dance or jump up and down but, because I couldn't do any of those things, my wheelchair teacher Craig pulled out a punching bag and put it in front of me. As I punched the bag and released some of the most wonderful emotions I'd ever experienced, I couldn't keep the smile from spreading across my face. *I did it, I actually did it.* For the first time in my life, I didn't just do what I had to or what was expected of me, I did *more.*

Learning to walk on crutches was one of the most notable stages in my recovery because although in the beginning I was only capable of a few steps at a time, I knew that one day it could become an achievable way for me to get around outside the hospital. Twice every day, I would go to physio and practice my walking, and each time I would aim to do a couple of extra steps. It wasn't only that it was hard physically; it was a mental challenge as well. Walking had gone from something that was automatic and thoughtless to something that required every ounce of my attention.

Although my legs had regained a lot of movement, I still hadn't recovered any feeling from the waist down. This tended to surprise people, and it surprised me too, in the beginning. I had assumed that if a body part was able to move, I should be able to feel it and vice versa. I was learning that this wasn't necessarily the case; our sensory and motor nerves are separate, so it is entirely possible to have one function without the other. I knew others who had complete feeling in their body but no movement at all—every spinal cord injury is unique, with the symptoms so varied that it seems no two are the same.

My lack of feeling didn't usually bother me, but I was learning just how much our bodies rely on the sensation in our legs for balance. Without it, it's very hard to know where your legs are in relation to the rest of your body and whether or not they are moving or touching the ground. Instead of walking being an instinctive reflex, it was now a deliberate thought process—*Okay right foot up, bring it forward, place it down, look at the ground to make sure it's touching, steady yourself, left foot up.* My brain was working overtime trying to remember all the cues I'd been taught, while simultaneously pushing myself to keep going when fatigue begged me to sit back down.

~

For months I'd been keeping my improvements a secret from Jemma. Although we spoke every day on the phone, I hadn't seen her since Switzerland and I'd been dreaming up a plan to surprise her with my healing when she got back home. The day finally arrived and when I knew she was on her way to the hospital, my mum and physios helped me execute my plan. I had given

Jemma directions to meet me on the ward, where I told her I was in my bed resting, but really I was waiting in my wheelchair by the door. When I knew she was only a moment away, my physio helped me up onto my crutches and my mum got out her camera. I took a few wobbly steps forward until I was out in the hall where I knew Jemma would be able to see me, and then I looked up. There she was. Running toward me with a huge smile on her face. Just like I'd pictured it as I lay on the ground in Switzerland all those months ago. Tears were flowing down her face and she ran into me with so much force I nearly fell over. As we stood there hugging and holding each other up in the hospital hallway, I knew this was all I needed. Even if I never got any better than this, being able to stand up and hug someone that meant the world to me was one of the greatest gifts I'd ever been given.

~

A few nights before I was set to be discharged, I was lying in bed when one of the best moments of my life occurred without any warning. It will always live on in my memory as the time I first learned to walk again—the moment I've never told anyone about. I was watching a movie on my laptop when I had the sudden and overwhelming urge for a snack. My room was overflowing with chocolates and other treats from visitors who had come to see me over the last few months and although it was an absolute dream, it was also not ideal. The nutritionist was constantly warning me that I had to be careful about what I ate now that I couldn't exercise or move as easily as I used to, because it would be a lot more difficult for me to maintain a healthy weight. Because of this, my mum had put everything on a table and moved it to the other side of the room so I couldn't sit in bed and mindlessly eat junk while I watched movies at night. At the time I had thought it was unnecessary (and, quite frankly, rude), but as it turns out, she had a pretty valid point. Because as I sat in my bed that night, that's exactly what I wanted to do. Naomi and all of the other patients had been asleep for hours and although the nurses would come to my room if I pressed the buzzer, it felt unreasonably late and also pretty non-essential to ask them to come in purely to pass me a snack. So, I did what any self-respecting, ravenous, twenty-year-old would do: I made it my mission to find a way to the chocolate.

I looked down at my wheelchair beside my bed. This was the obvious course of action, but my room was so small that I wouldn't have been able to fit the chair past the bed to get to the other side where the table was. I looked around for my crutches, but I was still in the early days of using them and I realised I must have left them in the physio rooms. The only other option was for me to stand up on my own two feet and use the bed and furniture to balance and hold me up. I took one final look around. Everything looked close enough together for me to hold onto and I assumed it would all be strong enough for me to lean the majority of my weight against. I lowered my bed so my feet could touch the floor and pushed myself upright. I leaned my weight onto the bed and used it as a crutch as I shuffled my feet and hands along to the edge. Next, I grabbed on to the drawers by the head of the bed and took tiny, wobbly steps forward, slowly creeping closer and closer to the tantalising table. When I got as far as the drawers would let me, I realised I'd made a huge mistake. The table was further away than I had anticipated and there was no way I could reach over and hold onto it from where I was. Also, alarmingly, the drawers I was leaning on weren't anywhere near as strong as I'd expected, so I couldn't put too much weight on them and my legs were starting to shake under me. I'd used so much energy getting here that I didn't even know if I had enough to make it back to my bed, all I knew was that I urgently needed to grab onto something that I could lean against properly. I was about to call out to the nurses for help, when out of nowhere, I heard a tiny, matter-of-fact voice within me ask, *What if you just let go and take a step forward?*

Could I? In physio I still felt so unstable on my feet that I hadn't even tried to walk without holding onto anything because it was obvious I wasn't there yet. But what was the worst that could happen? I'd fall a few feet? The voice spoke again: *So what? You've fallen from higher and survived.* In a split second, before I could change my mind, I let go of the drawers, picked up one foot and put it in front of the other. Then I lifted the other foot and put that one down too. I reached forward to grab the table and quickly leaned against it as I caught my breath. I was panting and dripping with sweat but as I reached for the chocolate, pride and elation flooded my veins. I couldn't believe it. I took two steps. I walked. With nothing holding me up but my own legs and my new strength.

Told ya, the voice said.

Learning to walk again after being told you never will is a story not many get to tell. It's a privilege that blows my mind daily, one I can't think about for too long without the risk of crying, but I never want it to be the takeaway from my journey. The way I see it, it was nothing but pure, beautiful and magical luck. Although I worked incredibly hard and am eternally proud of my determination and grit, I'm aware it was also predominantly out of my control. Perhaps the greater lesson here is something far more simplistic—if you have a hunger inside you, follow it. That sounds like a metaphor but it's not. Your love for chocolate could one day be the thing changes your life.

19

ADAPTABILITY

The first time I learned how I would have to go to the bathroom for the rest of my life, I nearly fainted. It was the most inconceivable, unimaginable and foreign thing I had ever been told and there wasn't an ounce of me that wanted to attempt it. Plus, it sounded so difficult that I doubted I was physically capable of it.

I already knew how catheters worked. I had spent the past few months with one permanently draining my bladder. I had a bag attached to my leg that the urine drained into and all I had to do was empty the bag into the toilet every few hours. To be honest, I didn't mind it at all. It was nice not having to go to the bathroom all the time and it was easy enough to empty. As for my bowels, a nurse was still giving me a daily enema and manual evacuation over the toilet. By now I was so used to it that I forgot there was ever a time I found it uncomfortable. I reminded myself that this was simply the nurses' job, they did it all the time, and to them it wasn't awkward, it was just a process that needed to be done.

I assumed this was how it would always be. I imagined I would have a nurse come to my house every morning who would help me to enema and shower and then leave for the day, and we would continue that routine for the rest of my life. That was until I had a meeting called by my medical team to discuss a plan for my future after hospital. This took me by surprise because I honestly hadn't thought about it. Up until that moment, my life was the next five minutes ahead of me and it was impossible to imagine anything beyond that, let alone a whole life *after* hospital.

The doctors decided I would need to learn how to manage my bladder and bowel routine on my own before I could be discharged, so that I was able to be independent at home. This meant learning how to evacuate my bowels myself, as well as replacing my leg bag with something called an 'intermittent catheter'. The independence sounded like a dream, but I was scared.

A few days later, an incontinence nurse walked into my room and said she was here to teach me. She was the kind of person who makes you feel instantly comfortable and safe because she is so at ease with herself. She was warm and eccentric and you could tell she didn't possess a shred of awkward energy. She was perfect for the job. She explained that an intermittent catheter was something you used only once to drain your bladder and then threw away, rather than having to keep the indwelling catheter (leg bag) at all times. It would give me more independence and I wouldn't have to keep the bag strapped to me anymore. She explained that while I was learning, I would insert the catheter lying down on the bed, but eventually I would be able to do it from my wheelchair straight into a toilet.

She instructed me to take off my pants and lie down on the bed with my legs spread. She attached a small mirror to my thigh so I could see a part of myself I've never had to look at so closely before. She then handed me something which looked like a thick plastic straw and told me to look in the mirror, find my urethra, put the straw inside, and drain the urine into a plastic container. I was equal parts horrified and confused. The hole was so tiny and the straw was so thick. It seemed absurd and unnatural. I felt a flicker of gratitude for not being able to feel down there because I imagined this would hurt. The nurse stayed with me for over an hour while I tried and failed and tried and failed a hundred times more. It was the most difficult thing I had ever attempted to do.

By this stage in my recovery, I'd already been through some pretty weird and uncomfortable situations. I'd learned to accept that multiple people would see me naked every time I showered, that nurses would have to help me go to the toilet and wipe me afterwards, and most days I felt as though my body had become more of a medical object than the home I lived inside. But this catheter experience was a whole new level. Not because of how bizarre it was having myself and a stranger examine and touch my private parts for a very extended period of time, but because I realised with a shattering and sudden clarity that this was how I was going to have to pee for the *rest. of. my. life.*

It seemed incomprehensible. It was nearly impossible to do it just once, so how on earth was I going to do it twelve times a day? It was so challenging even with a mirror guiding me, so how could I possibly do it from my wheelchair or sitting on a toilet? Was I going to have to find a bed, lie down, strap a mirror to my thigh, fumble for hours and drain my bladder into a plastic container every single hour for the rest of my life? How would there even be a 'rest of my life', when it seemed it would all be spent peeing? There was absolutely no way I could do it.

The nurse must have sensed my fear because she put her hand on my shoulder, looked me in the eye and said, 'Emma, you would be amazed at what you can adapt to.' I didn't believe her. Not even the slightest part of me believed that this is something I would ever adjust to. How could something so bizarre and difficult ever become normal? How could something so time and energy consuming ever become routine? I didn't want it to. I wanted to sit on a toilet and tell my bladder to pee and then stand back up and get on with my life without a second thought. I didn't want this.

After she left, I lay shaking on the bed, eyes wide with shock and cried myself to sleep. The future not only seemed bleak but utterly insurmountable.

~

To my surprise, life went on as it always tends to do, and now many years have passed. This morning I stood up from my bed, walked to the bathroom, picked up a catheter, drained my bladder into the toilet in a few seconds, went back to bed and thought nothing of it. It's as easy as brushing my teeth and as familiar as something I've been doing my entire life. The nurse was right. Of course she was, she'd seen it time and time again. Adaptability is something humans do incredibly well and we do it all the time. We adapt and we make 'impossible' situations a part of our everyday.

Sometimes life throws us a challenge we never saw coming. There are moments we are brought to our knees with the insufferable prospect of having to carry on with a new reality we didn't necessarily ask for. Moments the nurse hands you a bunch of catheters and says, 'Now go out into the world, you got this,' while you swallow the lump in your throat and blink in disbelief. Regardless of how unpredictable these moments are, one thing is for certain. We are capable of adapting to them. We might think we can't live with or without something, but we can. We might think something is impossible to ever come to terms with, but we will. And we might think something will break us, but, time and time again, it won't.

You will be amazed at what you can adapt to.

20

ENTERING THE UNKNOWN

I've always found it strange how a date can be nothing but a blank square on a calendar that slips by unnoticed for years, until one day we give it meaning and it becomes a date we remember. It's even stranger how that meaning can change with time. I woke up on what would have been mine and Ben's anniversary and realised that meaning had been superseded. It had now become the day I was being discharged from hospital and going home. It was time to leave the world I had known for the past few months and go back to the 'real' world to live out the rest of my life. The nurses were proud of me, the other patients were jealous and my family was thrilled, but there was one problem . . . I didn't want to leave.

Hospital felt safe. In the spinal ward, everything catered

to wheelchairs. The tables were the perfect height so we could effortlessly wheel up to them and fit our legs underneath. The bathrooms were modified and spacious enough that there was plenty of room to move around on a commode. The beds could rise and lower to help us easily transfer on and off them. The floors were perfectly smooth with no stairs or too-thin-to-navigate hallways. The nurses were only ever a button away if we needed absolutely anything at all. Every tiny detail had been carefully constructed to create the most accessible and comfortable environment for us as we adjusted to life on wheels. It made transitioning into our new realities far less scary, but it also meant we had been cushioned from how the rest of the world is built—for people on two legs. Over the past few weeks, I had begun venturing out of the hospital more frequently (as much as I could without missing any physio sessions) but I always looked forward to returning to the safe haven of the spinal ward after only a matter of hours. I didn't know what life in this body was going to be like beyond these walls full time, and I knew it would be easier to stay.

That wasn't my main concern though. I knew I would learn to adjust and adapt; what scared me most was something deeper. I didn't want to go home because I was terrified that the sense of purpose I had found and fostered in hospital would leave the moment I did. I was finally feeling so strong and determined—and oddly enough given the circumstances—the happiest I had been since I was a child. Every day, people I encountered (even strangers who passed me on the street) would tell me I radiated sunshine and joy, and that's exactly how I felt. Waking up each morning with the pure goal of healing my mind and body kept me inspired, enthusiastic and passionate. The feeling I used to have before my accident, the one that told me my soul was being crushed by living a life that was not mine and not meant for me, was completely gone because in here I felt purposeful. I was sad to be leaving the place that had forced me to bloom, because I didn't want to wilt back into the person I used to be. I couldn't tell if the environment was what was making me grow, or if it was all me, and I was scared to find out.

With tears in my eyes, I hugged goodbye to Naomi and all my friends, then I thanked each person who had played a part in my recovery. I took a final look at my shoebox room, which had witnessed so many emotions and milestones over the months, and hobbled my way out of the ward on my crutches. A feeling of profound gratitude washed over me as I realised I was walking out the very doors I was wheeled through back when I couldn't even sit up. I knew very few others ever got the chance to do the same and the unlikeliness of those odds was overwhelming. I felt lucky beyond belief and vowed to not waste the opportunity I was given. I wanted to make the most of my legs and use them to do everything I could, not only for me but for all my friends who couldn't. Even though I was leaving, I knew a part of me would forever remain with the people in here. Life would shift and move on, but my love and commitment to them never could.

My mum drove me the three and a half hours home to Canberra, and as our hometown came into view, I was surprised at how different everything seemed. It looked exactly the same of course, as it had only been a few months, but my eyes weren't used to it. I hadn't been home since the day I left for my trip nearly four months ago, and as we approached our street, I grew more and more nervous. I knew our house would be there, looking the same way it always had, while I was entirely different. I would be going back to a life that looked like mine, lying in the sheets I'd put on my bed, eating ice-cream from the freezer I'd bought months earlier, while nothing was the same at all. I no longer had a job to go to in the mornings, or the ability to go for a run after work, or the capacity to be left home alone to look after myself, or a person to keep me company and lie next to each night. It felt as though I was about to superimpose myself onto a world that was no longer there.

It reminded me of when I used to drive to my old childhood home and sit in the driveway, years after we'd moved. It was the house we had before my parents separated and the place I lived when I was young enough to believe the world could never hurt people and being a kid was something permanent. I would look at the house and try to imagine myself getting out of the car and walking up to the front door, twisting the handle and tiptoeing inside, and hearing the sound of every voice I knew and the warm smell of dinner bubbling on the stove. I imagined everything was as it always had been, frozen in time, just on the other side of the door. As I sat in my car looking at the brick walls, knowing I would never be on the inside of them again, I realised with an aching jolt how strange it is that we can return to a place but never to a feeling. We can go back to a house but never a moment in time.

We arrived home in the early evening and when I walked

inside, Jemma and my sisters were waiting for me with a big sign saying 'Welcome Home!' We spent the night chatting, eating food that wasn't cooked in a hospital kitchen, and feeling so blissfully happy to be together again. It felt odd not having a bedtime curfew or hearing the never-ending sound of machines beeping, but I felt a freedom I had almost forgotten. I was reminded of what life used to be like; an opportunity for endless possibilities and adventures, with no obligation to be anywhere or do anything I didn't choose myself. Life was something I didn't need a timetable for, because I could let it unfold however I liked. I just hadn't known how special that was at the time.

I had felt so much older than I really was in the past few months and forgot the autonomy and excitement that comes with youth. As we stayed up later than I had in weeks, and laughed without the fear of waking anyone else up, I wondered how there was ever a time I could have taken this for granted.

The next day a news reporter came to my house to interview Jemma and me. They wanted to do a story on the accident and our friendship, and when the station had reached out to us a few weeks earlier, it was such a bizarre concept that we didn't know what to say, so we agreed out of pure astonishment. We were both so nervous but the journalist told us not to worry and assured us that we could record it as many times as we needed. Jemma has always been incredibly well spoken and confident so she went first and of course answered every question eloquently. When it was finally my time to speak, I was shaking with nerves. For as long as I could remember I'd had a phobia of public speaking. It was so strong and debilitating that I had somehow managed to avoid giving any kind of oral presentation throughout the whole of high school without my teachers even realising. I had also never particularly liked being on camera and I definitely never imagined I would be sitting in front of one quite this large with an audience quite so big, but when I started to speak, something strange happened. To my complete shock and disbelief, I found I was somewhat enjoying it. Despite my trembling voice, I felt confident in what I was saying and sure of myself. As I spoke, I found I had so much more to share than I'd realised and when the interview ended, I was left wanting more.

~

As the days went on, I knew I was right to have assumed life in hospital would be easier. I missed the ease of the spinal ward and the camaraderie of the other patients who all silently understood. Where I used to walk through this same house without a moment's thought, it now took ten minutes to get from one room to the next. I would sit on the chair in the shower as the water washed over me and wonder how on earth I used to reach for the showerhead so effortlessly. I kept coming up against obstacles I wasn't quite sure how I would overcome, but time and time again, I was forced to find a way.

I'd felt the same way about coming back from Switzerland in the beginning, I realised. I had resisted and resented the change until I eventually let go, stopped living in the past and accepted the reality in front of me (which I grew to love even more). I imagined this feeling wasn't unique to me or even to hospitals, and that life is a series of chapters we need to move through, but we're also scared to turn each new page. We get comfortable where we are, hold on too tightly until we are forced to let go, then warily learn to walk in our new world. Until one day we look around and realise we're actually dancing in it. Then that becomes our new comfort zone, and when the next challenge arises, the cycle repeats. I'd faced the truth of this countless times in my life but was only now seeing the pattern more clearly.

It struck me that even though staying would have been easier, sometimes the thing that's the most difficult to do and the thing that's best for us are the very same thing.

21
HEALING

Life after hospital felt like being handed the keys to a new car, getting into the driver's seat and waving goodbye to the salesman, only to remember you have no idea how to drive. I kept looking around waiting for someone to pass me the handbook and tell me what to do next. I quickly realised no one was coming because there was no guide and no right way to heal emotionally. You simply do what you can and hope it works.

For me, my healing looked like this: I sat in the sunlight even when it was cold. I turned off the TV and read poetry about overcoming. I filled the pages of notepads with patterns drawn straight from my mind. I stayed in at night and didn't feel bad about it. I did my exercises and practised walking on my own two feet. I spent time with the people who had been there for me and distanced myself from those who hadn't. I went to my appointments and made it my mission to be the patient they most looked forward to treating. I became so fiercely independent that my broken heart began to mend. I buried my bare feet in the grass even though I couldn't feel it. I made sure I never missed a sunset even if it was only through a doctor's office window. I ventured out of my house bit by bit, until eventually the world outside no longer looked terrifying—it looked like something I wanted to be a part of.

I felt as though I was living that scene in a movie where sentimental music plays over a montage of the main character slowly but surely piecing their life back together. I could feel myself rebuilding, but I also got the sense that those scenes aren't entirely accurate and that they're missing a very crucial component. In between all the moments of triumph and strength, there is a whole lot of time that's spent not triumphing and not feeling strong. From what I could tell, recovery mainly looked like lying down, feeling exhausted and wondering how on earth you were going to get up again. No one prepares you for that. We're made to believe that healing in any form is something beautiful and all-inspiring. It's romanticised to the point where it looks like something we'd willingly choose to go through for the thrill of it. Truthfully though, a lot of the time it just looks like boredom.

Although I was out of hospital, I still very much felt like an in-patient who was recharging in the cocoon before emerging into the real world again. Whether it was on my own two feet or in my wheelchair, the idea that one day I might become an active member of society again was still such a far-fetched novelty. If someone had told me that one day there would come a time when I'd stroll through a Sunday market for no other purpose

Right: Feeling excited as I prepare to take the leap.

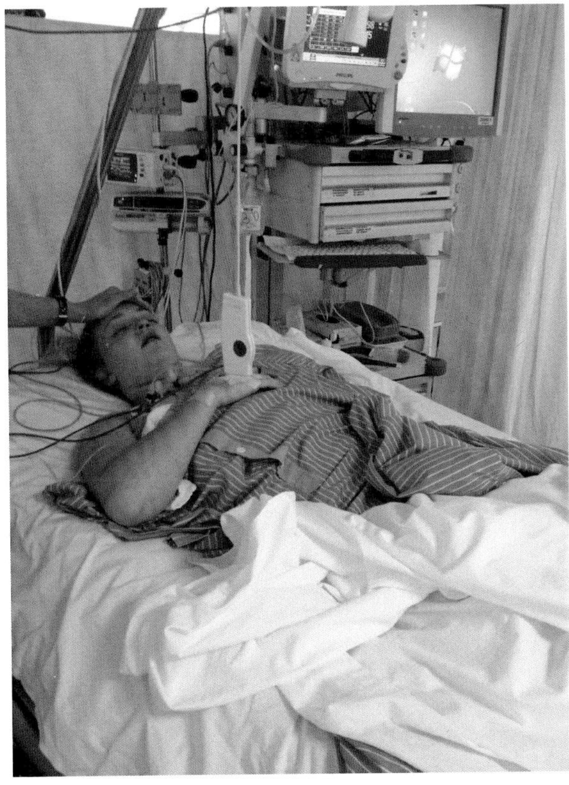

Left: The hardest days. My mum's hand on me after my second surgery.

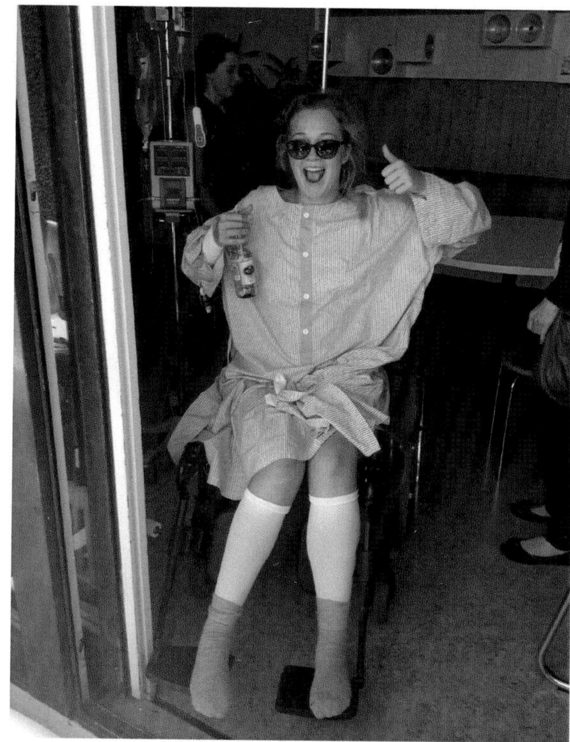

Left: Sitting in a wheelchair for the first time (I only lasted 30 seconds before fainting).

Below left: Catching a bus from the spinal ward in my chair.

Below Right: Tara and Mark carrying me across the sand so I could put my feet in the ocean.

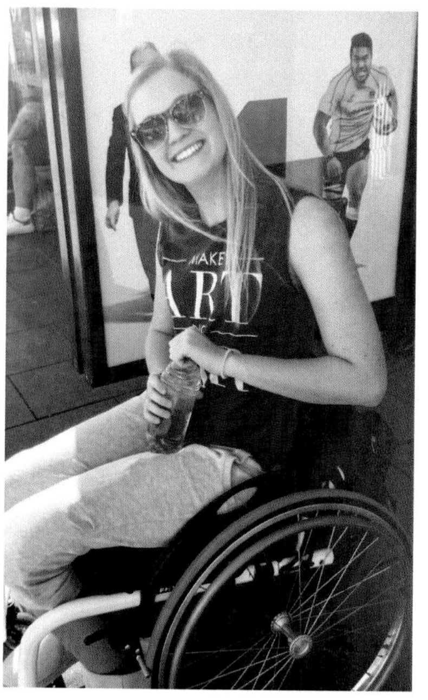

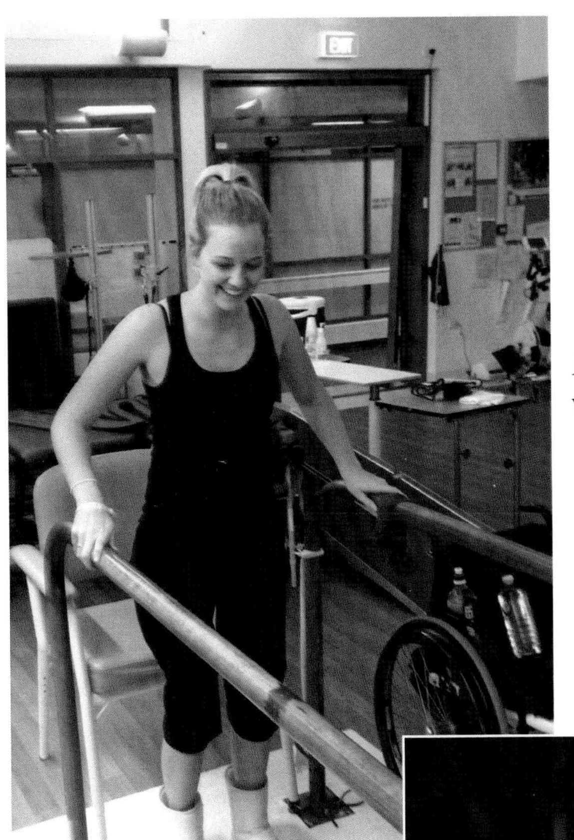

Left: Learning to balance with the parallel bars.

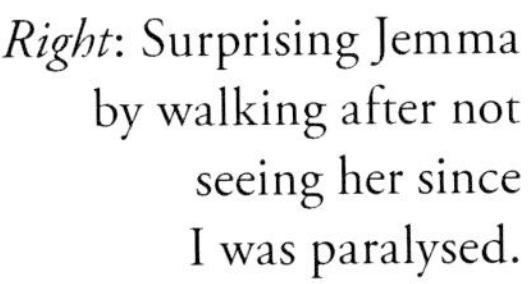

Right: Surprising Jemma by walking after not seeing her since I was paralysed.

Above: Our little light. Hayley, Layla and me.

Left: Making the most of my legs and taking them places I never dreamed possible.

A dream come true. Drawing my mural at Bondi Beach.

Swimming in an ocean pool while I was in hospital, then in Croatia five years later.

Left: Back in Switzerland. Finally walking the trail, five years on. If you can, you must.

Right: Smiling while rewriting a memory in the same helicopter that changed my life.

The ground where I fell, the ground where I stood.

Me and Sam nine years on from the accidents that changed our lives. Things got better.

than to pick up fresh flowers and sip on a hot chocolate, I would have laughed in their face. It still seemed so out of reach. I knew it was all just a part of the process though and I held tight to the belief that one day I'd have energy not only for healing, but for life as well.

~

After what I'd been through, I had become much more sensitive to my surrounding environment, which changed and shaped the way I interacted with the world. I'd learned empathy in a way I had never known and it seeped into all areas of my life. When I left hospital, I unintentionally stopped eating meat (something I had never even considered before) because subconsciously I didn't want to contribute to any more suffering. I had compassion for the metaphorical bad guy, because I understood that the only reason he was hurting people was because he himself was hurt. I felt real, tangible pain when I read the news, because for the first time I could begin to imagine how the devastation might feel. Of course, I couldn't relate to every horror that was occurring throughout the world, but I could begin to understand the sharpness of the hurt. I could relate to the sudden shock and disbelief that comes when the entire world as you knew it that morning no longer exists when you go to bed that very same night. I wasn't detached or numb to the stories like I used to be. I couldn't simply watch and move on the moment they left the screen, because I knew what it was like to be the name mentioned in a passing ten second segment. I understood that although to most viewers it's just letters and pictures on a page or screen, to someone with a heartbeat just like mine, it is their real life.

As time went on, I began to feel the disparity of the world I was in and the one from which I came. Coming home and finding lightness after living in the dark for so long seems as though it would be nothing short of wonderful. It is, but the light doesn't look the same as it once did. Even though I was now out of the thick of the smoke, I couldn't simply forget the memory of what I had found in the flames. How could I meticulously pick out a shirt to wear to dinner as though it mattered, when there were others who had no home to go to? How could I clean my teeth before bed knowing at that same moment there were people crying out in pain? How could I do all of the trivial, unimportant, insignificant yet necessary things in this light-filled world, when I knew there were still people in the dark, begging for a lantern?

It's hard to believe so much happiness and grief can exist at the same time, but my experience in hospital showed me that truth. Someone can be laughing until their cheeks hurt in the same hour somebody else is watching their loved one be buried. Kids can be frolicking on playgrounds in one corner of the earth, while in another a child is sitting in a doctor's office getting a diagnosis eighty years before their time. Love, heartbreak, excitement, dread, pride and disappointment can all exist on the very same day, at the very same time.

~

As the months passed, that spark I had found in the hospital was slowly starting to fade. The fears I'd had about leaving were all coming true. I hadn't even noticed at first because I was getting through each day with far more gratitude than I'd ever felt before, but it eventually dawned on me that something was missing. I couldn't put my finger on what it was because it had nothing to do with my disability or challenges, and it wasn't even that I felt sad exactly. It was something deeper that I couldn't put into words. Almost as if that profound and piercing aliveness I had experienced in hospital was fading into apathy. Before my accident I probably would have settled for apathy over sadness, but now that I'd experienced what it meant to properly *feel*, I wanted it back.

On one particularly low day, when I'd had yet another bowel accident and was in the shower washing myself off, I heard my phone ping. I half-heartedly checked it when I got out, assuming it would be some kind of appointment reminder, but when I saw the words light up in front of me, I had to do a double take.

Kayla Itsines liked your post.

Kayla is a personal trainer who has built a large following on social media sharing her workouts. I came across her page when I first downloaded Instagram the year before and, although I was perplexed by the concept of 'following' people we don't know, I was drawn to her and had been grateful for finding her ever since. When I was in hospital, I saw a post she had put up about one of her clients who was living with chronic health issues but was still training to the best of her abilities. Kayla explained that the benefits of exercise were about so much more than just altering the outer appearance of our bodies and that having the ability to move should be treated as a privilege, not a punishment. As I read her words from my hospital bed, paralysed and longing for movement, I could completely relate. I felt seen.

When I was in hospital, I'd started to write about what I was going through. I would write about whatever was on my mind and soon found that even if I had no idea what I was feeling before I began, by the time I lifted my pen off the paper, my feelings were clearer, as was my mind. I then started posting these snippets and musings, along with my drawings, to my Instagram page. I wanted future-me to have something to look back on so I could reflect on what I went through. I also wanted to share the truth of what living with a disability and through life-altering scenarios looked like in reality.

The photo she had 'liked' was something I'd drawn earlier that day. I had no idea how she came across it but I was filled with the warmth that comes from someone you admire acknowledging your existence. My phone pinged again. Kayla had left a comment. This time it was on a post where I had written a caption about perspective and how much I had gained through my experiences.

'You are amazing,' she wrote.

There's nothing quite like someone you look up to giving you the kind of compliment that could mean they look up to you too. I went to bed that night filled with gratitude that she had taken time out of her day purely to say something kind to me. It was only words on a screen, but when you're in the depths of a challenge and clinging to the little things, it felt like so much more.

I woke up the next morning to over 1000 people following my Instagram page. There had been less than a hundred people the day before and I had known every single one of them. It turned out that Kayla's many followers could see any comments she made and so other people had found my page as well. I googled an image of what a thousand people looks like and it blew my mind. Below each of my posts were new comments thanking me for sharing my story and for showing my strength. People were telling me about the things they were going through in their own lives and explaining that seeing my words had helped them feel less alone. *What?* I hadn't even realised I was 'sharing my story', I had simply been posting updates for my friends and family so they could see how I was doing. I had been writing captions under my photos that were straight from my diary and my heart, so that I could look back on them one day to remember how I felt. I didn't think anyone else would ever read them, let alone be impacted if they did.

Something about these messages touched me so deeply that I can still remember the names of the very first people who left comments. My mind flashed back to being in Switzerland where I would lie awake at night googling 'people who have had a spinal cord injury' and 'what to do when you've lost your identity'. Pages of results came up but they were clinical words on medical pages; they didn't mean anything to me. I had hoped to connect with real life people and see what their lives were like to help me feel less isolated. But I couldn't find anyone I related to, so after leaving the friends I'd made in the spinal ward, I felt entirely alone on my journey. As I read the comments from strangers around the world, who were all going through their own version of hardship, I was reminded of a quote I'd read many times before: 'Be the person you needed when you were younger.'

Could I? Could I be that person I had spent hours scouring the internet to find? Could I be the lantern for someone still in the dark?

Suddenly I felt it again. A spark. Something in the back of my mind whispering, *You're going in the right direction*. I was alight with passion and although I had no idea where it was going to lead me, the spark told me to follow it. Purpose—that was what I'd been missing.

I picked up my phone and wrote out all the things I'd longed to hear months earlier. I didn't know who would read them, but I hoped the words might somehow find their way through the ether and into the eyes of whoever needed them most. As I typed, a smile spread across my face and I realised something profound—I had something to look forward to again. And that was everything.

22

SECRETS

My whole life, I have kept a secret. It's something only a handful of people have ever known about me (until now, I guess), and before my spinal cord injury it completely ruled my world. It is that I wet the bed my entire life. Yes, even before my disability. Yes, even before I had any 'reason' to be incontinent. Every morning since my earliest memory, I have woken up to a saturated bed and soaked pyjamas.

It has always been my deepest secret and for me, it was debilitating. From the moment I was old enough to know something was 'wrong' with me, I felt disgusting. I had tried everything to make it go away; countless medications, pelvic floor training, hypnosis and any other therapy that was available to me. Absolutely nothing worked. I was petrified to go to sleepovers, school camps were filled with anxiety, and the excitement of a holiday was always outweighed by dread. Even at twenty years old while planning the trip of a lifetime to Europe, my secret kept me up at night crying and stressing and wanting to cancel. Not even Jemma knew, and she had been my best friend since I was four years old.

This secret consumed me. In so many areas of my life it prevented me from being present and enjoying the moment I was in. I lived in absolute terror that someone would find out and the anxiety from that crippled me. I can vividly remember being ten years old, crying hysterically and begging my mum not to make me go to a sleepover party. I remember being thirteen at a friend's house and wearing a nappy to bed, and when she accidentally brushed past me I was nauseous at the thought she might have felt it through my pyjamas. I remember being eighteen and telling my boyfriend I wanted to explain the reason why I never stayed at his house, and him replying, 'I promise you can tell me whatever it is, how bad can it be? It's not like you wet the bed or something weird like that.'

Well, now not only do I wet the bed, I wet everything. All day, every day.

It went from being a problem that only affected me at night to something that affects me twenty-four hours a day, every single day. You'd think it would be worse. You'd expect the anxiety would have multiplied tenfold. You'd imagine the fear would now be seeping into every little thing I did and contorting me into a constant hysterical mess begging my mum not to make me leave the house. But in reality, it's the complete opposite. It doesn't hold any power over me.

Yes, it's sometimes frustrating in the sense that I now have to use supplies to go to the bathroom, that I need to find a toilet every waking hour and have to shower and change my clothes a whole lot more than I'd like, but it doesn't *consume* me. In fact, incontinence doesn't make me anxious at all anymore.

There's only one reason for this gigantic and life-altering shift, and the secret is simple—I no longer keep it a secret.

When I left the hospital and got home to the real world, my bladder was the hardest thing for me to come to terms with. I was having accidents multiple times a day and had to change clothes constantly. Tests from urologists showed that my bladder could only hold 100mls, so any time it exceeded this, it came flooding out without warning, and I had no ability to stop it. The urge that warns us when our bladder is full no longer worked for me, so I was trying to master the guessing game of mentally measuring how much liquid I had consumed and when I would next need to go. As well as this, I was still getting the hang of catheters, so sometimes it would take me half an hour just to go to the bathroom.

In those early days, I felt the familiar sense of dread and anxiety seeping in. Besides those closest to me, no one knew about my new bathroom reality. I felt like I was ten years old again, only this time it wasn't just sleepovers I was insecure about, it was anything at all outside of my house. I rejected any invitation that came my way because I was petrified of being found out. I avoided letting anyone in and I eventually became a hermit.

As time went by, the weight of the reality that this problem wasn't going away began to dawn on me, and I realised that if I was going to get upset or angry *every* time I had an accident, it would mean that I would be upset or angry *every* day of my life. For the rest of my life.

That's when it hit me, something so obvious yet simultaneously mind-boggling—*I survived a skydiving accident*. Which also translates to: I survived the impossible. I didn't know how or why I was granted such an unexplainable miracle, but it certainly wasn't to live a miserable life in fear and isolation. I knew I owed myself more than that.

I had experienced so many huge shifts in perspective since my accident that, when I took a moment to zoom out, I couldn't believe I was still allowing something so comparatively minor to dictate my emotions. I no longer had the energy to hide something that, in the scheme of everything I'd been through, didn't matter at all.

In a moment of perfect clarity, I reminded myself of the truth: this was most likely a lifelong situation, there was nothing I could do to change it right now and if I was capable of preventing accidents I obviously would. This clear thinking enabled me to see how pointless my whole charade had been. I wasn't actively choosing to sit in my own urine every day, so why on earth should anyone judge me for it? Why would anyone laugh at or tease a misfortune that was completely beyond my control? I decided to take a chance and imagine they wouldn't.

I began to tell people. Gently and vaguely at first, but as I quickly gained confidence, I learned to bare it all. Nothing, and I can't emphasise that enough, has ever been more liberating and freeing than the decision to completely own every element of my disability, including my bladder issues. The moment I decided to stop hiding it from the world and truly let people into my life was the moment I felt complete freedom.

I realised that no one can hold something against you if you don't hold it against yourself. Nothing has any power over you unless you give it that power. I also realised that my hunch was right: no one cared. At all. People care about kindness and humour and loyalty, they don't care about the insignificant thing you're embarrassed about. I had been letting something that only made up the tiniest fraction of who I was rule the whole, when in reality I had so much more to offer.

Flash-forward to today and not only do I not mind people knowing, but it's a topic that is as normal, accepted and mundane as what I had for breakfast. Not only do I not care if anyone finds out, I actively tell people. In real life, online, with strangers I meet in cafes, on tinder dates and now in this book. I laugh about it daily, I leave a trail of catheters in my friends' cars and houses in case I ever need one, I speak about it on stage in front on thousands of people, and through all of it I don't feel even a hint of awkwardness. I want so badly for people to know that this level of emotional freedom is possible and it is so, so worth finding. I wish I could grab my past self and shake her by the shoulders, then hug her tightly and say, 'It's okay, you don't have to hide it anymore. I promise you, it's okay.'

When I was younger, I sincerely believed the only solution to my bed-wetting problem was to make it go away entirely. As a little girl I would clasp my hands together and pray to anyone who would listen, saying, 'I pinky promise I will never be naughty or sad ever again if you help me fix this one thing.

Everything in my life would be perfect if it wasn't for this.' It didn't occur to me, even for a moment, that there was another solution and another way for it to stop ruling my life. But there is. It isn't to eliminate the situation; it's to accept it. It really is as simple and as complicated as that. Although it doesn't technically remove the 'problem', the outcome is still the same because it means the problem doesn't have control anymore. I do. It can't hold me back, or limit me, or cause me any anxiety at all. It's as good as gone because I am free.

~

Only now, as I sit here to write this chapter, can I see something I've somehow never noticed before. I've never reflected on the unexplained bedwetting days of my life with gratitude or acceptance, because as I was experiencing them, they were nothing but torturous. It has only ever been a memory that I loathed and resented. But what if, in all its messiness, embarrassment and uniqueness, it actually prepared me? What if twenty years of bedwetting equipped me for a lifetime of permanent incontinence? What if I hadn't known how to handle wearing pads, changing sheets and washing underwear more times than I can count—if I hadn't already lived two decades of it? What if the very thing I had wished away every single night of my life was the one thing I needed the most?

I'm not saying I wouldn't love to know how it feels to sleep in a bed naked, or wear tight clothing without seeing a thick incontinence pad underneath, or drink water without limitation.

I would love to experience the thrill of all those things. I'm also not saying I think we need to find value in every tough thing we go through. I'm well aware that sometimes things are just hard without reason or merit. But I will admit, sometimes it's nice to find meaning. Sometimes it helps heal a part of yourself you didn't even know was still hurting. Sometimes it's liberating to find purpose in a painful part of your past so you can see it through gratitude-tinted lenses.

Sometimes it's nice to look back and say, 'Hey, that really sucked. But look at where it got me.'

23

LIVING IN LIMBO

Finding a lawyer is like finding a boyfriend. You meet up for coffee, give each other a brief rundown of your life, see what you each have to offer and then determine whether or not you're a good match. I went on *a lot* of first lawyer dates before I ever went on a second one. It turned out that finding someone I could trust enough to represent me in my personal injury claim was a lot trickier than I had expected. I nodded along with older men as I stared at their briefcases and suit jackets and pretended to have a single clue what they were talking about. I listened as they spoke technical legalese and I gave them polite smiles when they spoke about my body and life like it was just another number on a list, rather than the only thing I will ever have.

I had one particularly bad lawyer date soon after I came home from hospital. Using my crutches, I walked into an office where the lawyer looked me up and down critically. He then said, without even a hint of empathy or compassion, that if I was to select him to represent me, I would have to pretend to be completely paralysed for as long as the case went on. He said that he didn't want anyone to know I could walk, and that if I continued to improve, I would have to keep it to myself. My jaw fell to the floor. *What?*

As though that wasn't already the most insensitive thing someone could say to me, he then attacked my smiley and bubbly demeanour, the very thing I was most proud of. He told me I absolutely couldn't be seen in public like that. I couldn't be outwardly happy. No one could know that I was actually 'okay' and that I wasn't lying at home devastated and depressed and unable to cope. He explained that regardless of which lawyer I chose, there would be people watching my every move, both online and in real life, trying to catch me out. The opposing insurance company would hire people to 'prove' I wasn't actually injured and that I wasn't actually traumatised. He said that if I ever forgot that, even for a moment, and was seen doing something as simple as walking to catch a bus instead of using my wheelchair, they would take photos of me to prove that my entire case was a lie.

I didn't understand. I wasn't lying and I had no secrets to keep. What was there to catch me out on? What was there to prove? I was significantly injured, my entire life had changed, yet now my disability wasn't 'bad enough' to be valid? For months I had been working so hard to get the movement back in my legs and now I had to pretend I didn't have it? My joy and resilience were my greatest strengths, but now because I wasn't crying at home every day, I was going to be punished for them? He guaranteed me millions of dollars if I could stick to those 'simple' rules. I looked at him, smiled my too-bubbly smile, then walked out of his office and never called him back. It was the one and only time I've ever ghosted a date.

Even in my young and still-fragile mind, I knew enough about life to know that faking unhappiness would without a doubt lead to true unhappiness. I had survived something impossible and I had learned to walk again after being told I never would. I couldn't pretend to be unhappy even if I wanted to. And I most definitely couldn't let myself live in a wheelchair when I was one of the lucky few who got to walk away from one. No amount of money was worth that deceit.

I had seen my death and I was given the remarkable chance to live. I knew what a gift that was. I was alive in every sense of the word, and I wasn't going to give that up.

~

I eventually decided on a different lawyer, one who seemed far kinder and more considerate than the ones I'd met previously. We had several lengthy meetings where I gave him the rundown of the accident, my injury and the prognosis for my future. It was exhausting to talk about in so much depth, but it needed to be done. I gave him all my scans, doctors reports, hospital details and went on with my life, thinking that would be that. I assumed the lawyer would take all the information back to the insurance company and discuss what compensation I would need, and then it would be over. Straightforward, painless, fair.

I was told that I couldn't work or study while the claim was in progress because it would make it appear that I was 'fine' and hence lessen my need for any compensation. This didn't make sense to me because my disability was exactly the same, regardless of how I chose to spend my time, but I figured it was only going to take a few months and I wasn't yet in a position to work anyway, so I hesitantly agreed.

As time went by, I began to feel the weight of being in limbo. My days were filled with rehab and rest but without a job to keep me busy, I couldn't help but feel like now would be the perfect time to study while I was recovering at home. I had deferred university to go travelling and I'd also been in the middle of an online course, so I asked my lawyer if I was allowed to resume either option, but he sternly told me no. He explained again that studying would give the impression that I was physically unaffected and this would impact my claim negatively. From the outside, studying insinuated that I was planning on returning to work, which would mean I didn't need support for loss of income.

I was frustrated. I wanted to study because I wanted to *learn*; I wanted to use my brain and regain some sense of normality and routine in my life, plus I had plenty of time on my hands. I missed feeling like a twenty-year-old who got to steer her own ship.

I didn't understand why I was being made to feel like I was hiding something when I wasn't. If there was a lie to catch me out on, I sure didn't know what it was.

24

BRAVERY

I think we often look at people who have overcome adversity and assume that from day one they chose to fight. We put them on a pedestal made up of unattainable levels of strength and resilience and assume they possess something we don't. I've found that's not actually true at all. For every person we look up to, there was a time before things were good, before there was anything to be inspired by, before there was a story worth telling—a time when things were just plain shit. Before every pain that transformed itself into a lesson, there was only pain. I only realised how very human our idols are after people started looking up to me.

In the year after my accident, my social media following had started to grow quite rapidly. To my complete and utter shock, people started seeing my words, resonating with them and even deciding they liked them enough to follow my page and come along for the ride. It felt incredible. All of a sudden I went from someone who barely spoke to anyone, besides the few people in my inner circle, to talking to people from all around the world. People would send me well wishes and tell me they were rooting for me. It felt like I had this huge team around me. A community of people who wanted the best for me and who I could share anything with. I felt invincible from the amount of support surrounding me, like there was a warm blanket of love protecting me from the outside world.

Every day I was connecting with people just like me, and creating friendships through a screen. I would write about the sunsets that could bring me to tears from their beauty. I wrote about finding strength and hope in the people I loved. I would share pictures of my drawings, and to my surprise people began asking if they could purchase them.

What a lot of people probably didn't realise from the outside was that this relationship went both ways. People would share their own stories with me, or pass on poems or books they thought I would like. I couldn't believe I was lucky enough to have found a group of strangers (who felt like friends) who saw the world in the same awe-inspiring way I did. It was like I had been speaking another language my whole life and had finally stumbled into a part of the world that understood me.

Here's the thing though: with every unintentional social media rise, there is a transition phase; an invisible line that you never really agreed to cross. There's a moment where you go from a person posting about their life to a person whose life people look up to. Instead of just sharing your own struggles, people look to you for help with theirs. Without me really noticing, my accident and recovery quickly became glorified and idealised. I became a textbook example of what to do in a challenge, when in reality I often had no idea what I was doing. While everything I wrote was completely true—I made sure to share the struggles as well as the beauty—and I could smile and laugh every day and truly mean it, I also felt incomprehensibly lost.

On one particular day, I fainted while I was on the toilet and fell to the floor because my blood pressure had dropped so low (this often happened when I did an enema). I lay on the floor, half naked, in pain and in tears. I had no idea how I would physically get up from the ground in that moment, let alone get up from that period of my life to resemble a person who could have coherent thoughts beyond 'when do I need to do my next catheter?' I picked up my phone, which thankfully I had learned to always keep with me for exactly this reason, and called my mum. Before I clicked call on her number I saw I had a message on Instagram from a stranger. It said something along the lines of, 'How are you so happy every day? Please teach me so I can feel it too.' It didn't add up. Here I was on the bathroom floor, covered in my own poo, needing my mum to physically pick me up, and someone was asking me how to be happy? It didn't make sense that someone could be looking to me for advice and wisdom when I needed so much help myself. I felt like a fraud, even in the midst of my own truth.

Something I could never really seem to grasp was when people would call me 'strong'. They would say it as though it was a conscious choice, as though I had any other option. I wondered what *not* being strong would look like to them. I imagined it might look exactly the same from the outside. People would say I was 'brave' for using my wheelchair, 'inspiring' for learning to use catheters and 'strong' for getting up in the morning. These weren't deliberate acts of resilience; these were simply things that needed to be done. It seemed as though anything I did after my accident, no matter how mundane, would be viewed as part of my strength of character, when in reality it was just getting through. What other choice was there than to put one foot in front of the other, even when your feet no longer moved?

I definitely had small moments when I felt worthy of the titles people gave me. I was proud of myself for still being able to smile. I was proud of myself for venturing out into the world beyond the comfort of my home. I was proud of the fact that I could deal with so much trauma and ongoing pain and still find reasons to laugh. But despite all of this, I couldn't shake the feeling that stumbling upon calamity and a disability I never asked for didn't warrant the words 'strong' or 'brave'. Society tends to idealise trauma as this extraordinary gift that gives us strength and courage, but the truth was I didn't want to be strong. I wanted to be twenty. I wanted to be in Rome, eating gelato and dancing with my friends, like I should have been. I wanted the comfort of complaining about my boss and university deadlines and annoying housemates. I didn't want to be courageous. I wanted to be carefree. I wanted to be able to make mistakes that didn't stay with me for the rest of my life. If being weak was the opposite of this, that's what I would have preferred.

When I began to feel weighed down by this, I would think back to the girl I was in the Swiss hospital. The girl who wanted it all to end. I would remind myself of the moment I prayed for death but heard ambulance sirens instead. Maybe I wasn't brave in the way that everyone else saw me to be; maybe I was brave in a quieter way. I kept living when I wanted to die. Perhaps this was the epitome of strength.

All this is to say two things. Firstly, even notoriously happy people can feel that low. Even people who get asked on a daily basis 'How do you stay so positive?' have been in a place where they themselves didn't know. Secondly, things get better. Maybe not always physically, but mentally they always will. Nothing in this world is permanent. Emotions come and go even when they feel like they'll stay. If I left the world when I thought I wanted to, I would have missed so much of this life. I wouldn't have met most of the people who now fill up my heart. I wouldn't have met myself.

Something I find comforting to think about in my harder moments is all the beauty that is happening at that very same moment. I've learned it's possible to experience soul-lighting joy and genuine excitement for people we don't even know. Even if I can't see it with my own eyes, I like to imagine it's there for somebody else and that one day it will find me again too.

Here is a list of important things to remember when the future feels colourless:

Right now someone is seeing the sun rise over the ocean for the first time.

Right now someone is falling in love.
Right now someone is taking a bite of what will be their new favourite food.
Right now someone is curled up in bed cuddling their new baby.
Right now someone is on a flight they've spent years saving for.
Right now someone is dancing and singing in the front row of a concert.
Right now someone is sitting by a cosy fire place toasting a marshmallow.
Right now someone is closing a chapter that was hurting them and opening a new one.
Right now someone is having the very best day of their life.

Maybe today that isn't your story, but isn't it comforting to know that for someone else it is? Isn't it lovely to imagine that right at this very moment, someone, somewhere, is having a moment so perfect they'll never forget the way it feels? Maybe today it isn't you and maybe it hasn't been you for this entire year, but maybe tomorrow it will be, and isn't that nice to know?

If I am an inspiration for anything, it shouldn't be for my happiness or for learning to walk again, it should be for the fact that despite all odds, I found the tiniest glimmer of hope and held on to it as though my life depended on it. I suppose it did. Perhaps that's all bravery really is—the courage to look for hope where there is none and looking anyway.

25

REBIRTHDAY

I've always had an affinity for dates and an ability to transport myself back to the emotions and senses of certain moments, no matter how many years have passed. Even if I'm not consciously aware of what day it is, my body can somehow *feel* the presence and significance of the day's history before my mind has time to register why.

The ninth of June was not a date my mind could ever forget though, it was tattooed on my body and permanently imprinted on my soul, and when I woke up on a cold wintery Monday morning, I felt uneasy. There were so many thoughts and emotions flowing through me that it was hard to pinpoint what they were, but one stood out to me above the rest: *this time a year ago, I was fine.*

My mind kept retracing my steps from the year before; what I'd been doing, where I was, how I was feeling. I could see and feel it playing out so vividly, it was like I was back there, three hundred and sixty-five days ago. I remembered my excitement as the helicopter climbed higher, the endless possibilities that lay before me, and the innocence I hadn't known I possessed. The thing that struck me most when I thought about it now though, the part I couldn't seem to swallow even after so much time, was the extreme normalcy of that day.

Until my accident, I had always assumed there would be some kind of warning before life as you knew it ended. It seemed like the fair and generous trade off. I liked to imagine the universe would have the grace to say, 'Hey, maybe enjoy this version of yourself a little extra today, because after this you'll never go back to her.' I didn't know change could be so brutally abrupt.

As I lay in my bed on that first anniversary, I felt so much longing and sympathy for the girl I was only one year before. She had no idea what was just a few hours around the corner. Part of me wanted to be her again to experience the level of mental freedom she had before everything changed, and part me of wanted to hug her, prepare her and promise her that she would be okay.

The anniversary of my accident arrived unexpectedly fast. It was hard to believe that an entire year had passed since I stood in that Swiss kitchen making myself a sandwich, hands full of bread and salad, head definitely not full of expectation of my imminent metamorphosis. The memory of me there in that room, surrounded by the bustle of other twenty-something-year-olds on the opposite side of the world, was still so fresh and vivid in my mind that it felt like mere weeks ago. Everything had changed so rapidly I was barely keeping up, but at the same time, it also felt like the earth had decided to move breathtakingly slowly around the sun these past twelve months.

How was it only a year ago that I walked with ease, or went to the bathroom without thinking, or fell asleep on Ben's chest? It was all so foreign to my life now that I could barely believe I had lived any of it.

The day came and went and it was painstakingly ordinary. I wasn't expecting a parade to march down the street in my honour or the prime minister to knock on my door and congratulate me, but I thought I would at least experience some kind of monumental feeling to mark the milestone. It didn't feel possible that a date that had been so pivotal and transformative in the course of my life could simply pass by in the same predictable manner as any other. I had an immense amount of gratitude for an extra year of life and I also had an immense amount of sorrow from the pain I had endured, but none of it was really sinking in. I kept waiting for the Big Feeling to flow through me, or for my family or friends to check in and see how I was going, but nothing came and no one mentioned it at all. The chatter in my mind was so loud and insistent that the silence from everyone around me was deafeningly obvious.

Night-time came around and I couldn't take it anymore. No one had acknowledged the day and no one, including myself, had done anything to commemorate it. Eventually I stormed out of my room (as much as one can storm on crutches), ungracefully yelled at my family who were all sitting wide-eyed on the couch, slammed the front door behind me and got in my car.

I drove to a secluded carpark where I sat in the darkness and, for the first time in a long time, just let myself *feel*. I felt all of it, every bit of pain and anger, every bit of joy and appreciation. I let it pulsate through me until my eyes began to well with tears. I was surprised at how good it felt to cry, it wasn't something I had done very often in the past year and it was only now I was realising just how much I'd needed the release.

I had become so deliberately positive and upbeat that I was too scared to let it slip for even a moment, in case what I found in the depths of my mind swallowed me so completely that I couldn't climb back out again. My new-found happiness was so opposite to what I had always known that I still doubted its presence. It was as though I couldn't quite believe it was mine to keep, so I was constantly on alert, terrified of accidentally pulling out the one Jenga piece that would make the whole tower crumble.

But as my tears fell in that carpark, a year after my world was shaken to its core, I knew I would be okay. I knew there was more than one piece keeping me together and that I wasn't so fragile I could be knocked down by a few tears.

I finally understood that it was possible to be sad while also trusting that the sadness wouldn't last forever. The idea of that is so simple but it was strikingly different to what I had believed only a year earlier. Back then my sadness used to encompass me so completely that it didn't just feel like something I was experiencing, it felt like *who I was*. I'd finally learned that there was no need for me to fear sorrow, because my baseline was joy and I would always return to it.

I was so incredibly proud of myself. The Emma I was a year ago would have never thought she was capable of getting through a year like this one, yet here I was, getting through. In fact, I was more than just coping, I was *enjoying* my life and there wasn't a fragment of my old self that would have ever imagined that was possible. It dawned on me that probably very few people have any idea of just how strong they are until they are forced to be. We don't realise how much strength and resilience is hiding inside us, dormant or only surfacing occasionally for passing moments of stress or tension, until something big arises that wakes it up and makes it as familiar to us as the back of our hand. Our strength is as much a part of us as our humour or intelligence, as integral to our makeup as our values and beliefs, whether or not we've grown to know it yet.

I decided there in that carpark that I wanted a way to acknowledge the day that is the ninth of June. Not to be self-indulgent, but because not honouring it felt like a disservice to the girl who had worked so hard to get to where she was. But how do you mark a day that holds more than just one straightforward emotion? The majority of life's celebrations focus solely on the joy that comes from a particular life event, but what about the other personal journeys we are bound to go on that can't be defined in such a cookie-cutter way? What about the things we experience that feel as large and impactful as embarking on a marathon or committing to a partner, that don't provide a certificate or ring to show for our efforts? What about the mammoth and often invisible journeys that feel more pivotal and important than any socially acknowledged achievement we've had, that are more nuanced than a simple 'Congratulations, here's a present'?

I realised there was a handbook on ways to celebrate most of the big moments in our lives—birthdays, marriages, house warmings—but there was nothing for this. There were no designated balloons that read, 'We're happy you didn't die on this day, but we're sorry for all of the ways in which it hurt you'. If I wanted to celebrate the day, it was up to me to decide how to do that. I couldn't expect other people to read my mind and know what I needed when even I myself had no idea.

After an hour of sitting in the car digesting year-old emotions, I felt the weight of the world leave my shoulders and decided that this act of feeling and releasing was going to become a recurring ritual, an ongoing part of my anniversary. In order for me to celebrate in any other way, I first had to allow myself the grace of mourning what I so dearly missed.

As I drove back home, I prepared myself to apologise for storming out. I expected to be greeted with the damp mood in which I had left the house. Instead, when I opened the door I was surprised to find everyone with huge smiles on their faces and my favourite cake on the table. My outburst (although not the kindest method) had inadvertently given everyone permission to speak about and celebrate something they weren't quite sure they were allowed to. Without any of us knowing what the 'right' thing to do was, we had created it together. A cake symbolised celebration and as I looked around at my family surrounding me on the couch and my crutches leaning on the chair next to me, I knew that among a multitude of other emotions, what this day felt like most was a celebration.

Today didn't only have to be about reflecting and grieving, it could also be about sincerely appreciating getting a whole extra year of the beautiful, messy, confusing, wondrous thing that is my life. In an alternate world, one awfully close to this one, today would have been the anniversary of my death and I wouldn't have got the chance to eat delicious cake, or yell and apologise and forgive and laugh with my family, or any of the other very human things I got to do. That in itself seemed like enough of a reason to throw a party, sing from the rooftops, hug a stranger on the street and scream with the enthusiasm of a child, 'Oh my gosh, can you believe we're alive?'

As I tucked myself into bed that night, I watched the clock strike 10 pm (2 pm Swiss time). This time last year I was taking the leap off that helicopter ledge, flying blissfully above the clouds, thinking to myself, *This is exactly where I am supposed to be.* A year on, I felt like a completely different person to the girl I was back then, even before the flying became falling and the pretty landscape became a painful landing pad, but as I absorbed the beauty of the new life I'd created, I had that same feeling of being in exactly the right place.

That moment, that collision, that patch of dirt, had felt like a complete rebirth in every sense of the word and my second chance was becoming something that truly excited me. Rebirth, that was it. That's what this day was going to be from now on.

'Happy Rebirthday' might not be written on the front of a Hallmark card or be a universally recognised event, but it was what the ninth of June was always going to be for me. The anniversary of my accident was going to be a party, and as the day came to a close I couldn't wait to see who would be sitting around the table next year, thankful I had survived long enough to meet them.

26

FAMILY

One of the many side effects of nearly dying is that your ability to filter the things that really matter from the ones that don't increases drastically. Things that used to be hazy shades of grey become stark black and whites. Situations that seemed all-encompassing suddenly hold much less weight. There's an unspoken superpower in the worst having already happened; it enables you to see clearly.

A habit I've adopted since my accident is frequently taking the time to look around and ask myself a simple question: 'Would this have mattered to me when I was in hospital?'

What I'm essentially asking is, 'Would this have mattered to me even when my world was falling apart?' If the answer is yes, I know I've found something I need to put all my love and time into. I've come to learn there's only a few things that ever seem to make this list: my health, the safety of my loved ones and, most of all, my family.

I will never forget the way my family rallied around me when I needed them. It's easy to take the people we love the most for granted when we are so used to seeing them every day. When life is passing in the monotonous and repetitive way it often does, we can forget just how special it is to have a select few people who will *always* be on our team. I know not everyone is lucky enough to have that, so finding myself in a situation where having a support system felt essential was like having a spotlight beaming down on my inner circle, reminding me: *Here, this is what you have to be thankful for.*

Not a day went by, for the entire duration I was in hospital, that my mum wasn't by my side. She quit her job in Canberra, moved three and a half hours away to Sydney, and spent night after night away from her family in a cheap hotel beside the hospital. At the time I had just expected it; it seemed obvious that she would do that for me in my time of need. But it wasn't compulsory, it was love.

From the moment she boarded that last-minute flight to Switzerland, not long after receiving a midnight call telling her something was wrong, she hadn't gone home. She had completely uprooted her life without a moment's notice and so, in a way not too dissimilar from what I was going through, her world had completely changed as well.

My mum would cook for me and take me out for lunch so I didn't always have to eat the bland hospital food, she would come to every one of my physio sessions and patiently watch as I did the same movements over and over, she would understand the days when, even though she had no one else to speak to,

I didn't want to say a word. She did every little thing in her power to make what could have been a very dark time a whole lot brighter.

Being in hospital reminded me a lot of being a child and relying on outside help for almost every element of your day. I was grateful for a lot of things after my accident, but the main thing I was thankful for was that the help I got to reach for wasn't in the form of a stranger, but my very own mum.

My grandparents also visited me in hospital most days. They made sure I knew I was never alone, even in the moments where it felt like I surely was. For the first year after my accident, I travelled from Canberra to Sydney each week to go to a spinal rehab facility. The distance meant I got to stay with my grandparents for half of every week—precious quality time with them that I had craved since I was little. My grandpa would drive me to every session and stay by my side for the entire two hours, never once complaining or hinting he had any other place to be. My nanny is the most exuberant, friendly and talkative person I've ever met. These qualities have always been what I admire most about her, but never more than while I was in the spinal ward. She was a gift not only to myself but to all of the other patients as well. She would sit and talk to anyone who needed a kind listening ear, filling the place with warmth the moment she entered the room.

To this day, whenever people compliment me on my positivity, I want to tell them that it's only a fraction of the light that my nanny has. That the only reason I have any at all is because she showed me the way to live.

When I first got out of hospital, I wasn't able to go back to work, not only because of the legal case but because my body wasn't yet capable. Getting through the day was still physically exhausting, I was having accidents every half an hour and what a lot of people don't tell you about recovery is that it's a full-time job. My life for that first year consisted of countless doctors appointments as well as the weekly trips to Sydney for rehab. It didn't take long for the expenses to really add up.

Our family had enough money to get by, but we certainly didn't have any left over for something unexpected like this. If it wasn't for me taking out travel insurance in a last-minute rush before I left for my trip, I genuinely don't know what we would have done. My time in Switzerland and the flight home had cost over a hundred thousand dollars alone.

My sister Tara is only two years older than me, but the age gap has always felt a lot larger. She is far more mature, considered and put-together than I am. Because of this, she had the incredible forethought to organise a fundraiser for me so that I could afford to continue my rehab. She gathered all my friends, family and former work colleagues into a room for an eighties-themed trivia night. People reached out to any contacts they had and donated signed football jerseys, artworks and whatever else they could, in order to auction them off. I was lost for words when I saw how many people had come together to support me, and by the end of the night we had raised enough money for me to not worry about rushing back into work before I was ready.

Tara had been in a relationship since high school with a guy named Mark. By the time I had my accident I'd known him for almost ten years, and because he knew me from such a young age, he felt less like my sister's fiancé and more like my brother. Together Tara and Mark gave me one of my most cherished memories. They came to visit me in hospital and caught the bus with me to the beach. I sat in my wheelchair staring out at the ocean, longing to be immersed in it, when suddenly they picked me up, carried me across the sand, rolled up my pants and let my feet touch the water. It was one of the greatest gifts I've ever been given. I couldn't feel the water on my skin, but what I did feel was that I was the luckiest person in the world.

My dad is the kind of person who doesn't say much but shows his love in other ways. For me, it was typically through my sport. At school I'd get so excited whenever I would look at the crowd during a race and see him standing there cheering me on. I could always hear his voice from the crowd, even when I was underwater or on the other side of the oval. In hospital he gave me this same encouragement to push myself physically because he knew I loved to be competitive. Whenever he came to my wheelchair lessons he would spur me on to jump down the gutters and try the moves that scared me, and whenever he was watching I would nail it every time.

Once I got back home, I was going through all my photos and videos from the hospital and found footage of the first time I walked with crutches. After taking a few steps, I looked up and saw the phone Dad was holding out in front of him. I said with an eye-roll, 'Are you filming me?', because at the time it didn't really seem like something worth documenting, to which he replied in the most enthusiastic and proud voice I've ever heard him use, 'Absolutely.'

My dad is also the person who instilled in me my great love of nature. For as far back as I can remember, my sisters and I always spent a whole lot more time outside than we ever did indoors. He took us camping and taught us to look away from technology and up at the stars. Because of him I know how to set up a tent, drive on the beach, start a fire and do all the things which to this day make me the happiest version of me.

I'm not naive about the fact that what happened to me would have had a profound effect on all the people around me. In a lot of ways, I think seeing someone you love lie hurting in a hospital bed would be a lot more difficult than actually being the one in the bed. The domino effect of trauma is something you can't always see or understand, but for my younger sister Hayley, it was in plain sight.

Hayley Facetimed me every day while I was in hospital in Switzerland, but not being there physically was harder for her than we realised at first. She was so distraught by what had happened to me, and without us there to watch over her, she had got caught up with the wrong crowd as she tried to numb her pain. When I left for my holiday I said goodbye to my bubbly, naive and very youthful seventeen-year-old sister, and when I arrived back home, I was met by someone I didn't even recognise. She was still herself deep down, of course, but on the surface she was angry and harsh and playing a character that I knew wasn't her own.

A year later, I was sitting at home by myself when my mum walked in the front door looking like she'd seen a ghost. She dropped her bags in the doorway, stared at me blankly and, out of the bluest of blues, said: 'I just found out Hayley is nineteen weeks pregnant.' I felt time freeze over. The world stopped spinning and everything went silent.

My brain has never struggled to comprehend words as much as it did in that moment. It felt even more unfathomable and absurd to me than the moment I realised my legs weren't working. How could Hayley, my little baby sister, have her own baby inside of her? How could she be pregnant when she was only a child herself? How could we not have known something so life-changing and important for nearly five whole months? Why on earth didn't she tell us?

For seventeen years I had been my sister's idol and best friend. Everywhere I went she followed me like a little shadow. I had known her like the back of my hand and now, somehow, I didn't know the biggest thing that would ever happen to her. Life had already changed so much from the year before, but now it was so unrecognisable that I felt like I was being pranked. Nothing was the same as it used to be and I was struck once again by the bewildering reality that this was what life is. No one warns you about it when you're little, but change is the one certainty of growing up.

I went to my room and collapsed onto the floor. My entire body was shaking and I was struggling to breathe. The words 'Hayley' and 'pregnant' in the same sentence didn't make sense to me at all. It was so deeply unexpected that it didn't feel possible.

Not again, not again, not again.

The foundation of our lives had only just become steady; I wasn't ready for it to drop out from underneath us again so soon.

I wanted a pause. A moment to catch up and breathe without feeling like time was slipping through the hourglass of our life far faster than it should. As the shock wore off and reality sank in, my shaking grew worse and I realised I was having a panic attack right there on the carpet of my bedroom. As I clasped my hands to my chest and gasped for air, I wondered how many more times in my life I would find myself curled into a ball, crying on the floor in complete disbelief.

I knew I couldn't let Hayley see me like this, though. I knew that my emotions were not what was important in that moment and that I needed to pull myself together and be a big sister. I knew that there were only a handful of moments in everyone's life where you really need your family to be there for you, and this was one of them.

I called Tara and told her to come over, then I texted Hayley and asked her to come home to talk to us. I couldn't imagine how nervous she would be to confront us all if she had deliberately hidden her pregnancy for so many months. Right now she didn't need to know we were all scared and shocked, she just needed to know that we would always be there.

The moment she walked in the door I rushed over to her and pulled her into a hug, then I called the rest of the family to join in. For a few minutes we all just stood there in a silent embrace and let our presence tell her that it would all be okay. I didn't know how it would be, but if I'd learned anything in the past year it was that we have a funny way of surprising ourselves.

27

FINDING HOME

I've never been a planner or someone with detailed and specific goals. When I look to the future, the week ahead of me is typically as far as I can see; everything beyond that is nothing more than a hazy possibility. This is partly because I crave spontaneity and a life lived outside the lines, but I know it's also a residual effect of trauma. Since my accident, I've found planning to be a naive and pointless task—I now know all too well that life can be completely derailed at any time. The future seems fragile to me now and I figure if I can remain fluid instead of rigid, I won't break so badly if something goes wrong. Because of this, I've never known what kind of job I wanted to have or what kind of home I'd like to live in. I've never had visions of a big white wedding or wondered how many kids the future mum version of me will be holding in her arms. The only concrete dream I've ever had is an uncomplicated one, but it has been as clear as day for as long as I can remember. Growing up, photos of it filled my camera roll and the thought of it was an eternal reverie in my mind. The dream is simple and certain—to live by the ocean.

The place I was born and raised is a two hour drive from the nearest beach. Whenever we would travel to the coast I would spend hours in the sea, ignoring my parents yelling to me from the shore that it was time to come back in. I grew up swimming competitively, which meant I trained in the pool twice day and, as much as I loved the athletic challenge of it, it was always more about being in the water for me. Water, particularly the ocean, has always called to me and made me feel alive in a way that being landlocked cannot. When I dive beneath a wave or sink my feet into the sand, I feel with utmost certainty that I am exactly where I belong.

Within a few months of leaving the hospital, I gained medical clearance to get my scuba diving licence. I remember my first dive after becoming qualified; I swam down to the deep ocean floor, crossed my legs as though I was sitting on land, then looked up to the surface. I watched as perfectly formed bubbles escaped from my mask and floated upwards, taking so long to reach the top that I could barely even see them from where I was sitting. It was completely silent and all I could hear was the rhythmic and steady sound of my own breath. Fish swam around me and I became immersed in a bustling and colourful universe that you wouldn't know existed from the surface. I was thirty feet underwater, but it was the safest and freest I had ever felt.

I always knew I would live by the ocean. I had been dreaming about it for so long that it wasn't a question of *if*, it was simply a matter of *when*. The 'when' had always been a far-off dream, postponed even further by my accident, but it was something that arrived out of the blue one gloomy night as I was curled up on the couch at home. I suddenly closed the book I was reading, looked up, and thought, *What the heck am I doing?* Big life changes had always felt to me like something you happened upon; something the universe dropped into your lap when you least expected them. I'd forgotten they could also be as simple as making a decision and acting on it. I decided then and there, very matter-of-factly, that I was going to move to the Gold Coast. I have no idea what drew me to that particular area out of every coastline in Australia, because I'd only been there once for a few days with Jemma and all we saw were theme parks and the inside of night-clubs. But as I sat there on my couch, I had the most profound knowing that it was where I needed to be. Emboldened, I told Mum and Hayley that I was moving away. They knew it had always been my dream to live by the sea, so they supported me, but they were also cognisant that I wasn't exactly ready to live alone yet. A few hours later, to my complete surprise and elation, they decided that, after the year we'd all had, they wanted to come too. It would be a fresh start for all of us—a chance to rebuild someplace new.

Now that I'd thought of it, a sea change felt essential. Although I was happy with where I was at emotionally, I longed for newness. I had grown into a person that I loved and was proud of, but I couldn't shake the feeling that staying in the same place I'd lived my whole life was keeping me stuck. I would drive past the streets I used to run down and feel an ache in my chest knowing

I could only wheel or limp down them now. I would go into the chemist I used to work at but instead of serving customers, I was picking up medication to help with my incontinence. It wasn't only the physical contrasts that were difficult, it was the fact that every inch of the town had a memory attached to it from two decades of living there. Cosy cafes, places I used to go with Ben, even the roads and trees—everything already held significance. I wanted to be somewhere that knew no version of the old me. I wanted to be surrounded by faces and streets that held nothing but new beginnings. I wanted to create the version of me I'd been dreaming up my entire life.

The main problem with staying in Canberrra was that everyone had known me *before*. It is difficult for people to see and treat you in a new light when they are so used to you being a certain way. I had been the despondent, unenthusiastic, diluted version of myself for so long, that I feared I wouldn't be able to completely break away from that and embrace my new disposition while I was still in the same circle. It wasn't only that though. Everyone I knew was accustomed to me being able-bodied and so they could see how much I had lost physically. I heard their quiet whispers and glances of pity as I wheeled myself down the street in my chair. I didn't need pity though—I needed celebration, because, despite my new reality being different, I felt more 'me' and more alive than I ever had before. Without anyone intending to label me so, I realised I had become 'the poor girl who had a skydiving accident'. But that's not how I felt at all anymore. I wanted to go somewhere new so I could rewrite the narrative into something that better matched how I felt inside. I wanted what happened to me to be my greatest strength, not my permanent sob story. Where I was heading, no one could pity me because they didn't know any other version of me. There, I could become 'the girl who fell from the sky'.

The hardest part of leaving was the thought of being away from Jemma. Since we were four years old, the longest we had ever been apart was the few weeks after my accident when she went to Florence and I had to stay in hospital. Besides the occasional week here and there, we had spent every day together for over fifteen years. I genuinely didn't know life without her. She was my automatic and assumed point of call for everything: holidays, school partners, breakfast dates and all those moments where you feel like doing absolutely nothing at all. I couldn't imagine finding that level of comfort and familiarity with anyone else. With Jemma, I didn't need to explain anything about my life. She knew every version of me—the shy and curious child, the rebellious and sad teenager, the broken bodied and broken hearted adult, and now the healing and flourishing person I was becoming—and she had loved every single one of them. She had grown up beside me and despite the many changes in my life, she remained the one constant and ever-present thread. I know that's a once in a lifetime type of friendship.

Over the years people constantly told us that they envied what we had and how very rare it was to stumble across a best friend so young; someone you could live your whole life alongside. I asked myself if I was stupid for leaving something so special, knowing that not many people ever had the privilege of finding it at all. It wasn't that I didn't think our friendship would survive the distance—that didn't cross my mind for a second—it was that I wanted us to always live our lives side by side. I didn't want to hear stories through the phone of new jobs or boyfriends, I wanted to be able to put faces to names and know every little detail because I was there for those moments too. I knew we would be more than okay, but I also knew I would miss her with my whole heart and I wasn't sure how I would bear it.

A few months after that night I'd sat on my couch and decided to move away, the day came for Jemma and I to say goodbye. We stood beside the car that was packed with all my belongings and held onto each other as though our lives depended on it. The distance I was about to put between us felt unnatural, and tears streamed down our cheeks as the reality of it sank in. Our matching tattoos separated as we let go of each other's hands and as I got into the car, it felt as though my heart was being ripped from my chest. It hurt in the very unique way it does when you make a decision that you hope will be best for you, but also wonder if what you already have is in fact the very best thing you'll ever find.

My aunty was saying goodbye to us as well. I pulled her aside and said, 'I'm so scared things between Jemma and I will never be the same as they are right now.' My aunty had witnessed the entirety of our friendship and looked at me with eyes that said she'd been here before too.

'They won't,' she said, 'but that doesn't mean they won't be beautiful when they change too.'

I knew the intensity of my heartache really only meant one thing: I was lucky to have something so special that it was worth missing. Not many people get to meet their person when they're four years old.

~

Although moving to the coast was a life-long dream and something I wanted with my whole heart, the thing people often don't tell you about living your dream is that one day you actually have to *live* it. And that can be utterly terrifying. I couldn't fathom pulling out of the driveway, heading down the familiar streets and simply not returning. What if I didn't make any new friends where I was going? What if nowhere else ever felt like home? What if I wasn't actually running towards a fresh start and I was really just running away? All these thoughts circled my mind, and even as the car started I thought, *I'm not brave enough to do this, I know I'll be back in a month, it's not a real goodbye.* But as we hit the highway, my worries completely vanished. I felt a warm bubbly feeling rise up in my chest and it occurred to me that leaving always seems impossible until you leave, and then you realise the anticipation is often much worse than the reality. I looked in the rear-view mirror and saw the town that held everyone I loved and the only life I'd ever known, and I was filled with gratitude for everything it had brought me. Then I turned to look ahead at the long and empty road in front of me, and I felt a hope in my heart so large, I knew I was going the right way.

After fifteen hours in the car, Mum, Hayley and I arrived at what would be our new hometown. We had quite literally driven into the unknown. We didn't know where we were going to live or what we were planning to do, but the uncertainties were overridden by the certainty that this felt good. I walked out of our hotel and down onto the sparkling beach below. The water was perfectly calm and the colours of the sky were starting to transform into a rainbow painting above me. It had only just turned spring, but the sea breeze felt warm against my skin. I looked down the stretch of sand at the coastline; the whole Gold Coast was visible from where I was standing. There were grassy hills and palm trees breaking up the different beaches, and in the distance a city skyline was perfectly lit up against the darkening sky. I didn't know the names of any of the places I was looking at; I didn't even know the name of the beach I was standing on. Right now everything in front of me was a picturesque blank canvas. It was pretty, but it was all so unfamiliar that it didn't mean anything to me yet. I could see everything exactly as it was, because there were no memories attached to any of it. As I soaked in the view, I knew this was the last time I would see it like this. I wondered what would unfold here in the coming years and how very different this coastline would look once I had filled it with meaning.

I picked up a stick and drew a smiley face in the sand, then watched as the waves methodically lapped up against it. I couldn't believe that this wasn't just a holiday and that touching the ocean was now something I could do whenever I desired. It felt surreal, as though the younger version of me had just been handed everything she ever wanted. I was surprised to find that the Gold Coast immediately felt like home. The connection was so instant and palpable that it truly shocked me. Home isn't always where you grew up or where you have the most memories, it's wherever you breathe easiest.

I took a deep inhale and looked down at the smiley face I'd drawn at my feet. Despite the tide washing up against it time and time again, the mark was still imprinted deep into the wet sand, refusing to be washed away. That's when I knew I was exactly where I was meant to be.

28

LIGHTNING

Sometimes months go by and you don't notice anything changing. Nothing major happens and your days follow a fairly similar routine, so you assume you're the same person you have always been. Often it's only once you look back with hindsight that you can see all the subtle variations that add up over time, and you realise you're actually completely different to the person you used to be. But sometimes change doesn't quietly weave itself throughout your days—instead, it's a lightning strike. Occasionally, a single moment has enough power to change the entire course and meaning of your life.

I was struck by one of those moments in Switzerland, but it happened again on a warm and unsuspecting October evening, just a week after we arrived in our new home. A moment that I wasn't at all prepared for, but one that changed everything anyway.

By the time we moved to the Gold Coast, Mum and I were beyond eager to meet Hayley's baby and start this next chapter together. Something that had at first seemed terrifying was now the most exciting thing in the world. I wondered if life always worked that way; if beauty was always disguised as challenges, and our greatest paths always first appeared to be scattered with obstacles. I imagined they did.

The same week we arrived, Hayley had an appointment with her doctor and unexpectedly found out she needed to be induced the next day, weeks before she was actually due. When I woke up that morning, I knew my sister was having her baby—I knew that today was most definitely the day—but I wasn't at all prepared for how it would feel. I was still so nervous. Would Hayley be okay? Would she still get to have her own youth? Would I be capable of helping her look after a baby?

All these worries ran on repeat as I stood in the maternity ward holding Hayley's hand through her contractions. Uncertainty, anxiety and fear were filling the room, but then, all of a sudden, in the split second it takes for someone to take their first breath, there she was. A little girl lying on top of my little sister's chest. A new beginning, on top of a thousand other new beginnings. I felt time come skidding to a stop once again, but this time it was in the most beautiful of ways.

Oh, I thought to myself as I looked at my new niece. *So this is what everyone talks about. This is what love is. Oh.*

If there were doctors or sounds or raging wild animals in the room, I didn't notice any of it. She was all I could see. The moment she was born, I forgot every worry I'd had that morning. I forgot about the circumstances that had led us here. I forgot my own name. I saw her and I felt healed. Wholeheartedly, completely, indescribably healed.

I didn't know her name yet and I hadn't even held her in my arms, but I knew with the greatest knowing I've ever had that she was the best thing to ever happen to our family. I knew that miracles come in so many forms and she was the biggest one of all. More than anything, I knew that I would love her for the rest of my life.

Up until then, I hadn't known it was possible to love without a single condition, but when I looked at the tiny baby my sister had created, I felt emotion soar through me like a beam of golden light. I had the sense that this feeling was about more than the fact that she was my niece and we were related by blood. She was my soulmate.

Her name was Layla and her cry was my new favourite sound in the world. Her eyes held a wisdom far beyond her age and when she looked at you, it was as if every cloud in the sky parted to let the warmth come oozing in. In an instant I no longer cared about the things that had hurt me in the past. I didn't care about my heartbreak. It didn't matter that I was still on crutches. I didn't even care that I couldn't feel half of my body because, just by existing, she had taught me that I could feel so much more.

My mind flashed back to the last time my world had changed in a single moment, and I remembered the infinite darkness that had clouded my vision. I hadn't thought there was a way out of that period of my life, and although I'd started to see the sunshine again on my own, Layla had been the missing piece all along.

Looking down at the wondrous bundle in the hospital blanket I was holding in my arms, I understood everything perfectly. She was my light. She was what made everything worth it. She was the reason I was still here.

When I first found out Hayley was pregnant, my biggest concern was that my sister wouldn't be okay. That having such a huge responsibility so young would plunge her further into the darkness that was swallowing her. I thought it meant I was going to lose my sister. As time went by and I watched Hayley bloom into her role as a mother as though it was something always meant for her, I knew I couldn't have been more wrong. Having this baby brought her immense change and responsibility, but Layla was the very thing that saved her. Along with her tiny fingers and tremendous spirit, she brought purpose, peace and unconditional love.

I found it so strange to think that the thing I now loved most in the entire world didn't even exist until very recently. It was bizarre to me that I had lived a whole twenty-one years of my life without Layla in it.

If it was possible for me to experience a feeling I'd never had before after two decades of being on earth, I imagined it was possible for the rest of my life to be filled with other new and breathtaking experiences as well. There are people I will love with my whole heart who I haven't met yet. There are places I don't even know exist that I will one day refer to as 'my place'. There are mountains whose names I don't yet know that I will climb to the top of someday. There is so much goodness and love and joy ahead of me that I can't even see or imagine yet.

How wonderful it is to know that the best day of our life might be waiting for us somewhere in the future, and we have no idea how full our hearts are capable of feeling. That what we have and what we feel in this moment isn't all there will ever be—there is still so much more to come.

How wonderful to wonder how much more light you'll one day find. In the gentle, slow-moving orange sunrises, but also in the sudden, soul-shifting lightning strikes.

29

FRIENDSHIP

Despite being naturally shy, I have always found first dates to be exhilarating. The eternal romantic in me loves the thrill of possibility that comes with meeting someone new. Will the next hour be nothing more than a quick meal and some potentially bland conversation with a stranger, or will it be the first moment I lay eyes on a face I will always know? Dating, although sometimes turbulent and disappointing, always seemed to hold so much potential and mystique to me. I could often easily picture a vibrant future laid out in front me—the late-night talks, sleepy long-haul flights, patient perusals of department store aisles in search of the perfect fry-pan—before I'd even said hello. My imagination could run wild at the possibility of it all, yet for some reason I never allowed myself that same optimism on first dates with potential friends.

Somewhere along the line, I had developed the strong belief that unless you had nurtured a lifelong friendship, one that spanned the many decades and versions of yourself—like what I had with Jemma—you would always remain at a surface level distance. I didn't think adult friendships could evolve into anything more than close acquaintances or, at best, friends who went out for lunch every second Thursday—but never friends who cried into each other's laps at 3 am. So when I thrust myself into a brand new town, unable to lean on the familiarity of a best friend I'd always known, I knew that if I wanted friendship I would have to leave my comfort zone and make a very deliberate effort to connect with others. But I was also certain that I would just have to learn to live without the glow of a true, soul-level friend.

~

Social media understandably gets a bit of a bad rap, but in my experience I've found it to be an incredible tool for connecting with like-minded people. When I got home from hospital, I started following the accounts of people who were also living with disabilities or chronic health issues and it helped me feel part of a community. One of the first accounts I came across was a girl named Elle, who was using her page to share her story of living with scoliosis and overcoming chronic fatigue. Eventually we started speaking through messages and I had the sense that we would get along really well. She lived on the Sunshine Coast, which was thirteen hours from where I was in Canberra, but a year later, when I told her I was moving to Queensland, we planned to finally meet in person.

Something a lot of people might not realise about those who choose to share their life through a screen is that a large majority of us are introverts. A lot of us started accounts as a creative outlet and a way to share pieces of our life that we didn't necessarily feel comfortable sharing in person. The videos you see might depict people as confident and outgoing (and I'm sure that's the reality for many) but it's important to remember that these are often filmed in complete solitude where a person is their most comfortable self. So although you're seeing a true reflection of someone's personality, you don't get to see the version of them that quietens and becomes more reserved when they leave their own space.

All this is to say, when it came time to meet Elle, I was petrified. I even composed a mental list of conversation topics to bring up in case we ran out of things to talk about. I was expecting to meet her at a cafe, timidly chat for an hour or two and go home, but instead I jumped in her car and helped her run errands like we'd known each other for years. We spent the entire day together, and in all those hours there wasn't a single moment when I needed to refer to my extremely boring conversation points. We couldn't speak fast enough—it was as though we'd been mute for years and finally had the opportunity to get out everything we'd been wanting to say. We understood each other with such ease and immediacy that I went to bed that night with the overwhelming feeling that I'd found something I hadn't even known I was searching for.

One day Elle and I drove to what had quickly become my favourite spot on the coast. A lush green hill by the ocean, where on Sundays people brought picnic blankets and cheese boards and sat with their friends to watch the sunset. The place was beautiful on its own, but the first time I saw it filled with people, I was awed. The atmosphere was electric. Birds filled the trees above us and somehow sang louder than the hundreds of voices below, people of all ages paused to admire the beauty of the sky with the same reverence I did when I was alone, and music drifted through the air while waves lapped against the rocks to create the most beautiful symphony I'd ever heard. This. This was everything I'd always wanted. Community.

We found a spare patch of grass and sat down in our group of two, careful not to take up more room than we needed, and sat silently for a moment to take it all in. We looked out at the hill, an emerald canvas sprinkled with countless circles of friends. Some groups were singing and playing guitar, some were talking animatedly, some were drinking and dancing and laughing loudly. It felt like high school again. Everyone had a group and a place they belonged. I wondered how it would feel to be a part of it properly. To one day pull up to the carpark, get out of my car with snacks in hand and a blanket big enough to share and walk towards a circle I was welcomed into. To feel like I perfectly fit.

Elle must have been having a similar train of thought, because we turned to each other, eyes wide with the beauty of what we were seeing, and said to one another, 'I want this.' We didn't know how, but we decided then and there that we were going to create it.

~

About a month after moving to Queensland, once we were somewhat settled, I decided it was time to get back into my rehabilitation and focus on my physical healing. I had been doing exercises on my own at home but I knew I was still in the very early stages of my journey and wanted some more guidance. I noticed my strength only improved when I was putting in the work and that it would plateau or decrease as soon as I took a break. My calves had remained completely paralysed and my lower body still couldn't feel, but I had to continue to strengthen the muscles that *had* regained function so they didn't atrophy.

During the move I misplaced my crutches and was forced to walk without them for a while. At first it was daunting and I constantly had the sense that I was one rogue breath of wind away from being knocked off my feet, but after a while I realised to my surprise that I was actually okay. More than okay. I was walking on my own. It was unbalanced, slow and cautious, but it was walking nonetheless. I had been relying on my crutches out of comfort and familiarity, but I'd learned that comfortable and familiar isn't always what is best.

I made an appointment to have a consultation at a well-known spinal rehab facility. People travelled from all over the country for treatment there and, without even realising or planning to, I had moved a three-minute drive away.

I drove to my first appointment shaking with nerves. I wasn't nervous about the consult or the gruelling work I knew I was about to subject myself to—the anxiety pulsing through me was from the fear of having to meet and talk to people I didn't know.

The fear of entering an environment where I had no idea what to expect.

I intentionally arrived about ten minutes early so I could sit outside beforehand to mentally prepare myself. As I sat on a stoop out the front, a girl who looked to be about my age got out of a car and walked towards the entrance. Her hair was in two braids and she was wearing long colourful socks that burst out from her shoes. She looked like a little kid. I was instantly enamoured by her. She walked with a confidence that I deeply craved and it seemed like she had her own vibrant world going on inside her head. Without knowing a thing about her, I was certain that she was somebody who knew exactly who she was. I wondered why she was here, if perhaps she was the partner or sister of a patient, sent here to fill the room with her support and effervescence. She smiled as she walked past me through the doors.

When I eventually gathered the courage to go inside, I was surprised to find that the girl was one of the exercise physiologists who worked at the clinic. Her name was Bec and she welcomed me so warmly that I forgot to even be nervous. She was one of those people who had the ability to cut through the awkward small talk and dive straight into the good stuff. The session was hard, but in the best possible way. I loved the feeling of pushing my body to its limits and I'd missed the solidarity that comes with being surrounded by people all going through the same thing. I knew I'd made the right choice.

In every friendship, there comes a point where you go from 'people who hang out' to 'oh, now we're real friends', and I can remember that moment with Bec so clearly. I'd been going to rehab a few days a week for a couple of months and more often than not Bec was my trainer. She was incredible at her job so the work was physically exhausting, but I always looked forward to it because I loved spending time with her.

One afternoon there was a presentation on spinal cord injury research we both wanted to go to, so we decided to drive together. It was the first time we had hung out beyond the gym and again I felt a hint of nerves. I wondered if it would feel disconcerting seeing her outside of our usual habitat, like bumping into a teacher at the supermarket and not knowing how to act.

After the presentation, she drove me home and we alternated between deep chats, laughing and singing at the top of our lungs. Eventually I looked up to see that we were in my driveway and when I checked the clock, I realised we must have been sitting there for over an hour.

Time had passed without me feeling it move, and I knew I'd found someone who would become a sister.

~

When I first moved away, I had really wanted to find love. Despite living in an age where we are encouraged to be confident on our own and empowered by singlehood, I wanted to be in a relationship more than I wanted to be alone. I had this idea in my head that the happy ending to my story involved falling in love and finding someone who could accept and cherish all of me. Someone who would love me *because* of the things I'd gone through, not just in spite of them. I thought finding 'my person' would be the moment I found closure; that it would be the magical missing piece that made everything else worth it. Even though I was happy with who and where I was, I was still searching for something more.

As the months went by, I continued to feel like something was missing; something that I couldn't quite put my finger on. I had assumed it was a relationship, because that's what we're programmed to think. But that night when I looked out at the green hill sprinkled with community, and that day when I felt the warm wind on my face while singing loudly on the highway, I realised that it wasn't a relationship I had been craving at all—it was friendship. Real, genuine, soul-aligning friendship.

I vowed that I would never let myself forget how magical and important that was. That there would never come a day where I would discount all the platonic love in my life because I was waiting for the 'real thing'. My friends *were* the real thing.

30

TESTED

Something I quickly discovered about a legal case is that regular doctors and surgeon's reports don't count for much in court. You have to have reports from certified medico-legal doctors because they are bound by law to tell the truth and not exaggerate injuries for the sake of a claim. I had countless assessments from these kinds of doctors. Neurosurgeons, urologists, physiotherapists, occupational therapists, psychologists—you name it, I've got a fifty-page report from them.

These appointments weren't just an hour consult discussing my limitations and disability, they were whole day events. They consisted of talking in depth about the same things I'd spoken about more times than I could count; the same things that no one should ever be forced to talk about. Questions like, did I think I would ever be able to find a husband despite my 'condition'? Because if not, we would have to consider that I might need to be compensated for all the jobs a husband would typically do around the house. How many years did I think I would have before my disability worsened and I was back in a wheelchair? Where did I think I would live for each of the eighty-one years of my predicted life span and who would look after me at each point?

After the talking section of the assessment would come the physical exam. I was poked and prodded with needles and asked if I could feel them. The answer was always no. Next I was asked to move each individual muscle against resistance so they could rate my strength out of five. Then I was told to take off my pants and bend over so they could put their finger inside me to see whether or not I could clench around it. They would ask me to sit on the toilet while they watched to see if I could go to the bathroom naturally. They would ask me to do a catheter and enema in front of them so they could see how I did it.

Logically I understood why I had to go through these examinations, and I was willing to do them. I understood the insurance company needed clear reports explaining the extent of my injury and I understood why so many different specialists needed to be involved to cover all bases. What I didn't understand was why there had to be more than one examination from each profession. I couldn't fathom why there had to be up to five from each specialty when they were all finding the same results. If you added them all up, I would have spent weeks of my life undergoing these monotonous and degrading examinations.

I wanted to be young. I wanted to be able to relate to the awkwardness of a pap smear. I wanted to fill out a resume instead of a fecal chart. I wanted to be able to use all the joy I'd worked so hard for and spread it around the world. I wanted to enjoy the life I was so lucky to still have, without the constant and stark reminder of how much I'd lost. But I also needed to win the case in order to do all those things. Between my physical therapy, doctors appointments and needing to now spend money every time I went to the bathroom, my medical bills were not exactly cheap. In fact, according to Spinal Cure Australia, the average lifetime cost of a paraplegic injury is over $2 million. I wasn't too sure what type of work I would be capable of in the future with my disability, so I knew I'd need some form of support. As much as I wanted to simply move on, I needed the money to do so.

After countless examinations but no progress, I organised yet another meeting with my lawyer. While he'd initially seemed kind and sympathetic, as time went on it seemed like he'd lost patience with me. He'd begun to address me condescendingly, like I had no idea how the world worked. Like knowing law was what gave you life experience. So I decided to take my older sister Tara with me this time. Tara is the kind of person who doesn't take any shit and will say whatever needs to be said without question. We went into the meeting frustrated and wanting answers because I couldn't continue this way. My entire life had become consumed by the case and I was tired of living life on pause.

We talked for an hour and he went over the same things that we had already spoken about hundreds of times before. I didn't understand why he had to ask me these questions again; had he not already written the answers down? Had he not yet begun the case? I don't remember exactly how it came up, but something led him to the words 'Well, you're not *really* a paraplegic anyway'. This was a common misconception with my specific and very unique form of disability, so I wouldn't normally be offended, but after years of detailed doctor's reports and countless meetings, he should surely have been familiar with the medical name of my injury. If he was representing me and putting me through countless examinations, surely he understood what I was living with. My sister very quickly put him in his place and we moved on to talking about all the necessary equipment and medical supplies that I needed to live each day. When I mentioned catheters, he looked at me and said bluntly, 'Well no, we can't count catheters because they're a luxury, not a necessity.'

My jaw dropped. I swear my sister nearly threw a fist over the desk. I asked him if he thought being able to urinate was a luxury. I asked him if the fact that I would die if I didn't use them was indulgent. As he began to backpedal, I realised I couldn't take another word. My intuition was screaming at me to get as far away from this man as I could. When I got up to leave I saw that, ironically, I had peed through my incontinence pad and onto his seat. It was completely unintentional—of course, I have no control—but I absolutely wasn't mad about the timing. I left his office in a fit of rage.

I knew what I had to do, but it was such a difficult decision. I could continue on with a lawyer who I knew didn't respect, understand or fight for me, or I could forgo the years he'd spent on this case and start from scratch with someone new. It was a lose-lose situation, and I felt excruciating disappointment and a deep longing for it to be over.

With a warier disposition, stronger backbone and a whole lot less hope than I had a few years earlier when this had all begun, I switched lawyers.

31

IF YOU CAN, YOU MUST

I was lying in bed one night, not long after my disastrous visit to the lawyer, when I decided to go through the old notes in my phone. After so much time had passed, I was curious to revisit the stories I had jotted down in hospital. I scrolled down through the years as though I was flicking through pages of a diary, pausing occasionally to look at entries and remember the person I was when I wrote them. The year of my accident wasn't exactly profound at first. Just random notes like 'hospital Wi-Fi code: grüezi' and 'travel insurance policy #648395', but then I came across a note I'd written only a few days after the accident, while I was on suicide watch. It was so short that it didn't mean anything to me at first, but then I remembered.

If you can, you must.

I had written those five words to my future self to remind her to go for a run if she was ever lucky enough to be able to. It was strange reading them again after so long, now that I had actually become the person they were intended for. I wrote them when I was desperate to run again, and I was reading them now with the knowledge that I still couldn't.

On one hand it felt odd, because when I wrote the words all those seasons ago everything was still so fresh that reality hadn't had the chance to properly sink in yet. Even in the midst of my panic and despair, I don't think I ever *really* believed I'd never run again. The thought of it had seemed absurd.

On the other hand, reading the words was comforting. Remembering just how distraught and hopeless I had felt when I wrote them reminded me of how not-distraught and hope*ful* I felt now, even though I still didn't have the thing I'd been longing for.

I'd found acceptance in something that felt wholly unacceptable at the time. Something I was certain would never be okay, was. How simple and profound.

I read the sentence again and got goosebumps. The power of the words hit me with as much force as I had felt when I wrote them. Only this time the force wasn't heartbreaking or shattering, it was empowering. These words were about so much more than just running, they were about *everything.*

Here is what they mean to me now, after years of living in my second chance: if you can do something, and you want to do it, you must. For no other reason than the unbelievable and unlikely fact that you can. Write that song you've been keeping tucked away in your head, talk to that person you've been too shy to say hello to, travel the world while you're young and able, run that marathon you've been secretly training for. Basically, if you have the option and desire to do something, *anything*, you must do it while you can. We tend to think we have all the time in the world, but we don't. Opportunities don't hang around forever and you never know when the day will come that they'll pass you by for good and leave you thinking, *Damn, I should have done that while I had the chance.*

My past self wasn't just reminding me to embrace my legs, she was telling me to embrace it all. She had been lying there trembling with sadness over losing something she'd never realised was special, and she was begging the future me to never make that same mistake again. She was urging me to love things purely because I loved them, and not only because they'd been taken away. The words were a reminder of something we all know to be true but that we can far too easily choose to ignore: our time in these bodies and on this earth is finite. And our lives are often filled with blessings so plentiful that we forget to even notice them.

~

Something I've found interesting since being back on my two feet is the number of able-bodied people who, upon seeing my limp and questioning what happened, leave me with the same comment. 'You are so lucky to be walking.'

I nod along politely as I stand on un-feeling legs in the grocery store line or crowded cafe, because it's true, I am lucky.

Inexplicably so. But quietly, I always leave the conversation thinking the same thing . . . *so are you.*

The thing they view me as lucky for having is the very same thing they have themselves. You don't have to lose something in order for it to be important to you. You don't have to have gone without something in order to feel fortunate to have it.

I get nervous reminding people of that simple truth. I quieten my inner voice, swallow my words and smile politely in far more situations than I should. I know it can feel aggressive to receive such a sharp reminder in the middle of a Tuesday, and it's never nice to be called out for taking something special for granted. Especially by a stranger who knows nothing about your life, situation or level of thankfulness. So I dull my fire down and trust that people will understand without me needing to explain it to them.

But then my mind flashes to images from the spinal ward of the man tilting his head to the left and right, of the lady in the bed next to mine who screamed for hours each night from the pain, of Naomi opening packets of salt with fingers that wouldn't cooperate—and I see clearly again.

It's impossible for this message to be delivered too aggressively because it's one that needs to be heard. We all need a wake-up call occasionally. I gave myself one when I saw those five words glowing on the screen of my phone. Some of the time we know our own luck, and gratitude floods through our veins as we make the most of it, but far too often we don't know what we have until we don't have it anymore. What a waste and shame that is.

So from my past and present self, let me say this to my future self, and to you. Whatever that thing is that niggles away in the back of your mind, the thing you think about right before you fall asleep, the one that lights you up inside. Whatever it is you keep putting off for another tomorrow because you can't be bothered right now. If you are capable of doing it, and you want to do it, you need to. Before it's too late, before you get the chance to wonder *what if?*, before the parachute doesn't open.

Do it now—because if you can, you must.

32

SPINAL CORD INJURIES

It's a peculiar thing to suddenly lose the ability to feel and control your own body. Like most things in life, there are different stages in the realisation of it. Various moments of impact.

It starts with confusion. With doctors pressing on your body and asking if you can feel their touch, and your utter disbelief when the answer is 'no'.

Next is shock. The moment you look down and actually *see* their hands on you, and you realise they weren't playing a cruel prank when they said they were touching you before. You wonder if the legs attached to you are in fact even yours or some kind of uncanny, fake replica.

Then comes overwhelm. You reach down to touch your own skin for the first time and suddenly understand how someone else feels when they touch you. You can feel the giving of your touch with your fingertips, but you can't receive it at all. It's as foreign as touching a stranger.

There are so many of these small moments of impact—learning what you can and can't feel, learning what moves and what doesn't, learning how it feels to be inside a body you can't reach from the outside.

This book is testament not only to my personal strength but the human spirit as a whole. I have learned and witnessed time and time again just how much resilience and undying determination we are all truly capable of, and I've come to realise it is far beyond what we tend to give ourselves credit for. Throughout my journey, I have been lucky enough to meet the most remarkable and extraordinary human beings who have taught me the very meaning of hardiness and what it means to keep on living, even when you're certain you cannot. I have learned that a spinal cord injury, although devastating and life-altering, is not in fact world-ending. I have learned that life goes on and life can be beautiful, even after trauma and even alongside grief.

All these things are inherently true and are the key lessons I have taken from my time living with a disability, but there is something else which is also true. And that is the irrefutable fact that living with a spinal cord injury, no matter how accepted and well-treated, is more difficult than living without one.

Yes, living with this type of injury brings immense growth and character development and oftentimes instils a gratitude beyond comprehension. Yes, it is entirely possible, not to mention common, to live a completely fulfilling and joyous life with disability. Yes, there can be acceptance and forgiveness and no desire to go back in time to erase the past. But still, there is no denying the immense, axis-shifting weight that accompanies this type of unforeseen circumstance. To not acknowledge its heaviness would be a disservice to all those living with a spinal cord injury and would paint a half-done, sugar-coated and inaccurate depiction of reality.

If you were to google the effects of a spinal cord injury, you would find a list of possible symptoms including paralysis, lack of sensation, impaired bladder and bowel function, spasms, fertility issues, respiratory problems, and many more. But what does this really mean to a human life? How does this list translate into the everyday and what does it look like in the real world? Is the ability to walk what is most missed by those in wheelchairs, or is it the capacity to feel your child's hand on top of your own and be able to squeeze it back?

I want you to do something for me. I want you to read this chapter with a deep sense of curiosity, and instead of just acknowledging the words, I want you to really try and put yourself in these scenarios. Try to *really* imagine what it would feel like to experience them. It's so easy to hear about the pain of others but it's difficult to truly fathom the extent of it unless we take the time to properly digest and comprehend a person's reality; to actively exercise empathy.

Imagine it's the middle of the night. You're safe in bed but you've awoken in a sleepy haze by a chill coming through the window. The drop in temperature overnight has been enough to wake your body up to let you know you're cold. You instinctively reach down to pull the covers up and over you before you drift back to sleep, but you are reminded with a familiar yet still startling and always painful jolt that you cannot move. You cannot use your hands or arms (or any other part of your body for that matter) to complete the simple, menial task of pulling a sheet over your body to keep warm. So instead, you lay awake shivering, hoping sleep finds you again soon. But until it does, your mind wanders down corridors you normally keep firmly closed, like how very easy life must be for all those who didn't even need to wake up to pull the sheet over themselves tonight.

Now imagine having an itch and physically not being able to scratch it.

Imagine not being able to stand up, look at the person you love at eye-level and hug them tight.

Imagine having an injury where the frustrating period of time spent healing and out of action from your regular hobbies is not just six agonising weeks, it's the rest of your life.

Imagine a fly buzzing around your head, ever insistent on landing on your face or in your ear, and not being able to swat it away.

Imagine never being able to feel sex with your partner.

Imagine not being able to mindlessly scroll through your phone or send a text when you're bored.

Imagine having to spend money every time you go to the bathroom.

Imagine being in constant, inescapable pain.

Imagine getting to a friend's party and realising, only upon arrival, that you can't get inside the building because it's upstairs and no one thought to consider your wheelchair.

Imagine wanting to be alone, to revel in the comfort of solitude, but needing a carer with you twenty-four hours a day.

Imagine wanting to put your arm around someone you're dating and having to ask them to do it for you.

It's not just the wheelchair factor that is hard to bear, it's the million unforeseeable everyday moments that creep up on you and remind you of how much your life has changed. You never know when you'll stumble upon another one and it makes the loss not one solitary day but rather a continual series of blows you are forced to endure time and time again.

You see, it's not only losing the ability to walk; it's losing the ability to reach a cupboard in your kitchen which holds a crucial ingredient while you're midway through a recipe. It's wanting an early start to the day but needing to perform a three-hour bowel routine before you can leave the house. It's seeing your daughter crying in pain and not being able to pick her up to comfort her even though you so desperately want to. It's choosing clothes to wear based not on appearance but on their ability to keep you warm or cool because you can't regulate your own body temperature. It's craving the touch of another human and being physically unable to receive it. It's a friend instinctively reaching out to shake your hand, but you're unable to shake it back. It's having to rely on a machine just to breathe.

There are so many things the majority of people (myself included) do every day without thought or merit, but some people go a lifetime without them. Before my accident, I was so uninformed about spinal cord injuries that if I saw someone in a wheelchair I naively assumed that they couldn't walk and that was that. It never occurred to me that their legs were only a tiny fragment of what they were going through. I had no idea how many things accompany paralysis and how all-encompassing it can be.

I also never stopped to appreciate that not only would an individual be dealing with their medical struggles, they'd also still be facing the regular challenges and emotions that come with being human. When someone has a medical condition, we can tend to subconsciously think that it is the *only* problem that affects them; that they are somehow now immune to the woes that affect the rest of the population and that they are solely dedicated to tending to their health. Of course this isn't the case at all—whether it be financial stress, relationship troubles, mental health or the loss of a loved one, 'normal' life experiences don't stop just because your plate is already full. Instead, you are forced to withstand them all at once.

I have been living with my disability for nearly a decade and there are still days that are incredibly difficult or frustrating or where I long for the ease of my former body. Not because it was 'better', but because it was simpler. I say this even as someone who can stand up and walk whenever I want. As someone who frequently has bowel accidents but who is capable of cleaning myself up without help. As someone who has spent years in a wheelchair but who *still* cannot even begin to fathom the experience of others.

My heart breaks for all the people around the world who so

desperately crave what the majority already have and don't even realise is special. I ache knowing how thoughtlessly we get out of bed in the morning while there are others who are working towards that moment as their single lifelong dream. The things that some people deal with each and every day are so unimaginable to the uninformed that if you were aware of them all, you would realise the true strength and grit it takes to not only get through a day but to fill it with joy and kindness and enthusiasm. You would be awe-filled and almost starstruck by the individuals who are able to carry what they do.

All this is not to say that living with a spinal cord injury is unbearable or unlivable. In fact, every person I know with an SCI carries it with immense grace and a tenacious and infectious zest for life. There are countless people living with this particular disability who, even if they were given the chance, would choose not to change a thing. Who, if they were handed a cure tomorrow, would have absolutely no desire or need to accept it. I am confident that the pages of this book are enough to highlight our capacity as humans to not only overcome but to thrive throughout hardship and to accept our realities for what they are. I'm not insinuating that life is unkind or horrible for people who live with paralysis and I'm not assigning any intrinsic value or worth to the way a body functions, I'm merely pointing out the undisputable fact that it would, quite simply, be easier to live without it.

There's a quote that resonates deeply with what I aim to get across through these words. *Just because someone carries it well, doesn't mean it isn't heavy.* To all my friends (both known and unknown) who are living with a spinal cord injury, I want you to know that I see you, I love you, I marvel at your spirit every single day and I hope with a great ferocity that one day, if it's something you long for, you won't have to carry the weight anymore. You carry it so graciously, but I hope one day you'll be able to put it down.

33

CONNECTION

When I was younger, I remember watching TV shows and being amazed that the characters could walk out of their door and, without fail or any planning, bump into someone they knew. That they could step into a cafe and be greeted by a smiling face who, upon hearing their voice, looked up and said, 'Just the usual? How're the kids?'

I didn't believe towns like that existed in the real world. But the more roots I put down in my new home in Queensland, and the more I opened myself up to connection, the more I realised that this familiarity truly did exist. Not because of where I was, but because of who I was striving to become. Community isn't an automatic thing reserved only for small towns and mythical lands, it's something that grows when watered.

As I moved through the world and encountered strangers in day to day life, instead of just giving an obligatory closed mouth smile and nod as I passed them by, I started deliberately keeping myself open, ready to stop for a chat if they so wished. The encounters and friendships that this simple shift in attitude led to were cosmic.

Doctor's receptionists, nextdoor neighbours, grocery store workers—dozens of people who I hadn't known just months earlier were now regular characters in the story of my life, people I didn't necessarily know all that well, but whose presence was woven into my everyday to create a colourful tapestry.

~

My world had started expanding so rapidly that I felt like I was living in a film I'd dreamed up. Elle and Bec had moved in with us, so along with Mum, Hayley and Layla, there were six of us living under the one roof. There weren't even enough rooms in the house for each of us to have our own, but we were all so close that it didn't matter. Sharing beds and memories was exactly what that period of our lives called for. The affinity we all had was instant and, somehow, although our worlds had only collided in the past year, I knew it would be permanent too.

I thought I'd reached my maximum amount of soul-level friends until, one unassuming morning as I walked into a cafe, I found another one. A girl named Chloe who was the kind of person whose energy levels make you feel as though you've never made the most of a day in your life. Chloe taught me how to wake up at the crack of dawn and feel excitement for the added hours, how to water-ski on legs I never imagined would be able to and how to trust, implicitly, that whatever path I walked down next, I would turn into the right one. I was learning that, although rare, soulmates were something you likely never stopped stumbling upon.

I felt like a magnet as I moved through my new life, as if the things intended for me were finding me without any effort or force. I wondered if I was now seeing the world in a better light because of this, or if perhaps the magnetism was happening because of how I now saw the world.

Elle and I bought an old kombi and started taking trips up and down the coast. Along with the rest of our friends, we would sleep by the ocean, cook breakfast on a gas stove and see where the road would lead us the next day. We visited waterfalls and mountain tops, rode bikes and attempted to surf, and embraced any and every adventure we stumbled upon. We were in that very rare but thrilling period of our lives where our entire friendship group was single at the same time, and we were soaking up every moment of it, knowing there would come a day, without any warning, when we couldn't experience this again.

Life is full of chapters. Pages turn, new stories are written and, in my experience, each one tends to get better than the last. But this chapter—the one where my friends were my family and I never went more than an hour without genuine laughter—was one so special and beautiful that even as I was in it I knew it would forever remain one of my favourites.

With every trip I went on, every new place I got to visit and every friend that came into my world, one thought repeated in my mind. *How lucky am I to be here?* I was never more acutely aware of my improbable second chance than the moments I stood somewhere my wheelchair wouldn't have reached, looked beside me at a face I hadn't known in my Life Before and realised with sheer disbelief—*Holy shit, I almost didn't get to see this.*

I'd heard the saying that grief doesn't shrink and instead life grows around it, and I was learning that this was true. When you're in the eye of your storm, it's hard to imagine there could ever possibly come a time where it isn't as all-consuming and suffocating as it is in that moment. People tell you the pain will pass and that time will someday allow you to heal, but you don't believe it, not really. How can something so devastating ever become something ordinary? But there I was, years on from the peak of my hurt, laughing and living and thinking, *Huh, it really did happen.* Someday was finally here.

The things I missed were all still missing—my body had healed as much as it probably ever would—but it didn't matter because my life was growing regardless. Things didn't need to be perfect in order for me to be happy, I'd realised. My grief was still there, but somehow it didn't feel anywhere near as large or looming, and there was room for joy and love to sit right beside it. It occurred to me that my heart wasn't just rebuilding to the size it had been before everything changed, it was expanding.

~

One night when I was in hospital, a lady I didn't recognise came into the ward and asked if she could give me a psychic reading. Most of the patients were already asleep and the nurses were busy helping with night-time routines, so without much else to do and no one around, I said, 'Sure, why not?'

She read my cards and told me lots of things about my future. When I think about it now, I realise that all the parts I can remember have since come true. She said I would learn to walk again and that my purpose was to share my story and words with the world. But it wasn't the reading that stuck with me the most, it was something she said briefly before she left.

'I want you to know a secret about the world,' she told me. 'You can go and sit under the sky, or put your hands on a tree, or bury your feet into the grass, and borrow nature's energy whenever you need it. The only thing you have to do in return is make sure you give that energy back to the world in the best way you can.'

I have no idea where this woman came from, and like a genie that clicks its fingers and disappears into a puff of smoke, she left immediately after our conversation. It was so bizarre and random that sometimes I wonder if she was real or just a figment of my medicated imagination. At the time I had laughed it off, storing the encounter in the 'well, that was odd' category of my memory, without giving much thought to her words. But I never forgot them.

As the years went on and my love for the outside world became one of the most fundamental elements of my happiness, I slowly realised that what she had told me was in fact true. Diving into the ocean or stepping outside to feel the warmth of the sun piercing my skin has not once failed to make me feel more alive. Because of this, I now actively put myself in the way of nature. I swim in it, walk amongst it, marvel as it changes colour, fill my home with flowers and plant my palms on tree trunks as I pass them. Being outdoors, even for five fleeting minutes, energises me in a way nothing else can. All I have to do is make sure that when I'm okay again I return that energy to the world in the most beautiful way I can.

Nature teaches us so much: how to bend without breaking, how to be patient with growth, how to rebuild after a wildfire. The metaphors and lessons are endless. Whenever I'm alone, I always seem to find myself sitting on cliff edges and watching on in awe as the waves continuously smash against the rocks. Or staring at sunsets wondering how I went twenty years without ever noticing how flawlessly the gradient of the sky melds from blue to pink.

What I love the most about nature is that it doesn't care whether we look at it or not. It will keep moving and shining even if nobody bothers to watch it. The waves will keep crashing, the leaves will keep falling, the colours will keep changing, even if no one is looking.

Time has shown me that if you're really lucky, you might come across a person like that too. Shining not because it wants to be seen, but because it can't help but glow. Beautiful not because it's showing off but because it just is.

34

A SINGLE SECOND

Something I learned very soon after my accident is that people want to ask me a lot of questions about skydiving. Would I do it again? What did it feel like when I was falling? If I could go back and *not* jump from that helicopter, would I? Would I recommend it to other people? I understand the very human element of curiosity about an intriguing and unique story, so I'm not at all offended or surprised by the influx of questions. Although it does feel odd, and somewhat boring, to be repeatedly asked about something that you actually care very little about. Despite what happened, I barely think about skydiving at all. I know next to nothing about it and I've only ever done it once. Of course I resonate with the growth and lessons that have indirectly come from the experience, but not with a two-minute period of my life that happened almost a decade ago.

I used to have such a strong desire to skydive again because I felt like I 'needed' to. I wanted to prove to myself that I wasn't afraid, and somewhere along the line I had formed the belief that reliving the experience was going to be pivotal in closing that chapter of my life. I've never been worried that something would go wrong again (I mean, if it did I'd simply have to take the hint that maybe, just maybe, it's not the sport for me), I was more concerned about how doing it would *feel*. Would I have a panic attack on the way down as the memories resurfaced? Would I even be able to enjoy the thrill? And if not, what was the point?

As more time passed and I realised how unrelated skydiving was to anything I was going through, I knew that I had absolutely nothing to prove and even if I did, this wasn't the way to do it. Skydiving felt incredibly irrelevant to my now very full life, so I knew it wasn't going to be an essential part of my journey or healing. Over time, the idea of jumping again went from something I felt like I *needed* to do to something I would possibly one day do, but only if I ever found myself *wanting* to.

So when Bec came to me and told me she was going skydiving on an ordinary and cloudless Sunday, I decided to go along with her. Not to jump, but to see how being there felt. She had planned a tandem jump with an instructor who was a good friend of ours who we trusted completely, and I felt so excited for her. I remembered how much joy and freedom the fall had brought me before it all went wrong and I loved knowing that she was about to experience that feeling of elation for herself. When we arrived at the drop zone, I asked our friend if I could go up in the plane with Bec to watch her jump out and, to my surprise, he said yes. But there was one condition—I had to get geared up and strapped to an instructor just in case there was an emergency and we had to jump out. I agreed without thinking much of it, but when the instructor began to put on my harness, I learned that the body remembers what the mind forgets.

I'm able to recall my accident so vividly and with such perfect clarity that I assumed I'd left no memory unexamined after all these years. But in that moment, I realised the smaller details must have faded over time. Because as we climbed into the plane and flew toward the clouds, my ears remembered the sound of the air rushing past as the door opened, my eyes remembered the way the earth looks from 14,000 feet, my heart remembered the heavy beating in my chest as we got higher and higher, and all of a sudden I was back there. I was twenty years old again, unaware that a single second was about to change the entire course of my life. My body had a physical response. I was shaking as I stared out the window, my eyes frozen in place as if what I was seeing was instead a vision of a memory long gone. The man I was strapped onto must have sensed my distress, because he squeezed my hand tightly.

When the plane touched down again I shook myself off, plastered on a big grin and found Bec, who thankfully had loved every moment of her jump. Together we sat and watched on as other skydivers went up in the plane and drifted down to the ground again like little snowflakes on a calm day. When they landed, I noticed everyone giving their instructor a quick hi-five before turning and walking away from them, and suddenly the reality of it hit me.

One second. That was the difference between me and my

instructor exchanging a simple hand gesture and an almost entirely silent exchange in a hospital bed.

I looked at the TV playing a reel of tandem videos beside us and saw the huge smiles on everyone's faces as their parachutes obligingly opened. *One second.* That was the difference between my video being a happy memory I'd probably watch a total of three times in my life and it being used as evidence in the investigation of our near deaths.

I watched on as people got in their cars and drove away five minutes after they landed, and it astounded me that the whole experience was over for them so very quickly. That fun and fleeting experience could have been my own, if just *one second* had gone differently.

~

To accurately answer the question 'knowing what I know now, if I could go back in time to that helicopter in Switzerland, would I still choose to jump?', I would have to assume three things. One, that it's physically possible to force yourself out of a safe helicopter and into the abyss below, knowing with certainty the fear and pain that lie directly in front of you. Two, that had I stayed in the helicopter I wouldn't have one day suffered a traumatic injury in some other way. And three, that there's even a point in pondering or answering the question as though it would make any difference to my current reality.

This question, and the surprising persistence of it, has always bewildered me because I don't believe it's something that is humanly possible to answer, nor is it necessary or helpful to try. If I knew what was going to happen, of course I wouldn't have jumped. Who in their right mind would willingly put themselves in that kind of danger and through that much hurt?

Is that the same as saying I would *want* to take it back? No, not at all. I have no desire to erase the past or change what happened.

Although these facts are contradictory, I believe both can be true.

I've often wondered whether people ask themselves this same question, with the same intense curiosity, about the many turning points in their own lives, or if it's something that is reserved only for the glaringly visible forks in the roads. Although my skydive experience is a very obvious example of how a life can go one way or another based on one decision, this profound domino effect happens to all of us every single day, without us even realising. Every second, each choice we make is changing and forming the rest of our lives in ways we can't yet fathom. Missing a bus, turning right instead of left, smiling back at that guy in the gym, stopping or going through an orange light, saying 'bless you' to a stranger's sneeze. These 'sliding doors' moments that seem so minute and uneventful as they are happening, they are the very things that are weaving the fabric of our identity and writing the story of our lives.

Isn't that one of the most terrifying and amazing things you've ever heard? Terrifying because we have no idea where each decision will take us, and amazing because we have *no freaking idea* where each decision will take us. We don't know which new friend is hiding around the next corner, ready to become someone we will one day not be able to imagine a life without. We don't know what lessons and stories will come from the nerve-wracking job we just started or unfamiliar street we moved into. We don't know what unique gifts we will uncover by walking into a restaurant at the precise time we did. Who's to say the path you choose won't be leading you to a life beyond your wildest dreams? One far more fulfilling and enlivening than anything you would have chosen for yourself if life held no surprises?

The concept of one single second changing the course of my life rattled me deeply when I was first coming to terms with it. It seemed unimaginable that a moment so fleeting could have such a lasting and permanent effect. Now, more than anything else, it excites me.

As humans who naturally like to be in control, we tend to think that change is synonymous with 'scary' or at very least 'hard', and in a lot of ways that can often be true. We're also inclined to believe that certain types of change (i.e. the ones we desperately want) are somewhere far ahead in the future—weeks or years or other worlds away.

After experiencing so much of it myself, I take comfort in the knowledge that change can often be the most wonderful and dearly needed gift we can receive, even if it seems like the very opposite at the time. I've also learned that the things we want most might not be nearly as far away as they seem. One second is all it takes to change a life.

How remarkable, unfair, thrilling, frightening, magical and true—all at the same time.

35

NUMB

A year after switching lawyers, I was told I needed to go to Switzerland to meet with the opposing insurance company. I had never met anyone from their team, and I wondered how it would feel to put a face to the corporate name that had been filling my inbox for the last few years. They also requested that I undergo tests with a local medical team while I was over there, so they could be certain the findings were trustworthy. I couldn't fathom needing more examinations but was happy that at least something was happening. The case wasn't stagnant anymore, which meant I was one step closer to it finally being over.

Once I got to Switzerland, I had a meeting with my lawyer and a woman representing the insurance company. I watched the entire thing unfold from above like a movie. A receptionist ushered me into a room with a long wooden table that was larger than my entire kitchen, and I felt like I was five years old pretending to be an adult. I could feel accusatory eyes on me as I walked in, judging whether or not my limp seemed legitimate and whether or not I was a person who could be trusted. Once I sat down, I was bombarded with questions that made me feel like I was covering up a ghastly crime. It was as though I was hiding a huge secret, one that had hurt millions of people and ruined countless lives, when in reality, all I was doing was being was honest. Wasn't I the one who had been hurt?

After about an hour of torturous questioning, the woman from the insurance company paused, looked at me, and said 'You signed a waiver the day you went skydiving, so technically we aren't even liable to compensate you.'

I have never felt tears spring to my eyes faster. Not at the prospect of not being compensated but because if they knew they weren't going to do so, then why on earth was I here? Why did they not tell me that from day one? Why would they make me endure this distress for years if it was all for nothing?

The next two days were filled morning to night with specialist appointments. I was emotionally prepared for the same kind of examinations I'd had in the past, but I was not prepared for what actually happened. The tests seemed relatively straightforward at first, similar to the ones I'd done time and time again, but then they asked me to go into a room and lie on a bed for some more testing.

I was told to strip down so all I was wearing was my bra but no underwear, and then lie down with my legs in stirrups. Three male doctors came in, speaking to each other in another language. I couldn't understand a word of it. They put sticky pads all over my body and told me in English they were going to put something on my head which would send electric shocks through me. The pads were meant to measure where the electric current stopped, and in turn, where my sensation stopped. We had just tested my ability to feel with pin pricks, so I wasn't sure why we had to do it again, but I knew this was the last examination I would need.

They told me the test was about to begin, but before I had time to register what was happening, my whole body was thrust up from the bed. The shock was so painful and forceful it physically jolted me. The current continued to rip through me four more times. They then moved the contraption from my head to different parts of my body and continued the electric shocks. The worst pain of all was when they got to my back, an area filled with metal rods and a cage. My body jerked up off the bed in agony.

After several more of these shocks, they told me they were now going to pierce my anus with a metal needle to see if I could feel it. *What?* Surely this was some kind of sick joke. It wasn't. As they inserted the needle, I felt sick to my stomach at the thought of what was happening but of course I couldn't feel a single thing. I closed my eyes and waited for the doctors to tell me it was over, but instead I heard the words, 'We are now going to send an electric shock through the needle, just so we can be sure.' As though my lifeless response to the current wasn't enough of an indication that I was numb, they asked if I could feel anything. For the first time since I crashed-landed into that field, I was glad that I couldn't.

I felt helpless as I lay there, naked, vulnerable and soul-tired. I couldn't believe I was doubted to the point where I had to be almost electrocuted to prove I was sincere. None of this was my fault—the accident, the disability, the loss of feeling—yet somehow, I felt like I was entirely to blame. How did I get myself here?

I felt silent tears start to run down my face. I didn't know which was worse, the humiliating experience of it all or the realisation that I truly didn't have a speck of sensation left. Until this intense testing, I'd only let myself feel incredibly lucky to have regained as much movement as I had—I'd never let myself acknowledge the severity of what I'd lost.

I gathered myself and assumed the worst was over, but then they told me they had one last thing to check before we could finish. One of the male doctors looked at me and said, 'We need to check the feeling in your vagina. Would you prefer to rub your own clitoris, or should I do it?'

If I wasn't entirely numb before, I was now. It wasn't even shock I was feeling. It was helpless resignation. My body was nothing more than a medical prop. I had been touched and poked and stared at by so many people over the years that my body didn't feel like my own anymore. Tears were streaming now and I shook my head to let him know that I wasn't doing it. I knew I couldn't feel anything there and the idea of touching myself made me feel pathetic. The doctor proceeded to touch my skin, pierce me with the needle and send the electric shocks through me.

I was numb. In every sense of word.

~

I want to point out that I don't believe any of this was done inappropriately. The doctors were professional and I'm sure it was all just standard protocol. Perhaps without a language barrier and with more explanation and forewarning, it would have been far less traumatic. That's not what made me upset; what angered me was that although it may not have been inappropriate, it was entirely unnecessary and simply cruel.

Why could they not believe my X-rays and scans, where you can clearly see the lesion in my spinal cord? Why could they not believe the first ten examinations I had from medical professionals? Why could they not believe my limp and the fact I am clearly incontinent? Why could they not believe my own word?

I couldn't understand how a system put in place to help people in need had become so obstructed and overcomplicated to the point where people whose lives had already been rattled to the core were forced to endure so much added trauma.

For years my lawyer had told me that insurance claims are deliberately dragged out with the intention of getting people to give up and forfeit their claim before it ever reaches the end. I thought I had understood him before. I thought I could see why people would give up when their life was on hold for countless years. I thought I had already been experiencing what he meant, but it was only now that I truly understood. These claims weren't just dragged out in the time sense, they were dragged out to the point that you were at the end of your emotional tether and you had nothing left to give. I was almost four years in now and I truly didn't see the point anymore. All this was for what? To be paid money to which I was rightly entitled to cover the costs of a disability I didn't ask for or cause? I doubted it was worth it. I knew I was fortunate to even have the possibility of compensation when so many others don't, but if I could have backed out at this point, I would have without question. I knew I couldn't though, or I would have been left with years' worth of lawyer fees and no way to pay for them.

These should have been the best years of my life after surviving the impossible, but as I lay there naked, legs spread, listening to words I didn't understand, being touched in places I couldn't even feel, I knew they were undoubtedly the worst. This wasn't what my second chance was for.

I didn't know why I had survived, but I knew it wasn't for this.

36

SUNFLOWER

Something I find baffling is the ease with which I leaped out of that helicopter. Despite all the risk, fear and my inexperience, I was more than happy to plunge into the ether without a moment's hesitation. I looked at the ground below, saw the danger laid out in plain sight, took my chances and (I only know this from watching the footage back) threw a double-shaka as soon as I felt the fall.

I wasn't scared at all.

I've had friends share stories with me about their own jumps and how they had to muster all their courage to just get themselves into the plane. They then flew all the way up, clutched onto the railing beside the door, peered down at the formidable ground, felt the pounding of their heartbeat and said, 'Absolutely not.'

No matter how hard they tried, they just couldn't make the leap.

I've never been afraid of heights, but I've been left white-knuckled and clutching to the safety of something solid, saying 'Hmm, maybe not for me', more times than I can count. I've arrived at parties, shopping centres and networking events, taken one brief look inside and turned right back around. Despite knowing all I had to do was walk through the door and open my mouth to say 'Hello', I couldn't make the leap.

My fear isn't heights, it's talking to strangers.

Social anxiety is something I have experienced for as long as I can remember. When I was younger, it paralysed me more than any physical injury ever could. I had the sense that I'd fallen asleep during an essential how-to-be-a-human class and was left not understanding something that made perfect sense to others. I remember playing a game of bingo in primary school and having my winning number called out, only to keep it to myself because I couldn't bear the thought of raising my hand. As a teenager, phoning a restaurant to order a pizza often felt like the most daunting task in the world. Even into adulthood, the knowledge of an upcoming event, no matter how far in the distant future, was enough to keep me up at night, trembling from the dread and nerves pulsing through me.

Despite the stakes in these situations being a whole lot lower than that of a freefall, they scared me far, far more.

I have always marvelled at the kind of person who can waltz into any given room and flawlessly exchange words and lightness without so much as a stutter or hint of awkward energy. Those effortlessly vibrant people who can approach a table full of people at a party and instinctively know the appropriate way to greet each guest. Do you announce your arrival to the entire room in one swift moment, or is it a hug for him, a kiss on the cheek for her and a handshake for someone else? Charm and the ability to breezily interact with the world seemed like something you either had or didn't have. I naturally (and very clearly) was lacking it, and it left me wondering how very different my life would look if I didn't need to muster up every ounce of my courage each time I left the house.

I think a common misconception about being shy is that however you present to the outside world is a direct reflection of your internal world. That just because you don't necessarily have much to say out loud, your mind must be free of opinions and humour and vibrant ideas bursting through the seams. This isn't the case at all. Shy is not necessarily synonymous with timid. It doesn't always mean a lack of self-confidence or exhilaration or courage—in my experience, you can be quiet and still overflowing with all of those things.

In fact, despite my shyness, I've always intrinsically been a 'yes person'. Do I want to go scuba diving with sharks? Absolutely. Do I want to walk on a runway wearing nothing but lingerie despite never having modelled before? Sure, why not? Do I want to wake up at 2am to hike to the top of a mountain in the pitch black and freezing cold? Of course.

But do I want to be standing in a change-room and have to ask the shop assistant to please grab me a different sized dress? No, thank you.

It isn't always the case that someone who is shy is also introverted, although I happen to be both. I revel in solitude and crave it after any interaction, no matter how easy or fun it may have been. In the same way some people gain energy from being surrounded by people in a bustling room, others find it hiding in the cubicle of a public toilet, once they have closed the door behind them and know they have the next two minutes to themselves. Because of this, I've never felt overly compelled to alter this element of my personality or tried to become someone who thrives in social settings.

But when I returned to Australia after being poked and prodded for what I hoped was the final time, my zest for life and love for spontaneity grew exponentially. Something was calling me to change. Staying still began to make me restless. I was being pulled into more and more situations where I desperately wanted to take a leap, and where the only thing stopping me from free-falling was my pounding heart.

~

Having a following on social media, I'd learned, sometimes means being invited to events and experiences that sound unbelievably appealing. Free holidays, brunches where you can mingle with all the people you follow online, and countless other opportunities that before the age of social media would have been completely out of my reach. So many of these invites excited me and I felt immensely lucky to even be receiving them, yet I declined every single one that came my way. For no other reason than the fact that my fear was overriding my ability to take the leap.

One event invite that showed up in my inbox was a three-day

trip to Byron Bay with a group of content creators. The days would be filled with activities like hot air ballooning at sunrise, hiking mountains and horse riding along the beach—it sounded like a dream. I looked up the other guests who had been invited, none of whom I knew, and when I looked at their profiles they all seemed to have huge, outgoing personalities. My immediate reaction was to say no, as I so often did, but there was something about this email and the timing of it that made me reply 'yes' instantly, before I could give myself the chance to back out.

Unless you relate to the experience of social anxiety, I imagine it would be almost impossible to understand or empathise with just how nervous I was in the lead up to this trip. It seems frivolous, but it agonised me. When the day finally arrived a month later, I understood why I had said yes in the first place. It was because I was so tired of this fear ruling my life. I had spent the weeks leading up to the event consumed with worry while I was in the safety of my own home, and I was exhausted from the needlessness. It was time for a change. I headed out the door, hands trembling, with a reminder playing on repeat in my mind: *This isn't the hardest thing you've done. This is easy.*

I was sitting in the reception room with the other guests, trying to listen to our briefing while simultaneously wondering where to put my hands, when we heard the sound of a door bursting open followed by loud laughter, and everyone's heads spun around to see who it was. A girl who looked to be around my age walked in.

I have never, in all my life before or since, witnessed what happened next.

Each person in the room lit up one by one. Joy radiated off this girl and visibly spread across the room like a Mexican wave. I didn't know who she was and oddly I don't think anyone else did either. But we didn't need to have met her before to instantly know the kind of person she was. People throw around the term 'human sunshine' pretty casually, but seeing her, glowing while walking in late and emitting the energy and excitement of a toddler on Christmas morning, while having an immediate connection with every person she spoke to, I understood. She was contagious.

Her name was Liv and although her confidence was obvious, I soon realised that her charm wasn't purely her assertiveness, it was her sheer love for life. I didn't look at her big personality and exuberant levels of enthusiasm and think, *She's loud and outgoing*, I thought, *She is someone who is so in love with the world that she's going to make the most of it.* She was like a sunflower, constantly turning towards the light. And that's when it hit me—my shyness wasn't necessarily what I desired to change about myself, it was its frustrating ability to make me wilt, to hold me back from outwardly expressing that same level of joy I felt inside.

Liv and I became friends immediately and as time went on, both at the event and in the years that followed, we were inseparable. I began noticing little parts of her in my mannerisms and words, as though I'd accidentally got too close and caught them off her like a cold. Here was someone who was so exactly and unashamedly who she was, it was impossible to not be your true, weird and authentic self too. I don't often use the term 'inspiring', as I think its overuse has diminished its meaning somewhat, but there is truly no other word to describe the effervescent way she moves through the world. Her name fits her perfectly—she deeply, truly *lives*.

From the moment I saw her beaming and moving chaotically in the doorway, I knew she was the kind of person I wanted to become.

~

One of the greatest things about being human is that we aren't set in stone. We can choose to move, grow and rebuild, as readily and as frequently as we like. I've always loved the concept of the phrase 'You are under no obligation to be the same person you were five minutes ago,' but I didn't necessarily believe it. Some things (like being shy) felt too innate—as much a part of my identity as my eye colour or lactose intolerance—to ever change. I somehow forgot that my very existence was living proof of transformation.

I used to think the only reason I became someone new after Switzerland was because I had a near-death experience. That the one fleeting minute I spent nearly dying was solely responsible for the many years that followed. It wasn't, of course. Nearly dying doesn't magically instil newfound purpose and meaning into someone's life, and not everyone is changed by it. The accident opened my eyes to a lot of things I hadn't noticed before, but the actual *change*—the consistent and deliberate actions that led to a new version of myself—that wasn't the fall, it was me. Transformation isn't a given, it's intentional. I figured if I had the power to do it once, then there was nothing stopping me from doing it again. I didn't need a near-death experience to have a new life experience.

Building your confidence is an ongoing thing. You don't just wake up one day and all of a sudden, you're no longer anxious or shy and instead speak fluent 'Effortless Interaction'. It's a choice you actively make and work at every day. I knew that, in order to go somewhere I'd never been, I had to choose paths I hadn't walked before. That meant saying yes to things when my instinct was to say no, pushing past my usual threshold of comfort and acting confident even my heart was pounding.

At first it can be tiring to live in a way that feels unnatural after decades of doing something different, but it becomes a little easier and more ingrained each time. Then one day, if you do it often enough, you'll notice the bar of what you can comfortably say 'yes' to has shifted. You'll surprise yourself by willingly waltzing through doors you used to keep firmly locked. You'll look ahead and realise you're not in your bedroom rehearsing a phone call before you dial the number anymore, you're on a stage in front of thousands of people, sharing your story. Shaking, but showing up all the same.

I'm never going to be the loudest person in the room or someone so eloquent that I'm not at least somewhat awkward, but I don't need to be. I used to think my shyness was an affliction I had to conquer. That being quiet and more reserved must be something negative rather than simply my preferred way of moving through the world. The older I get, the more I have grown to respect and appreciate this element of my personality.

It sometimes makes me tongue-tied but it has also made me perceptive and empathetic, curious and insightful. I am a wall-flower, and I love that about myself.

But now I know, I can be a sunflower too. Turning not away but towards.

37

A CRACK IN THE GLASS

I used to live with the unconscious belief that once something 'bad' happened to you, you were in the clear. Similar to the way people feel safe swimming alongside shark attack victims (because what are the chances of lightning striking twice?), I had a surprising sense of security after my accident. Despite being more aware of the fragility of life, I also felt somewhat invincible because I thought I had already experienced my *thing*.

Not surprisingly, I learned that this wasn't the way the universe worked at all. Time was capable of handing you more than one thing to hurt you, that you could learn and grow from. Life wasn't a test I could pass and then sit back and enjoy the rewards of, it was ever evolving.

When I was twenty-three, my life looked like the 'after' photo of a before and after trauma campaign. I had designed and created the exciting, full and colourful life I had always dreamed of making my own. Everything I had longed for when I was growing up, and hoped for in my most challenging moments, was now a reality that I could reach out and touch. I was so aware of the magic and vibrancy surrounding me that I felt a constant surge of gratitude in every waking moment. I felt like I had finally done it. I had overcome my obstacle, closed the chapter and was moving on toward a life of utter bliss, ease and eternal contentment.

Life had shown me time and time again that nothing was actually out of my reach, and so in that spirit I decided to aim for something else I had always dreamed of doing. I applied to paint a mural at the famous Bondi Beach; a goal that had always seemed 'too big' and 'too scary' for me to achieve. When I opened the email to find my application had been accepted, my heart swelled with pride. The mural would be in the heart of Bondi, on a wall right in front of the beach that thousands of people walked by each day. It was a wall that I had admired and taken countless photos in front of ever since I was little, and I couldn't believe that my artwork was now going to be the one that people stopped to look at.

It felt like a full circle moment in my healing. Drawing had been something I only ever I did on my own in my hardest times, but now it was something I got to give back to the world while I was at my strongest. It had gone from something I did in hospital while daydreaming about someday being on a beach, to something I got to do at the very same beach I used to daydream about.

Painting the mural took almost an entire month and that month holds some of the fondest memories of my life. I began in summer, a few weeks before Christmas, so the energy in the air was contagious. Bondi was jam-packed with locals and tourists who were all out soaking up the sunshine, humming with the liveliness and thrill that comes with a new year approaching. And I was too. I knew the year ahead was going to be my best yet.

As I worked on the mural I played music through a speaker, and friends and strangers who passed by would stop to dance with me throughout the day. I was in my element and had that familiar sense of being exactly where I was meant to be. I would spend hours down by the beach each day, adding tiny detail after tiny detail to my artwork, until eventually the blank wall in front of me transformed into a huge, turquoise and patterned picture of the world map. It was one of the most fun, healing and fulfilling experiences I've ever had.

On the final day of drawing, I noticed a few spots of blood on the concrete beneath my feet. Being at the beach in the peak of summer (and also being a staunch non-shoe-wearer from Australia), I was barefoot for the entirety of the mural, so I wondered if perhaps the blood was coming from me. Because I have very minimal feeling from the waist down, I can't feel pain in my legs and feet so I don't always immediately know when something is wrong. I checked the bottoms of my feet and sure enough noticed a small cut on one of my heels. It didn't look bad at all and I only had a few hours until I finished the mural, so I wiped my skin clean, put a sock over my foot to prevent any dirt getting into the cut and kept drawing.

I finished the mural and flew home, only to wake up the next day to an incredibly swollen foot that was burning hot to touch. I was confused because the cut was still tiny, but I knew that my body responded to things differently now, so I went to the emergency room just in case. The doctors told me my foot was infected and gave me a few rounds of IV antibiotics to help clear it up. It didn't seem to help though, because for weeks the same thing kept happening—my foot would grow increasingly swollen and hot, I would go to the hospital, be put on antibiotics, and be sent back home—until eventually I was referred to an orthopaedic surgeon for a more thorough examination.

I thought it was odd to see someone who specialises in the musculoskeletal system for a skin issue, but I trusted the referring doctor's judgement and was happy to be getting a second opinion after all this time. By now I had been dealing with my foot issue for over a month so I was more than ready to make the most of my legs again and get back to all the activities I had grown to love so dearly. I booked an appointment with the surgeon and after a brief consult, he told me he was going to treat my cut in the same way he would treat a diabetic ulcer. He put a hard cast on my foot, all the way from my toes to just below my knee (exactly like what you would have for a broken leg), then asked me to come back in a week to take it off and see if it had healed.

The next week I headed back to the surgeon's office, filled to the brim with anticipation and bubbliness as I prepared to have the cast removed. I bounced through the hospital and made jolly chitchat with the surgeon as he cut the cast off with what looked like a little saw. When he was finished, a phone starting ringing in another room, so he left me on my own for a moment to take the call. While I was alone, I excitedly checked the bottom of my foot to see how much the cut had healed, and prepared myself to walk out of the hospital and into the sun-filled horizon that was the rest of my life.

The moment I saw it, a lump in my throat formed and I felt my stomach drop to the ground like smashed glass. I didn't know anything about diabetic ulcers but I knew this wasn't what healing should look like. There was now a much larger and deeper wound where the cut had been, and even more concerningly, the rest of the skin on my heel had gone white and was soft to touch. The surgeon came back into the room and I told him I was alarmed by what I had seen. I reasoned that the summer heat combined with the confined cast must be leaving my foot constantly damp so it couldn't heal. He took a very brief look at my foot, shrugged and said, 'We'll put a new cast on today and leave it for twelve weeks. If it isn't better by then, we will most likely have to amputate your foot.'

My ears filled with the sound of ringing. The room kept moving around me but I was frozen, unable to digest his words. He'd said them so casually, so unperturbed, as though I hadn't just spent the last three years learning to walk again. As though the perfect snow globe world I had so meticulously built hadn't just shattered on the floor. As though single moments don't have the power to maim you.

Something in my body felt off. My intuition had grown so strong in the last few years that I now trusted it more than logic, and this situation had my alarm bells sounding on high alert. I questioned the doctor over and over and was met with condescending non-answers that proved he wasn't listening to a word I was saying. I started to panic because I was alone with no one to back me up and share my concern for what I had seen. On one hand I had a surgeon with years' worth of experience telling me what to do, but on the other, I had my soul screaming at me that something wasn't right and that this was much more serious than I was being led to believe. I told the doctor I wasn't comfortable with him putting another cast on, and he said that I couldn't leave his care until he did. By now my heart was racing and I knew I had to think quick. I sneakily snapped a photo of my foot while he wasn't looking, then agreed to let him do what he had to do. As he prepared, I started googling 'how to cut off a cast at home'.

A fiery rage filled my chest as I sat watching a new cast being wrapped around my leg as though it wasn't a part of me. I had the deep and unmistakable feeling that something was wrong, so I sent the photo of my foot to a friend who also had a spinal cord injury to see if she had any ideas. Thankfully she knew of a wound nurse who specialised in spinal patients and she passed the photo on to her for advice. Within minutes my fears were validated. I got a text from the nurse that said, 'Your skin is turning necrotic (which means it's dying), if that cast is on for even one more day you're going to lose your foot. Get it off however you can and see me tomorrow.'

I left the hospital in total shock. When I got back to my car I felt like a shell of the person who had driven there only an hour earlier. I had thought today was going to be the end of an already frustrating road, but now I had the foreboding feeling that it was actually the beginning of a far, far longer one. I drove home blasting music, still in disbelief at how something so seemingly insignificant had escalated into something potentially life-altering in the space of a day. When I walked inside the house, the reality of what I'd heard began to sink in and I let my emotions catch up to me. I dropped to my knees as though I couldn't take one more moment of carrying my own weight and started screaming on the kitchen tiles. The feeling of desolation and cold ground felt terribly familiar.

My mind flashed back to hospital floors, hotel bedrooms and airport bathrooms; all the floors I had found myself on in the past. But I was surprised to find that there was something distinctly different about this one. The emotions were raw and painful and exploding above the surface, but there was another feeling among them, too. Beneath the pain and despair, I had the strong and all-knowing sense that this wasn't actually going to be forever. The knowledge that there would be other times and other moments beyond this one. Whether or not I lost my foot, there would be days where this didn't hurt anymore and I would be somewhere else, smiling in the sun with a book in my hand. Days where I didn't give this moment in time a passing thought because life had gone on, as it always manages to do.

I knew instinctively that great things were coming, they just weren't here today. And that was okay.

I thought I'd hit rock bottom again, but even through my tears I could see that I was far from it. I was simply experiencing the emotions of being human and I had the invaluable knowledge that I was capable of getting through them. I realised that what had haunted me in the past wasn't simply sadness, it was being incapable of seeing that the sadness would ever end. It wasn't the difficult road ahead that I used to fear, it was the belief that there was no road.

There on that floor, I knew with all my heart that there would be a light at the end of my tunnel, even if the tunnel was daunting and unexpected and involved me striding through life on a single foot. I knew the light was there and that one day I would be basking in it again. I'd finally learned my strength.

38

SITTING BACK DOWN

Once I cut the cast off my foot, I met with the wound nurse, Amy, who as it turned out, happened to be one of the kindest and most wonderful people I've ever met. She explained to me in the most empathetic way possible just how serious this situation really was and what it would mean for my future. She told me that any part of my body below the level of my spinal cord injury would always heal much more slowly than it used to, so I would need to dedicate a lot of time, energy and money into healing my foot. It wasn't something I could simply set and forget and hope it cleared up on its own eventually, like a cold sore or an ear infection—this wound needed constant and consistent care. Healing my foot was going to have to become my full-time job and although it wasn't exactly how I had hoped to spend the year, I intended to commit wholeheartedly. We mapped out a plan which involved me visiting the wound clinic every few days for treatment to help speed the process along, and Amy estimated that it would take around twelve weeks to heal. She then looked at me apologetically, as if she didn't want to say whatever she had to say next, and confirmed the news I'd been half-expecting but dreading: I would need to keep all weight and pressure off my foot until it healed.

In other words, I needed to get back in my wheelchair.

I had always seen my wheelchair as a form of freedom and something which pushed me forward both literally and metaphorically, but this time it felt different. Years earlier I had accepted life in a wheelchair—I understood it was a potential path for me and I'd learned to be okay with that—but then I got to stand up again. It felt unfair that I now had to return to a stage of life I had just emerged from, one that the world had seemingly promised me I was finished with for good. I had only just begun to feel safe in my own body once more and had finally relaxed into trusting my legs and embracing all they allowed me to do, and it seemed cruel for that trust to be broken again so quickly. I was angry—at myself, at the surgeon, and the situation in general—but truthfully, an even greater part of me was filled with deep guilt for feeling that way.

Who was I to be frustrated by this journey when realistically I knew I would one day get better? Although the situation wasn't ideal or at all what I had planned, I was still going to get the chance to stand back up someday. I didn't feel like I was entitled to feel annoyed by this fleeting inconvenience when for so many others, including many of my real-life friends, this was their forever. Survivor's guilt tugged on my conscience, begging me to gain some perspective, and I became stuck in a cycle of anger, annoyance and shame, none of which was particularly helpful.

Apart from the mental challenge, my main concern with being back in my wheelchair was losing all the muscle I had spent so many years regaining and strengthening. I knew how fast it could deteriorate when it wasn't being used, and after putting so much time and energy into my rehab, I was terrified that this wound would end up reversing my walking progress as well. I had no idea how long my foot would take to heal but I knew the long journey of regaining muscle and learning to walk again like the back of my hand. I could feel the preciousness of time as it ticked on by—I had mountains to climb and foreign cities to wander—and I had the sense I was losing so much of it while staying surrounded by antiseptic and old hurts.

Months went by and it became obvious to everyone that this wasn't just a twelve-week thing. This was far more serious than expected. The wound, which I now referred to simply as a 'hole' because that's exactly what it was—a large, deep, gaping hole in the bottom of my foot—was taking far longer to heal than anyone could have imagined. Every few days I would go to see Amy, excited to peel off the bandage and see how much had changed, only to be disappointed and heartbroken every time.

Each time I had an appointment, I asked (despite knowing it was an impossible question) how much longer she thought it would be until I could walk again. Did she think I would be able to start rehab again next month? Would it be healed in time for summer? Could I swim in the ocean again soon? She always gave me her most optimistic answer. Although I appreciated and desperately needed that positive reassurance, in hindsight I think Amy knew what she was doing. I don't think she ever believed it was only going to take three months. I think she understood the realistic timeline from the very first day we met and decided to drip-feed the truth to me. If I had known from the beginning just how long this gruelling journey would take, I don't know how I would have handled it, and I might have been shocked into total desolation and given up on healing altogether. Although I was still definitely tired and frustrated, staying naive kept me hopeful and bright-eyed. I wondered if sometimes lying is actually the kindest thing we can do.

Eight months later, I was still seeing Amy every week. Like a record that can only play the one song over and over despite how much you want to skip it or turn it off, I was on repeat. Going to the clinic, watching as Amy used a scalpel to cut off the dead parts of my skin, squirming as she sliced the living areas to draw blood and then applied creams and oils to promote healing. Our routine was the same as it had been all year, although in the past few months I'd gained a new accessory as well. I now had a machine attached to my foot that was like a little vacuum, loudly pulling the fluid from the wound and into a container that I carried around like a cannibalistic flesh-filled handbag. If you were to google 'ways to heal a wound', I can guarantee I tried every single one of them, no matter how abstract or peculiar.

Although I had complete faith in my medical team and I knew the wound was healing slowly, to an untrained eye like mine it honestly looked worse than ever. After so much time, I couldn't fathom looking down at my foot and seeing nothing but healthy and unbroken skin. I couldn't imagine waking up in the morning, swinging my legs off the side of the bed and planting my feet on the ground with my only thought being, *Do I feel like pancakes or toast?* As the months passed by, I realised with exasperated resignation that I had been in a wheelchair longer now than I ever was when I was paralysed.

~

The thing about healing an injury, or grieving a loss, or literally anything at all, is that the world doesn't stop spinning and wait for you to get through it. Although the wound was taking up a huge majority of my time and mental space, it wasn't the only thing that was happening in those months. Despite it being one of the most challenging times in my life, it was also one of the most fun, exciting and friend-filled years I've ever had. It never ceases to amaze me how so much joy and pain can occur in the same stage of life, let alone in the very same hour.

I was on a road-trip with my friends (one of countless that year), when we parked our vans up along the coastline of a quiet and cosy beach town. We gathered around the back of the vans, watching the waves and listening to the boys play guitar, and then everyone decided they were going to head off for a skate along the esplanade followed by a surf. I couldn't do either of those things, which I'd long ago come to accept, so instead I lay in the back of our kombi, face turned to the glistening water, and picked up my diary and pen. I wrote my future self a letter.

Dear Emma,

One day you won't remember how it feels to have a hole in your foot, so I'm writing you this letter to make sure you never forget.

Right now you are lying in the van, listening to the sound of the waves and writing in this book. You are happy but you also have the sense of missing out. Your friends are in the ocean or riding skateboards and you want to join them but you can't. For the past ten months you have experienced this feeling of not being able to do all that you want to, it's what you experienced four years ago as well, back when you thought it was permanent. Today you are lucky and you only have a short time left of this feeling but I need you to remember it. Right now you would do anything to move around freely, jump in the ocean, and set your feet on every inch of this world. You would do anything to feel twenty-four and carefree.

So from the Emma who has been sitting on the sidelines for the past ten months, from the Emma who was told she might have to have her foot amputated, from the Emma who had to lie on her back for a month straight in hospital, from the Emma who was told she would never walk again—when you are lucky enough to get back on your feet and use your two legs, you better not take them for granted. You better soak up every single moment, say yes to every adventure, and move until your body aches and your muscles are sore and you are absolutely exhausted. Simply because you can. And if you can, you must.

If you are reading this right now and you are deciding

whether or not you should get up and go to the gym, or go for that walk, or get in the freezing cold ocean, promise me you'll say yes. Say yes for the you who once prayed for the things you have now, say yes for the you who wanted to die when she realised her legs didn't work, say yes for all of the people who don't even have the option of saying no.

Never forget the value of this lesson because it's going to take you places and show you things you can only dream of now.

Love, Emma (with a hole in her foot). The girl who would do anything to be you right now. The girl who has no idea how you got through it but is so glad you did.

39

BURNT

While my foot was healing and I was in my wheelchair, I took every opportunity to immerse myself in nature and soak up the ever-calming sea breeze. Just like when I was in the spinal ward, my key focus was on preserving and nurturing my mental health, and for me, being outdoors was the simplest and most effective way to do that. On one particularly beautiful sky-blue morning, I took a book down to the ocean with my friends and found a lush grassy spot to perch upon for the day. I was in my bikini, lying on my stomach reading, when my friends noticed a tiny red patch of skin on my bum. It didn't look like anything sinister, just a very light, small mark, almost like I'd been sitting on it too long and it would go away if I stayed off it for a few minutes. I wasn't concerned in the slightest but happened to mention it in passing to Amy when I saw her the next day. She took one look and was absolutely horrified. She told me it was a burn and that over the coming days it would get much, much worse. Honestly, at that point I just thought she was being extremely dramatic.

In the spinal ward, the importance of consistently checking our skin had been drilled into us like nothing else. We were taught to lean forward in our wheelchairs every twenty minutes to give the skin under our sit bones a chance to breathe. We were instructed to examine our body every night before bed, searching our skin for any early signs of a wound. We were given mirrors to help us check our blind spots for scars we couldn't have otherwise seen.

At the time, I had thought I understood the importance of all of this. Logically it made sense that without being able to use pain as a guide, we had to physically search ourselves to pinpoint our hurts. I respected this new reality and looked over my body each day with the same care and concern with which I would check a friend's teeth for food before a first date. What I hadn't anticipated though was what came next. What happens when you do find something that doesn't look quite right? I hadn't realised that I'd not only lost the ability to feel when something was wrong, I'd also somewhat lost the ability to heal it.

Sure enough, Amy was right. In a matter of days the tiny mark had transformed into a very obvious and much larger burn that was piercing through layers and layers of skin. I didn't have a clue how it got there, or what had been so hot that I could possibly have burnt myself on it without noticing. Did someone sneak into my room and brand me with an iron rod while I was sleeping? Did I miss a patch when putting on sunscreen and lie in the sun too long? My best guess (which I'll never know whether or not is the truth) is that while I was wearing minishorts one day, I sat on a metal bench that had grown warm from hours in the sun and didn't realise it was actually incredibly hot. Because I didn't feel any reaction to the heat, I must have sat there oblivious, with my skin directly touching the bench for far longer than I should have. Far longer than someone who has the ability to feel pain would have been able to withstand.

The burn itself wasn't that big of a deal. I would just need to visit a wound nurse for the next few months for treatment, which, conveniently and ironically, I was already doing. What wasn't convenient, and what shattered my very last ounce of hope and strength, was the fact that in order to allow the wound to heal, I couldn't put any pressure on it. Which meant I couldn't sit down.

I could no longer use my wheelchair.

Somehow, in the middle of my brightest new beginning and self-proclaimed 'best year yet', I was bed-bound again. As I lay on my stomach, eyes unblinking as I stared at the white wall of my bedroom, watching as it changed from dark to light to dark again with the passing of days, all I could think was, *How on earth did I get back here?*

~

I've heard the words *'you are learning from this'* time and time again since the day of my accident, not only from myself but from most people in my life. Years ago when I was in the spinal ward, I found this phrase to be extremely comforting and validating. I loved the idea that all the heaviness I was experiencing would one day make me stronger, because at that point in my life I didn't feel overly brave or capable. Now though? Hearing it was as jarring as nails on a chalkboard.

While I appreciated the sentiment and blind optimism, a huge part of me was overwhelmingly tired of hearing the same words repeated for nearly half a decade. I wondered when I would get to stop learning and just start living? I didn't want another lesson. I didn't want something more to grow from. Hadn't I learned and grown enough? Hadn't I been adequately tested already? Wasn't it my time to just enjoy it all?

Besides, what was I even learning? Not to trust doctors? Not to wear mini-shorts? How long it takes to heal a wound when you have a spinal cord injury? People would constantly tell me that I was inspirational and brave, but truthfully I didn't want to be either of those things. I wanted to be reckless. I wanted to have faith in my own body. I wanted to be able to relate to my friends.

I wanted a fucking break.

~

I was lying in bed one evening, filled with self-pity, when I picked up my phone to send a text to Bec. 'I'm so sorry I can't make it' were the words I hesitantly typed out. It was her 25th birthday and she was having a party to celebrate another lap around the sun, but instead of being by her side, I was lying stomach-down on my bed at home. Stuck in the same place I would be for the foreseeable future.

I imagined being told just a few years earlier that there would one day come a time when I looked forward to using a wheelchair, where I longed for the ease and freedom it brought. I wouldn't have believed it. Nothing had humbled me more than the realisation that even something I once didn't want at all could be dearly missed.

I wanted to believe there was some kind of purpose to it all, that these days spent back in a bed would make me a better person, or friend, or instil in me some great otherworldly wisdom, but I didn't feel that way at all. I just felt bone tired and painfully lonely. I noticed my diary on my bedside table and decided to try to write, knowing that words could usually help me figure out what my heart already knew but my mind didn't yet. No words came, so instead I drew a picture of a flower to try to find some semblance of calm. Before I knew it, the words I had been told on repeat for the past few months came to the front of my mind. I decided to write them out multiple times in the hope that maybe I would start to believe them like I used to.

You are growing from this.

You are growing from this.

You are glowing from this.

I put the pen down and closed my eyes. I felt like I was losing my rosy view of the world, and I desperately hoped that one day I would be able to find it again. Later that night, I opened my diary to continue writing and came across the page with the flower. I reread the words and realised that, without meaning to, I had changed the last sentence. *You are glowing from this.* I don't know if it was the meditative drawing, my sleepy mind or some kind of deep subconscious knowing, but the words were there, written by me, written *to* me, and I liked them.

I thoroughly liked the notion that you could not only grow from hard times, but perhaps one day even glow from them too. That they could not only make you stronger, but make you shinier as well. More luminous, more radiant. That all this wasn't simply to make me strong—I felt sufficiently tough enough already—but that it could make me more sunshiny as well. I held onto this thought and resolved to carry it with me for the remainder of my healing journey. I didn't know how or when, but I had to hold onto the hope that there would come a day where I would look back on this chapter and think, *Look at how much light you gave me.*

I went to sleep that night with the belief that somehow, someday, I would make it through to the other side of this obstacle, but reasoned that it was okay to be sad while I was on my way there. I knew that one day I would overcome, write and maybe even laugh about this period of my life. That there would come a time when I would turn the bruises into poetry and the hurt into purpose. But for now it didn't have to be anything eloquent or meaningful. I didn't have to find the silver lining while I was still beneath the thick grey of the cloud, soaked and shivering from the downpour—I just had to survive it.

40

PAIN

Twelve months, two weeks and three days—that was how long it took me to be wound-free once again. I was surprised, or, more accurately, humbled, to learn just how slowly my body healed now that I had a spinal cord injury. I was warned about it in hospital, I'd seen friends become bed-bound from pressure sores, and I knew medically that it was a possibility, but I hadn't believed it. Not really. Since regaining the use of my legs, the outside world tended to view me as 'healed' and oftentimes I found myself attempting to fit into that identity too. Not because I felt shame about being in a wheelchair, but because I never wanted to act as though I could wholeheartedly relate to the challenges that come along with it, when realistically my short experience only just scratches the surface. I found myself in a weird in-between place that felt not only confusing, but also kind of lonely. Where did I fit if I couldn't relate to my friends who were also living with disability, but I most definitely didn't relate to a life without one either?

The year of healing my wounds highlighted the severity of my disability and reminded me, quite ungraciously, that I wasn't in fact 'healed' at all. Just because I could walk didn't mean the rest of my body suddenly worked any differently to how it did before I stood up out of my chair. I was still functioning exactly the same on the inside, with a spinal cord that had been severely compressed. I knew my bladder and bowel were paralysed and I'd accepted that, but because I'd regained more function and mobility than many ever do, I'd felt as though I wasn't allowed to mourn or acknowledge the fact that my legs didn't work in the seamless way they used to. The way that would have enabled them to heal a tiny cut on my foot in a week, rather than a year. Or that would have enabled me to sit on a scalding hot bench and actually know it was hot. For years I had been minimising this huge element of my identity, so afraid of offending or not appropriately honouring the community I was a part of that I forgot just that: *I* was a part of it too.

I'd seen four whole seasons, aged an entire year and grown two new scars since my journey began back at that turquoise wall in Bondi. I felt like a completely different girl to the one who had eagerly picked up a paintbrush and danced barefoot with passing strangers the summer before. Throughout all the hardship and countless appointments, I imagined the day my wounds healed would be the happiest moment of my life and that my diary would be filled with positive exclamations about how preposterously wonderful and perfect the world is. But neither of those things really happened. I didn't feel any kind of overwhelming relief and my diary remained empty. Of course, I was grateful and more than ready to move into the next stage of my life, but there was definitely no sense of victory or celebration. How could there be when I had absolutely nothing left to give?

I realised that sometimes endings, even the ones we want the most, are less like closing concert curtains that demand loud applause and a standing ovation and are more like a quiet and solitary shutting of your book at 3 am when everyone else is already asleep. You wake up the next morning puffy-eyed, ready to head back into the world after living out such a profound storyline, only to realise that nothing monumental has changed for anyone else and that you're actually just exhausted from losing so much sleep.

~

I personally don't believe that we need to take a lesson from every difficult life experience, or that we have to turn each patch of dirt we come across into gold. I think sometimes we should be allowed to just see hard things for what they are—hard—and look back on them however the heck we want to. In saying that, The Year Of The Wound did teach me a very valuable lesson that I wish I had known sooner: the immeasurable importance of pain.

I don't think I ever truly grasped its value until losing the ability to feel it cost me my health and a whole lot of time and stability. Despite how deeply pain can hurt and how much we might wish or medicate it away when it's there, it's actually often one of the kindest gifts our body can give us. Its purpose is purely to protect us and keep us safe from harm. I like to think of pain as my body saying, 'Hey, sorry I had to get your attention this way, but I love you and I just want to let you know that something isn't right. Can you please take care of us before it gets any worse?'

We listen to our physical pain so well. If something feels too hot to touch, we pull our hand away and run it under cold water. If we feel a sudden jolt of pain while exercising, we stop. If music is so loud that it hurts our ears, we turn it down. So, I wondered, why is it that we don't acknowledge and respect our emotional pain in the same unquestioning way? Regardless of what form it shows up in, pain is still pain and it serves the very same purpose of warning us when something is wrong. So why do we so often choose to ignore it?

I've heard people (myself included) say things like, 'I love him but it hurts,' or 'I just don't feel right when I'm here,' and, honestly, I think there might be a pretty strong reason for that. As human beings, we are much more in tune and aware of our surroundings than we give ourselves credit for, and often our body and heart know a whole lot more about what is good for us than our mind does. If being around a particular person or being in a certain place doesn't feel right, it's probably because it's not. The pain is there nudging us to pay attention to something, we just have to learn to listen to the signals and then find the strength to acknowledge them.

Now that I can't feel pain in half of my body, when something is wrong it takes something drastic for me to realise and I end up getting far more hurt than I would have otherwise. My foot and burn are prime examples of that. We tend to forget that the same thing happens when we choose to ignore our emotional pain and inevitably something will have to break in order for us to take notice. But what if we searched our minds in the same way I was taught to search over my skin while I was in hospital? What if we gave ourselves a break every now and again to take a deep inhale and let our mind breathe? What if we examined our heart every night before bed, searching it for any early signs of a scratch or bruise? What if the things that trigger us are actually mirrors to help us find the blind spots we wouldn't have seen otherwise?

Imagine we then had the courage to listen to those aches and tend to them as quickly as we would a physical hurt. Like running a burning finger under cold water, our inner pain calls us to nurture our wounds before they have the chance to form into something deeper and longer lasting. Pain can be uncomfortable, unbearable and sometimes unforgiving, but I think it's important to remember that it is a gift and a privilege to feel.

If this year of my life taught me anything, it is to listen to pain when it comes. To pull my hand off the hot plate, turn down the music and save myself the hurt.

41

ABLEISM

Going from a wheelchair to walking (twice) has given me a very unique insight into what it's like to live with both a disability that is outwardly obvious as well as one that is predominantly invisible. The first time I left the hospital in my wheelchair, I was terrified. People stared at me brazenly. Others came rushing to help. My line of sight was at a lower level to what I was used to and it made the world look entirely different. I felt self-conscious in a way I'd never experienced before, like I was naked in a crowd with a spotlight bearing down on me.

I ventured out slowly, only going a street away from the hospital, and decided my first outside-world encounter would be something simple like ordering food from a cafe. When I got to the front counter, I realised the bench was taller than me. The waitress didn't even know I was there. I timidly called out to get her attention and when she eventually saw me, she looked at me with an odd expression that somehow mixed shock, pity, compassion and intrigue. A surprising combination that I would soon become very familiar with.

After months of going about the world in my wheelchair, I noticed a lot of differences in the way I was treated. Some people became more reserved because they didn't know what to say, others asked unsolicited personal questions in the produce aisle at the supermarket, others would come up behind me and push my wheelchair forwards, assuming I needed help rather than asking if I did.

By far the biggest shift I noticed was that people became inherently kinder. Strangers suddenly granted me an unearned patience and generosity that I'd never received on my feet. At first this relieved me because I desperately needed warmth in a time where I felt like my path was made up entirely of eggshells, but over time it started to irritate me.

Initially I had assumed that people could somehow sense I was living the hardest days of my life and that's why they were offering me compassion, but once I was confident and thriving again I realised that people weren't being kind because they could *sense* I was going through something difficult, they just *assumed* I was. They were being kind because they thought no one else would be. They expected my life to be awful just because I was sitting down.

I quickly realised that despite the disabled community making up about twenty per cent of our population, there were still a whole lot of people who associated 'disability' with something negative or less than. Who believed that just because one body functioned differently to another it automatically meant one was 'worse'. When in reality, a body simply works how it does or doesn't, and there is no value attached to it. It just is. I constantly got comments from people that, whether conscious or internalised, were deeply rooted in ableism. Strangers would say things like, 'You're too pretty to be in a wheelchair,' as though having a disability made me less attractive to them. As though it was such a shame that I was now a wasted commodity. I also often heard, 'But you don't look like you have a disability,' as if that was a compliment. People's attempts to comfort me very rarely included trying to learn more about my differences, and instead involved them convincing me that I didn't match their preconceived idea of what a disabled person *should* look like, therefore they could still like me in spite of it.

One night recently, I was out at a bar with my good friend Sam from hospital (who uses a wheelchair) when a stranger came up to him and handed him a hundred dollar note. He didn't speak to Sam, didn't explain why he was giving him the money—he actually didn't even acknowledge him at all. Even though I knew the answer, I asked the man what it was for. He told me it was because he thought Sam was inspiring. I could feel my hands clenching inside my pockets. Sam *is* inspiring, he's brilliant, but this stranger didn't know that. In fact, he didn't know a single thing about him. For all he knew, Sam could be the shittiest person on the planet.

We passed the note back to him, but the man persevered, again insisting that Sam's presence alone was somehow something to be marvelled.

Don't get me wrong, there are a whole number of reasons why Sam is admirable, but being a thirty-year-old guy out at a bar with his friends sure as hell wasn't one of them. It wasn't brave, it was ordinary. No more impressive or noteworthy than this man being at the very same bar.

The gesture wasn't saying, 'Take this money, you're an incredible person and you deserve it,' it was saying, 'I'm sorry your life sucks, this is the only thing I can think of to make it better.'

What irked me most was knowing how the man would remember the encounter. That he likely would have walked away genuinely believing he had done a good deed. When in reality all he had done was create an entire identity for one of the most interesting people I know in a matter of seconds, and completely missed the privilege of actually knowing him.

~

Once I reached the stage in my recovery where I could alternate between using my wheelchair and crutches, I noticed that something very interesting happened. I realised I could stand up out of my wheelchair and in five seconds flat transform myself from someone who received automatic kindness to someone who wasn't even acknowledged. I was exactly the same me, still living with the same disability, still facing the same challenges, yet my experience in the world was completely different. I was still going through a tricky time, yet because I looked 'fine', nobody knew.

I found the difference in people's treatment of me to be infuriating, not because I wanted involuntary warmth, but because it highlighted the societally ingrained belief that disabled people are a variation from the 'norm', and therefore must be unhappy and treated softly. In saying that, I could easily tell the difference between someone being ignorant and showing me pity, versus someone offering me compassion and genuine care. Oftentimes the way people treated me was completely well-intentioned and actually quite heart-warming.

Humans are beautiful in the sense that when we see someone in trouble, instinctively we want to help. Being in a wheelchair was like having a sign on my head that said 'Life hasn't always been kind to me,' and so naturally people became more inclined to tread gently. This benevolence is touching and would be a wonderful thing, if only it was how *everyone* was treated. If only compassion and grace became our automatic attitude towards each other.

In any given room, I imagine people are often going through their own version of hardship, even if we can't see it from the outside. It seems like such a waste that our humanity, the very best version of ourselves, is usually only reserved for people who we *know* are struggling, or who physically look like they need it. Why couldn't we extend this kindness and generosity to everyone we crossed paths with? I wondered what would happen if we collectively moved through the world tenderly, with the knowledge that even though we might not be able to see someone's pain, everyone is dealing with something we know nothing about.

~

Once I no longer needed my crutches and walked on my own two feet, I learned that prejudice wasn't only reserved for visible disabilities. I was now subject to an entirely new set of judgements and opinions that I was not at all expecting. Unfortunately, our society has the tendency to form assumptions about people based solely on their physical appearance. Based on what we see, we might conclude whether or not a person is sick or healthy, capable or incapable, and way too often these projected identities are completely false. This is where the struggle of an invisible condition comes in: 'They *look* healthy, so obviously they can't be *too* sick, right?'

From the moment I looked like I was 'healed', I started fielding comments like 'You're so lucky you don't have to work,' or 'It must be nice to sleep all day.' It occurred to me that in a culture that idolises hustle and hard work, we hold some very dangerous and inaccurate views on what it means to live with a disability.

Until I experienced this judgement myself, it never occurred to me that chronic health conditions could be viewed as an 'easy' option. That being potentially unable to work and earn your own living would be the desired choice. I didn't realise living in a body that doesn't function with ease might ever be considered lazy or weak.

I also learned that the more I got 'better', the more respect I gained. Suddenly I wasn't inspiring for my resilience, I was inspiring for 'doing the impossible and proving doctors wrong'. As though my biggest accomplishment while having a disability was 'beating' it.

When people tell me they admire me, I never know how to graciously accept the compliment, but I always hope that whatever it is they look up to me for is something within my control. I am proud of myself for a lot of things, such as my strength, my sunny disposition and my adventurous spirit, so if someone was inspired by any of those, I would feel immensely honoured. What I can't take responsibility for, and what doesn't sit quite right with me, is being praised for something that is ultimately out of my control. Something like leaving my wheelchair and learning to walk again. Something that wasn't even a negative in the first place.

Almost every day, well-meaning people will comment on my ability to walk. More often than not, they note that I must have regained movement due to my positive attitude. That my gratitude, determination and sheer belief that I would heal meant that I eventually did. I truly believe these words are said with the best of intentions, but there's a huge problem with this kind of dialogue. It completely belittles and undermines the entire community of people living in wheelchairs.

Believing that my healing came from anything other than pure luck is indirectly believing that other people just mustn't be trying hard enough. That if they could just be a little more upbeat, or dedicate more time to rehab, or manifest a teensy bit harder, then they too could one day walk again.

Throughout the years of sharing my story, I have made a very conscious effort to ensure I *never* insinuate that I hold a secret cure to healing. I deliberately brush over the specifics of rehab and timelines because I know how it feels to be lying in a hospital bed the day you're told you'll never walk again, scouring the internet for any semblance of hope, and holding onto that promise for dear life. Yes, I put a lot of work into my physical therapy, but no amount of sheer willpower can force a nerve to work when it is severed. I will never pretend to have answers I don't.

One thing I know for sure is this—if positivity, resilience and determination were all it took to heal a damaged spinal cord, not a single person I've encountered in a wheelchair would still be sitting down.

42

TWO WORLDS

It's an odd and perplexing thing to live multiple realities at the same time. My legal case had been going on for over five years now, and for its entire duration there were two distinct and contrasting versions of me that just didn't add up. On the one hand, there was the twenty-something-year-old me who saw the world in rainbows and butterflies and who radiated joy. I was the girl who lived in constant wonder and appreciation, spurred on by the sheer unlikeliness of being alive. Then, on the other hand, there was the part of me that was forced to swallow all of that and be small while my case was ongoing. I was the girl who was told one too many times that no one would love her, that her life was going to get harder with every passing year and that she would never amount to anything.

After I left the hospital, I had a fire inside of me. I considered myself to be quite literally the luckiest human on planet earth, and to this day I still do. How many people can say they've survived a freefall from 14,000 feet? How many people can say they were told they would never walk again, yet now walk on their own two feet daily? How many people can say they've done both? I knew my luck. I felt it with every fibre of my being. I didn't want to waste the remarkable gifts of life and body that I'd been handed, and I couldn't hold in my gratitude even if I tried. I wanted to devour every inch of the world and leave no stone unturned; I wanted to create a life full of endless colour and adventure. So I did. I beamed with joy, I explored nature, I travelled, I wrote, I met new people, I moved to the ocean.

I relished everything I did, but for every building block I gratefully added to my life, there were people telling me to tear them down; to remain stagnant.

I was flying above the weight of the world with thankfulness, only to be pulled back down to reality every time I checked my emails or got a call from my lawyers. They told me my attitude was 'cute' but I was naive in my happiness and obviously didn't understand the extent of the damage done to me. They said not only was I refusing to embellish my injuries for the sake of the case, but I was actually doing the opposite: I was presenting to the world as perfectly happy when in reality I was severely injured.

I didn't understand. Couldn't I be both of those things? Why did I have to choose one or the other? Yes, I was injured and it was affecting my life in a lot of really hard ways, but I was also capable of seeing the good in the world. I was learning that duality was beautiful and vital to a life well lived, but I was also learning that the legal realm doesn't want to admit that shades of grey exist. Instead, they wanted a cookie cutter example of what they imagined a disability 'should' look like.

There were days when I would write a heartfelt diary entry expressing my happiness and post it online because I was proud of it, only to get an email moments later telling me to take it down. There were times I would get asked to share my story on major international platforms that had the potential to reach and inspire millions of people, and be told not to. There were moments I would go to the gym and film a video of me doing chin-ups, something I'd worked so hard at, something which doesn't involve any injured part of my body, only to be told to delete it immediately. I was living in a paradox and I had no idea how to navigate it.

There was such an obvious misalignment in my life and the worst part was that I couldn't tell anyone. Legally I wasn't allowed to talk about the case so I had to keep it hidden. I wasn't allowed to hint at my growing impatience or the insurance company would use it against me, knowing they could easily sway me into accepting an offer that was less than what I deserved. To the outside world, I was the smiling, bubbly, inspiring, happy-go-lucky girl from Instagram who had survived a miracle. This was true, but I was also in an impossible, secret and heartbreaking bind.

At first I was so capable of separating the two worlds and was very clear on who I was. I was impenetrable and nothing could take away my blissful state. I could objectively see the lawyers and insurance companies for what they were: businesses who needed to make money. I could logically detach the things I was told about my life from the things I knew in my heart to be true.

But, like any consistent force, over time the words began to seep in. It happened over so many years that I didn't even notice it at first. It began with me addressing my lawyers in hushed, apathetic tones because I knew I wasn't meant to seem happy or enthusiastic. It grew to me downplaying incredible triumphs of my recovery because I knew any physical improvement would be looked down upon. It eventually changed me from a person who knew I could do absolutely anything I desired in life to someone who wondered how on earth I was ever going to find a single purpose or passion. I felt like I was being left behind. When you're told something so frequently, for so many years, by so many powerful people, there comes a time when you start to listen. Like a slowly leaking tap left unnoticed for five years, I soon realised I was overflowing with a negativity that I knew wasn't mine.

Without me ever really acknowledging it, I had been conditioned to view any misfortune in my life as 'good'. After my break up with Ben, my lawyer told me it was positive because it further proved that I was hard to love and would likely end up alone, therefore I'd require compensation for a gardener and handy man. When I got the hole in my foot, I was told it wouldn't be the worst thing in the world if they had to amputate because it proved just how severe my injury really was. When my lawyer realised I was now capable of walking full-time without my wheelchair, his only response was, 'Well, that's not very good for the case.' My life celebrations became less about achievements and more about hardships.

Somewhere along the line I had subconsciously subscribed to

this view without ever meaning to. I would catch myself dimming my light for things I should have been able to shine bright for. I would find myself feeling relieved and secretly thrilled when something bad happened. I was trained to believe that bad things = good, and good things = something to be ashamed of and hide.

It can take years to recognise a deeply ingrained belief like this, and even longer to rewrite it. Even now I sometimes find myself self-sabotaging any success I might have in order to avoid any sense of achievement. I still catch myself feeling an undertone of comfort at any misfortune that comes my way. I have to actively remind myself that I'm allowed to film myself walking up a hill or riding a bike or doing push-ups without having to hide it from the world. It has taken me years to realise that I am allowed to be happy if that's what I'm feeling. *I am allowed.* What a simple but liberating sentence. There is so much freedom in being able to take back your own emotions, but there's still a major part of me that feels so much disappointment that there was ever a time when I was forced to hand them over to someone else.

The thing that hurt me the most from this whole experience was uncovering the existence of a different kind of person. A person who doesn't seem to have empathy or compassion or perspective. Up until this legal case, I had never encountered this before and I didn't expect I ever would. I had always assumed that humans *felt* the same inside, regardless of how hard someone's exterior may seem. I truly didn't believe that anyone was inherently selfish or money-hungry or cruel, and that if it came down to it, a person's conscience would intervene before causing anyone harm. That sometimes circumstances would lead people astray, but their personalities were never intrinsically lacking humanity. Between the insurance company and the many lawyers, doctors and other people I met along the way, I discovered there really are people who are capable of putting wealth and power ahead of kindness. Maybe this seems obvious, but I had never known these types of people existed. I wish I could have continued walking naively through the world without this knowledge, because seeing it scared me. It made me cautious.

Even now, years on, I still feel a hint of sadness, frustration and disbelief that I had to go through what I did. I still feel enraged at the time I lost to a system that I know is hurting so many others in their most vulnerable moments. I guess that means I'm not entirely over it yet. To be honest, I'm not sure I ever want to be.

The more I reflect on that period of my life, the more I realise that the situation wasn't okay at all and I don't think I should have to quietly accept it as being so. My case was dehumanising and time consuming, I was made to feel like I had done something wrong and I was doubted at every single turn, even though someone had openly admitted from day one that they were at fault. Even though there were multiple people at the scene and surgeons who quite literally saw the inside of my damaged spinal cord. Even though I had hard, medical, indisputable proof of my injuries.

I can't help but wonder just how much worse the torment is for people in situations where no one admits responsibility, where there are no witnesses, or where a clear diagnosis isn't possible. I can't help but wonder what happens in a sexual assault trial where it is purely one person's word against another. I can't help but wonder what additional condescending tones, accusatory stares and blatant lies people are forced to endure in situations like that.

That's why I'm not over it. I refuse to accept a system as sufficient when it is as flawed as it currently is. I refuse to accept that anyone needs to go through more hurt after their life has been irreversibly changed.

When I write about my accident and injury, I can do so in a tone of gratitude and wisdom because I have spent years processing and moving past the hurt. Although these experiences are still present in my life, they don't negatively affect me anymore. However, when I write about the legal battle, I can still feel the rawness of the wound. The scab hasn't fully formed yet. I'm learning to be okay with this. I don't think we need to be over things in a particular timeframe or experience a linear recovery. Who's to say how long any particular emotion should take to process? Is it one month for a break up? Two weeks for a job rejection? Five years for a death? There is no rulebook for these things. There is no correct timeline for healing.

It's okay to not be over something you thought you *should* be over by now. It's okay to be angry at the things that hurt you. They hurt because they changed you. You're allowed to grieve that change. You're allowed to miss who you were before it. You're allowed to move forwards but still wish it didn't happen.

43

CLOSING THE CHAPTER

When I was twenty-five, I decided to go back to Europe. My friends and I were talking about going overseas for a month to dodge the Australian winter and when we were deciding on a place, I felt compelled to go to Switzerland. I'd been back there before, once for the legal case and another time for a quick trip, but I'd never been back to Lauterbrunnen, the town where I had skydived. I'd never really had the longing to go back, but suddenly it felt important that I did.

Over the years, my accident had become something I speak about so frequently, both intentionally and by chance (as my limp attracts questions most days), that when I do, the words roll off my tongue like a rehearsed and memorised speech. I can easily feel no emotion about what I'm saying and I often feel so dissociated that it's as though I'm talking about something that happened to someone else. I love sharing my story with the world and I'm so thankful I made the decision to do so, but that's just it—the whole thing had started to feel like a 'story' and not a very real and traumatic thing that happened to me.

Now that five years had passed, I wanted to revisit the place I had my accident. I wanted to see the ground I had landed on and the sky I fell from, I wanted to hear the language I'd grown to somewhat understand and the sounds of the waterfalls flowing through the Alps. I wanted to experience it all. I didn't exactly know what I hoped to get out of going back, and I accepted that perhaps it wouldn't be anything monumental or impactful, but at the very least I hoped it could give me the simple reminder that *this is real and this happened.*

I booked the plane ticket only a week before we left, because the thought of flying overseas, particularly to Europe, made me physically sick. It was as if everything in my body was screaming at me not to go back there, to the place where it had got so hurt, and to stay where I was safe. It wasn't that I was particularly worried about something going wrong or having another accident, it was more the thought of coming back home that scared me. When I was twenty and left the country, I came home to an entirely different world. Not only was my body forever changed, but every other aspect of my life was as well. It was like my identity was something as easily misplaced as a lost T-shirt; something I could leave home with and somehow arrive home without. This of course ended up being the catalyst for a lot of good, but I didn't want to leave anything behind this time. I was completely enamoured by the life I had spent years building, and I felt I had a lot to lose.

Although I was scared, an even bigger part of me was desperately longing to go, to stop overthinking the trip so much and to finally enjoy a European summer for what it should have always been: fun.

I headed off with a suitcase full of catheters, a diary ready to fill and the profound desire to create new memories. As the plane took off, the fear I had felt in the lead up was quickly replaced with wanderlust and anticipation. Travelling has been my greatest passion and desire for as long as I can remember and it felt so grounding to be reminded of that. Two flights later, we touched down in Zurich in the late afternoon and excitement flooded my veins. Fuelled by jetlag, we dropped our bags at the hotel and decided to explore the bustling city before we left the next morning for Lauterbrunnen.

I had forgotten how magical this country was and as we stepped out onto the street, I was awestruck by its beauty. Even though it was 9pm, the sun was only just starting to set and the air was the perfect level of warm where you can't tell where your body ends and the rest of the world begins. Music filled the streets and everyone was gathered by the lake to watch the sky change colour. My heart instantly felt so at home, almost as though I had left a piece of it here somewhere all those years ago and was just now finding it again.

The next morning, we hopped on a train and headed to the town I'd stayed in five years earlier. Lauterbrunnen is so breathtakingly stunning that it makes you feel like you're in some kind of fairytale. I truly don't think there's a place on earth quite like it, one that physically stops you in your tracks from the sheer beauty of it. No matter which direction you're facing, every single inch of the town is like a perfectly crafted postcard. I inhaled deeply as I soaked it all up. The mountain air was so crisp and fresh that it felt like I'd never taken a proper breath before in my life. As I looked around, I thought, *How could I possibly be mad at a place this magical?*

I had imagined that if anything on this trip was going to make me emotional, it would be coming back here. I thought I would see the familiar landscape and be reminded of all of the 'lasts' I had experienced here. It was the last place I ever walked without a limp, the last place I could feel my legs, and the last place I was in my old life. As I looked around at the picture-perfect wooden homes and the lush green grass filling every empty space, I knew I had been wrong. This place holds a lot of lasts for me, but being there five years on, with an entirely different disposition, I realised it also holds a lot of firsts. Things that were far too raw for me to see and appreciate at the time. This is the first place I discovered my strength, the first place I learned what it really means to be alive, and the first place I realised that I get to decide who I want to become. Each of those things is far more valuable than the ability to put one foot in front of the other without stumbling. I thought being here would hurt, but I didn't feel sad at all; I felt complete. The last time I was here I'd thought I was never going to feel happiness again, but as I stood there five years later, I felt it in every breath.

Until that day, I don't think I had ever realised that we are capable of changing our memories, of re-wiring the way we see something and deciding how we want it to make us feel. Just because this was once a sad place, didn't mean it always had to be. I was going to use my time here to rewrite all the memories I kept filed in the 'tougher moments' category of my brain, and I figured the best way to do that would be to go back to all the spots that hurt and create new stories. Ones that would allow me to look back on this enchanted town with the appreciative lens it deserved.

The first stop on my list was the walking trail I had planned to run along the morning of my accident. The one I had felt too lazy to explore and then hugely regretted a few days later when I was told I would never walk again. The place that was responsible for me pulling out my phone and writing a five-word note to my future self.

After all this time, I still couldn't run—not even close—but what I could do was walk, and that meant everything to me now. My friends walked beside me, helping me with a push or a pull whenever I needed it, and slowly we zigzagged our way along the trail. It weaved up a grassy mountain, which was scattered with yellow flowers and cows with bells hanging from their necks. As we climbed higher and higher, we could see the snow-capped mountains in the distance and the tiny, perfect town below us. It turns out I had been right all those years ago; this really would have been one of the most spectacular places in the world to run, and I felt overwhelmed knowing that I'd finally got to see it for myself.

The heat from the summer sun beat down on us and as we walked on, I could hear the sound of my own breath, racing from exertion. My body was growing tired and I could feel sweat trickling down my forehead as I used everything in me to keep walking. I loved the feeling of pushing my body and mind to their limits. Over the years, I'd become very familiar with the sensation of knowing it would be easier to stop, but feeling capable of continuing on anyway. I instinctively clutched the necklace on my chest and read the words I'd had engraved on it.

'If you can, you must.'

For years I had been saying this, but as I felt the blood coursing through my veins and looked down at the legs that had carried me this far, I realised I was doing it.

I *could,* and so I *did.*

The next day we explored the town a little more. I showed my friends the cabin Jemma and I had stayed in last time, which was now filled with other young twenty-somethings beaming with excitement as they set off on their own adventures. We made our way through the little shops and cafes and admired the pristine waterfalls we could see flowing in the distance. Then, we turned a corner and I saw something that stood out to me like a single beam of light in the darkness. The skydive shop. My heart started to race and, before I had time to think about it, I opened the door and led my friends inside. The bell chimed as we entered and a lady looked up from the desk to greet us. Her face immediately went white and she froze to the spot.

She remembered me.

'Emma?' she whispered. The next thing I knew, I was in her

embrace and tears were filling her eyes as she said, 'I'm so glad you're here and that you're okay.'

Somewhere in the back of my mind a hazy memory surfaced from my first day in hospital. She had been there. She had held my hand. I didn't know it at the time but this woman and her husband owned the skydive company and although they weren't working the day of the accident, they had come to be by my side and make sure I wasn't alone.

We stood in the shop and talked and talked, as though we had years worth of words built up and we couldn't get them out fast enough. Eventually she told me her husband would love to see me too and so we organised to have dinner later that night. My friends came along and, in what felt like an out-of-body experience, we ate and laughed and shared stories of what had happened over the past five years.

When it was time to go, they asked my friends and me if we would like to go up in a helicopter the next day to fly over the Alps. It was the very same helicopter I had jumped from five years earlier. I'd never really spoken about it, but I'd had a slight phobia of helicopters ever since the accident. I hadn't hesitated to join Bec on her skydive flight in the plane, but the sound of helicopters would instantly transport me back to the ground where I had crash-landed. I could be standing on a sunny beach in Australia, toes dipped in the ocean, but suddenly I'd be back there, bruised and broken in the field, listening as the rescue helicopter came down beside me and blew dust into the blood that covered my face.

Before I could answer, and as if they could read my thoughts, they asked me another question. They asked if I'd like them to drive me to that very spot.

A lump grew in my throat but I swallowed it down.

Rewrite the memory, I said to myself. 'Yes, please,' I said to them.

44

FLYING AGAIN

The deafening beats of the propellers matched the thundering of my heart. I felt electric as the ground shrank beneath us, snow-capped mountains disappearing into the landscape—a patchwork of green, brown and white as the grey sky yawned open around me, large and endless. The town below looked like a dollhouse, and then an oil painting, as we rose. I'd been here before. This wasn't the first time I'd peered out this window and towered above these mountains, but this time it all felt new. How peculiar to experience the same thing twice but to be an entirely different person each time.

It turns out I wasn't scared of helicopters at all. In fact, I loved our time in the air so much that I hoped the next half an hour would unfold in slow motion. Believe it or not, a flight is much more enjoyable when you know you don't have to fall out of it later. Funny that.

Our pilot flew us above the mountains, where summer had been replaced by a white winter wonderland. We flew past trails only the most experienced hikers can trek to, and cliff edges where base jumpers leave solid land to spread their wings and fly. I didn't even feel like I was rewriting a past trauma, because the fear and memory of my last flight wasn't in my mind at all. How could it be when I was living an experience most people can only dream of? While I was looking at heaven on earth with my very own eyes? I was nowhere but *exactly* where I was.

After a few minutes of silent appreciation and astonishment, our pilot spoke into our headphones. 'Are you ready?' he asked. I looked over at him to catch his grin and before I knew it, we landed on the top of a glacier. We got out of the helicopter and our jaws dropped in unison. How was this real?

You never realise how large a mountain is until you're standing on its peak, looking at your trail of footprints in the snow and realising no one else in the world will ever see them. They were barely visible, sunk deep in the surrounding snow that looked like a speck of white in comparison to the rest of the glacier, which in turn was eclipsed by the towering alps surrounding us. There were no homes or buildings up here; there were no powerlines or connection to the rest of humanity, there weren't even any trees or signs of life. There was only white snow and the blue of the sky for as far as we could see. It occurred to me that I could scream and no one, besides the three people standing right next to me (who would think I was incredibly strange) would hear me. I screamed anyway. The nothingness surrounding me made me feel tremendously full and alive. It was one of those moments that reminded me in the very best way of how incredibly small and insignificant we are.

When we landed, the man who owns the skydive company was waiting for us at the hanger to take us to the field. He looked at me with eyes full of meaning I couldn't interpret, and said, 'I need to tell you something you don't know about the day of your accident, but I'll tell you once we get there.'

Goosebumps erupted on my body. I had gone over that day countless times in the past five years, so I couldn't possibly imagine what I didn't yet know. All I knew was that I was desperate to find out. We climbed into his car and got ready to go back to a place I never thought I'd see again. A place I never even thought I'd survive.

It's odd seeing something again after a long time has passed. There are studies that suggest that despite the clarity of our recollection, our memories aren't recalling original events—they're remembering the last time we remembered them. So you never really know if a place is actually anything like it is in your mind or if you've warped it into a different reality. I had often wondered if this spot would be unrecognisable because of how much time I'd spent thinking about it and how much I'd built it up in my brain over the years. I wondered if it would be like going back to a garden you played in when you were little, where the branches towered over you and you daydreamed about all of the fairies who lived in the enchanted roots below. But when you stood in the yard decades later, you realised the trees weren't actually that large at all and the roots were rotting. As the car slowed to a stop and I saw the familiar sight of the green Swiss grass, I instantly knew this wasn't going to be like that.

We got out of the car and I didn't even need to be shown where I had landed because I knew. I remembered with perfect clarity. Before I could let myself look around properly or absorb where I was though, I needed to know whatever it was this man knew that I didn't. My friends stood beside me as we waited, holding each other's hands as we prepared for the worst. He opened his mouth and then closed it again, unsure of how to begin. He looked nervous, as if the words he needed to say had the power to destroy me and he wasn't sure how to best get them out.

'You nearly died that day,' he eventually blurted.

A pause.

Wait, was that all? I let out the breath I didn't realise I'd been holding. Having fallen four kilometres to the ground, this didn't exactly feel like a revelation.

The man looked agonised. There was something else.

'Five years ago when you had your accident, this field that we are standing in was a home for cows,' he continued carefully. 'The morning of your skydive, the farmer who owns the cows decided to move them to another field. If he hadn't done that, by pure chance, you would have died without question.'

Huh? Now I was lost.

He searched our confused expressions for a sign to stop, before telling us the part he'd been holding back: 'The cows here are so large and territorial that if you had entered the field, whether by foot or by falling, they would have trampled you to death.'

The silence lengthened.

He looked me in the eye nervously as he awaited my response. It was obvious that this was something he'd been holding in and dreading speaking aloud for half a decade.

Of all the things I'd imagined he might say, this was certainly not one of them. I looked at my friends in complete astonishment, paused while I let this new information sink in and then burst out laughing.

The whole thing was so utterly absurd that it was hilarious. Imagine surviving a 14,000-foot freefall only to be killed by a herd of cows stomping on you. It was the most bizarre and, honestly, the most *me* story I'd ever heard.

The man breathed an audible sigh of relief when he realised I wasn't distressed and joined in on our laughter. Life is so outrageously weird sometimes that you have to see the humour in it. I'd already learned on this trip that you never really know how certain things are going to make you feel, so there's no point in even trying to anticipate your emotions. I had come here ready to feel whatever I needed to feel, but nothing had come, apart from a deep belly laugh and the knowledge that I was even luckier than I'd thought.

I understood very early on in this whole journey that your joy in life is mainly based on one thing, and that's perspective. There's a big difference between whether you see a skydiving accident as something you're lucky to have survived or something that is unlucky for happening in the first place. Whether you are grateful for being able to walk or are ashamed of having a limp. Whether you are thankful that you landed on grass or resent not landing on your feet. People often ask me how I choose the glass half full option and to me it's simple: I would prefer to be happy.

When I looked around the field, I was surprised to find it didn't look monumental or life-altering; it looked like a patch of grass. The same as any other around here. When the thick of the smoke has cleared, you can see things exactly as they are. And all I could think was *How the heck did we survive?* The field was surrounded by alps, trees, cliffs, lakes and, two metres from where I landed, a hard asphalt road. Not to mention cows. That's when I realised something I'd never considered before. This ground didn't break me, not at all. It caught me. It was the best-case scenario in a situation that could have been far, far worse. We never really know what worse moments our bad moments have saved us from, but now suddenly I did.

As I stood in the field that held the oldest and newest parts of myself, I realised how lucky I was to be standing there. *Standing.* On the same two legs that had stopped working in this very spot. A friend once told me something I've never forgotten. He said, 'The ground was hard enough to change you but soft enough to keep you.' I like that a lot.

Before we left, I asked my friends to take a picture of me standing in the field. I wanted to compare it to a photo I had from the day of my accident. Before we skydived, I had given my camera to a girl from our tour group who was meant to jump after me. I had asked her to take photos of Jemma and I as we drifted down with our parachutes to land. When our tour leader was eventually informed that something had gone wrong, she drove out to find me along with the other girls who were supposed to be jumping next. When I looked through my camera months later, I realised that the girl *had* taken a photo for me. Just not the one I'd originally envisioned. In it you could see me and my instructor sprawled across the ground, Jemma crouched down next to me, along with the paramedics and the policemen who held my hand. The ambulance was on the road beside us, as well as the couple who had been out walking, whose phone we had borrowed to call my mum. The rescue helicopter was in the photo too, hovering just above the ground, about to touch down and fly us to a new world.

Half a decade later, once we had said goodbye to the skydive shop owner and returned to our cabin, I looked through my phone at all of the photos from the day. I pulled up the one of me standing in the field, then I found the one from five years earlier and placed them side by side. There were a lot of differences in the two images, many which would be obvious to anyone who looked, but most were only visible to me. One difference stood out as clear as day though. The sky. In the older photo, the sky was so dark and grey that you couldn't see even a sliver of blue or sunlight. In the photo from today, the sky was so blue and bright that you could barely see a cloud. And that's exactly how it felt.

There I was, in the field that caught me—standing and shining.

45

LETTING GO

A week after we arrived in Switzerland, we gathered all of our new memories, got on a train and headed to Italy to continue our adventure. I could have quite happily stayed in Switzerland for far longer than we did, but I was also bursting with excitement to see the other places I'd never quite made it to on my last trip. Our plan was to head to Milan where we would pick up a car, then drive through Italy and on to Croatia. The past week had been incredible and cathartic but it had also been big. Now, I was ready to release it all and have fun.

Late one night after we'd spent the day exploring the cobblestoned streets of Lake Como, I went for a walk on my own. It was 11pm and I was still wide awake, so I walked out onto a pier and lay down. The air was blissfully warm and I could hear people laughing and speaking Italian in the distance. The stars were twinkling bright against the dark canvas above me, and the water was gently rocking the pier up and down beneath my back. I was floating and, in more ways than one, that's precisely how I felt.

Since returning to Switzerland, I felt like I'd let go of something. Something heavy I didn't even know I was holding until I put it down. I was surprised by this because the whole time we were there I'd only felt emotional once, for a brief moment when we first arrived, and then that was it. I had been waiting for other emotions to surface while I was up in the helicopter or down in the field, but they never came. As I was looking up at the stars and reflecting, I realised there *had* been a moment I'd forgotten about until now. The moment was so small and fleeting in comparison to the bigger things I'd done on this trip that initially it had barely registered as a blip.

It was the morning we headed to Lauterbrunnen. We were at the train station, about to head to the Alps, and the illuminated sign on the platform said there was six minutes until our train departed. Suddenly, I'd sensed that I was peeing myself. I looked down at my pants and I was right, they were wet. I couldn't feel it happening of course, but by now I'd grown so familiar with my body that I knew when my incontinence pad was overflowing. I didn't think there would be toilets on the train and it was a two-hour journey, so I knew I had to go to the bathroom now otherwise an overly-full bladder could force the urine back up into my kidneys and cause a nasty infection.

I left the platform and went up the stairs as fast as I could, then found the nearest bathroom and tried to do a catheter. Annoyingly, I couldn't seem to get it right for about two minutes.

I very rarely had any problems using catheters anymore, but while I was travelling I had stuffed a handful of them into my bag and they had gotten bent, which made it tricky. Eventually I figured it out, then hurried out of the bathroom and checked the time. I only had one minute to get back to the platform before the train left. As I was racing back, I was suddenly filled with an overwhelming frustration that my legs could only move at the one pace. No matter how hard I tried and how much I wanted to, I couldn't speed up to run to the train.

I was frustrated. Frustrated that I was peeing myself in the first place, frustrated that I had to use a catheter and frustrated that I couldn't just hurry up and run so I didn't miss the train. This feeling of intense annoyance was so foreign to me that it caught me off guard. Maybe I had every right to feel this more frequently than I did—maybe it's to be expected that you'd be upset about losing control over your muscles, maybe it's fair to be sad that your body doesn't work the way it once did. But I very rarely felt that way. I never felt like I had the right to since I'd learned to walk again. I only ever felt immense gratitude for the way my legs moved, until this one tiny moment. For the first time in years, I was sad at what I had lost.

I was so angry that I was nearly crying, but I was still walking as fast as I could. I rushed down the stairs to the platform and just as I got there, the train was driving away. I could have screamed. Not only because I missed it (it turned out there was another train two minutes later so it really didn't matter), but because the past five years had been filled with tiny, inconvenient moments like this one, and suddenly I realised that this wasn't something that was going to pass, this was my life. It was as though all of a sudden I became acutely aware that what I was living with was permanent. Consciously I had known this—of course I had. I understood that my body probably wasn't going to heal any more than it already had, but somewhere deep inside was a hopeful version of me who thought she'd one day get better. I was surprised by the simple and harsh truth of the matter, and my heart ached at the realisation.

I strongly believe I am the luckiest person in the entire world, and being in Switzerland only cemented that belief even further. People call me an angel for surviving what I did, but I'm not. I'm human. And for the first time in a long time, I realised that I have every right to be frustrated that I can't run for a train. I can be angry that I didn't get the carefree and youthful twenties I had hoped for. I can be jealous that my friends get to experience things that I can't. And I can be hurt knowing that somewhere out there, there is a man I barely know who is responsible for these losses. As I stood crying on the empty platform, I finally understood that I can be all of these things and I can still know my luck.

It was the smallest, shortest moment of anger but as I lay on the gently rocking pier I had a feeling it was important. For those six minutes I grieved my old body and in those same minutes, I think I was able to truly let go of the loss of it. I finally accepted my reality for what it was and I gave myself the grace to grieve it if that's what I needed. I don't know if I would have done that if I hadn't gone back to Switzerland. I sensed going there healed me in ways I didn't even know needed healing until I felt my heart stitch back together. It felt very full-circle, and that enabled me to viscerally feel the contrast between who I was all those years ago and who I am now. It made me realise that although my body might not be what it once was, *I* am far, far more.

There's one word that has continued to circle my mind no matter how many years pass or how good and full my new life is. It is the word 'should'. I *should* be able to do that. This *should* be easier. It *should* have been this way. It's so easy to get caught up in the thinking that things could and should have gone differently. This idea that if things had played out in a slightly different manner, if that tiny thing hadn't happened, if one single second could be altered, then *everything* would be better than it is now. Mentally I time travel to an alternate world all the time, one where my life looks exactly as it does now, but my body is healed. I imagine how much more fun I would have if I could surf and skate. How much more spontaneous I would be if I wasn't incontinent. How much simpler life itself would be if I could run for a damn train. I've found myself subconsciously caught in this trap so many times over the years, conveniently forgetting that it's impossible for that world to even exist.

You can't take away one thing without also taking away all of the subsequent good that has come from it. My life—the one I love and embrace and cherish beyond words—would look nothing like it does now if it wasn't for the one moment I'd been longing to change. Perhaps instead of wishing that moment away, I should wholeheartedly thank it for helping me uncover a life that I might have never had the strength to find otherwise.

The truth of the matter was simple and suddenly I could see

it as clear as the glimmering sky above me—it did happen and it is like this. Perhaps it shouldn't be, perhaps mistakes were made, perhaps things would have been easier another way, but this is how it is, and that's really all there is to it. Five years on, as I understood this with a newfound clarity, I realised that accepting things for how they are instead of fantasising about how they could have been is one of the most valuable, brave and transformative things we can ever do.

As I lay on the pier in the warm Italian air, I realised it felt a lot like the beginning of summer. You know when it's been winter for so long that you can barely imagine what the sun would feel like touching your skin? When your bones have been cold for too many months that you can't even remember what warmth feels like? Then one day you notice you don't need a jumper anymore and the smell in the air is different. It feels as if the trees have only just lost their leaves, but when you look around you realise the flowers are in bloom again. You feel so much excitement and anticipation about what moments and memories lie in the warm months ahead. You know it's going to be magic.

That's exactly how I felt staring up into the starry night sky. Like the winter was finally over and I couldn't wait to see what the summer would bring.

46

MOVING ON

There was a long period of time where all I did was lie still in a hospital bed and quite literally watch the clock tick by, counting the panels on the ceiling above me because it was all I could do. It was excruciating and exhausting but I had no choice but to be there and live out those days. Months later, when I first got to leave the hospital for a few hours, I asked if I could go to the beach. It was the place I had daydreamed about in every difficult moment, and the place I knew would make me feel a surge of gratitude for being alive. The beach was only a suburb away from the hospital, so my family helped me onto a bus and pushed my wheelchair down the street until we saw it.

There it was, the big blue, glistening in the sun. I closed my eyes and breathed in the salty air, I listened to the waves and felt the wind on my skin, and I savoured every moment of the experience. I was so happy. I'd come so far. I couldn't believe I was able to sit up long enough in my chair to see the ocean. I was irrevocably proud of myself.

I opened my eyes and saw a girl nearby who looked to be about my age. She was in workout clothes and was stretching her legs on a bench, getting ready to do some sort of exercise. I was shocked at how disconnected I felt from her. The fact that she was in tights while I was wearing a nappy. How she was alone while I had to be cared for. Knowing she would go home to a house while I would go back to a hospital. It was disorientating to see the disparity, but still I was so thankful to be where I was. I took another deep inhale.

A few minutes later, I noticed the girl had finished stretching. I watched with curiosity as she walked from the grass to the sand, and then, with the ease of a graceful gazelle, started to run along the beach. I felt a sharp pang in my chest. A jealousy I hadn't expected.

That simple act of running freely—feet on the damp sand, alongside the ocean, combining both of my favourite things in the universe—has always been my greatest wish. Whenever I'm asked to 'picture a happy place', it's where my mind immediately goes. I imagine it would feel euphoric. This girl was living my dream, right in front of my eyes, and it physically hurt to watch. The journey between me and her, between wheeling and running, between rehab and life, felt unfathomably long and painful from where I was sitting. Life beyond the sidelines seemed so inconceivable and far away that I couldn't even imagine it. I would have given anything to be the twenty-year-old she got to be. And she didn't even realise.

A couple of days ago, years after that moment, I walked along the beach by myself and didn't think twice about it. I was walking, I was alone and I live now two minutes from the ocean.

I didn't even realise.

Something that was once so far out of my reach was now normal. It was something I'd thought I would never take for granted, but, just a few years later, I did.

~

My European holiday was coming to an end. After a few blissful weeks in Italy we headed to Croatia to finish our trip in the sunshine. The night before I flew home, I was lying in bed when my phone pinged with a memory. There on my screen was a photo of me from that very same day, five years earlier. I was in an ocean pool in Sydney holding onto the ledge and looking up at the camera with a huge smile on my face. My hospital band was around my wrist because at this stage I was still living in the spinal ward. Looking back on the photo filled me with instant warmth because I was reminded of what a special and wholesome moment that was.

But then I gasped, because I noticed how similar it was to a photo someone had taken of me that very morning. In this one, I was floating in the crystal blue Croatian water, looking sun-kissed after a month in the European summer, and the only thing around my wrist was a hair-tie. I hadn't intended to recreate the picture—to be honest I didn't even know the first photo existed—but they were so eerily similar, it looked deliberate.

As I considered both of the memories, it was astounding to think about just how different the two days were, how different the seasons of my life were.

I could remember the day in Sydney perfectly. It was the first time I'd swum in salt water since my accident and I was almost bursting with excitement. It was the middle of winter and the water was ice cold but I didn't want to wait another moment. I couldn't walk on my own yet, so my uncle helped me down the few steps into the ocean pool. I couldn't exactly swim yet either, so I just held on to the edge and floated for a while. It's impossible to explain just how much it meant to me to be submerged in the sea after everything I'd been through. It had been my greatest wish for so many months, and after not knowing if it would ever be a possibility, I didn't take a single second of it for granted. In that moment I genuinely felt like I'd won the life jackpot. I was meant to be in Spain or Greece or somewhere on the other side of the world and instead I was living in a hospital, but in that moment, it didn't matter one bit.

I remembered feeling wholly content, just as I had that morning in Croatia.

Isn't that crazy? That floating paralysed in a freezing ocean pool honestly felt just as liberating as diving into the warm sparkling Croatian water? That even though on paper, one situation was undoubtedly better, they both felt equally fulfilling? That even though emotions often seem circumstantial, they're ever-changing and malleable? It's comforting to think that this Croatian water is where I was meant to be all those years ago but life took me somewhere else and I was just as happy there. I hadn't gone where I originally planned and despite my new path looking nothing like what was intended, my heart had ended up full either way.

I looked at the photo from that morning and realised that even as the moment was happening, it didn't feel like a milestone and it certainly didn't feel like I was conquering something big. The contrast of how my life had looked five years earlier never hit me. I wasn't consciously rewriting a memory by jumping into the water, and it wasn't at all a deep and thought-provoking swim in the sea. It simply felt like I was young and carefree, travelling Europe with my friends, and floating in the ocean because I felt like it—which was exactly how I'd always wanted it to feel.

Something I often find myself thinking about is how contradictory it is that we can experience so much gratitude and normalcy at the same time. That we can be appreciative beyond words for what we have, yet still sometimes find the miraculous mundane.

No one tells you this, but after any of life's upheavals and subsequent rushes of survival, there will come a day when the monotony of life seeps in again. When the fact that you survived the un-survivable becomes less shocking and your sisters can yell at you for stealing their clothes once more. When seeing you alive doesn't make anyone's heart swell with overwhelming joy, it's just normal. When jumping into the ocean isn't a deliberate rebellion against all odds, it simply is what it is.

Gratitude, I've learned, doesn't always look like tears of joy and an unwavering smile. Sometimes it looks like a regular day. For me, that's one of the most sincere forms of gratitude: the fact that I'm lucky enough to do something so often and with such ease that I forget to even be grateful for it.

When I was paralysed, I read a quote that said, 'Life is so subtle sometimes that you barely notice yourself walking through the doors you once prayed would open.' As I lay there counting the panels on the hospital ceiling, I couldn't imagine that ever being true. I couldn't imagine not noticing when you got the things you'd always dreamed of. I thought it meant a lack of gratitude or an inability to pay attention to magic, but that's not true at all. I understand it now because it keeps happening to me—I think it means you're moving on.

47

MINE

There are so many ways to fall. Off a ledge, down the stairs, in love, from the sky.

Falling is scary because it insinuates a lack of control. Leaving the platform we were once standing safely upon and moving towards an unfamiliar one is a leap of faith that takes us outside our comfort zone—because we don't know if we'll make it to the new step intact and we don't know if we'll like how the world looks from a different view. The status quo will always feel safer than the unknown.

But in the same way that the sun dropping below the horizon will inevitably be met with the shine of a new morning—what if falling simply means having the remarkable opportunity to rise?

~

The anniversary of my accident came around again, but for this particular year's rebirthday, I decided I didn't want to have a big party, I wanted to do something simple that felt more like me. A sunset picnic by the ocean.

With every year that passed, I was amazed by how effortlessly my friends and family dropped whatever else they had going on in their lives to be there with me to celebrate. Each year I watched with wonder as the circle of people sitting beside me continued to grow.

We drove to the hill and set up our blankets on the grass. The sun was low in the sky, casting a golden glow onto everything it touched. The waves gleamed like smooth glass as they rolled gently by in the distance. Even after so much time, I never stopped being awed by the view in front of me. I couldn't believe a place so astoundingly beautiful could exist, let alone be my home. I walked to the top of the hill to get a better look at the ocean below and took a deep breath to soak it all in.

When I turned around to head back to the group, I stopped in my tracks.

The view in front of me stood out like a wish from the past come true. Right before my eyes was everyone I loved, sitting in a circle on the grass, talking and laughing—waiting for me.

I had found somewhere I belonged.

As I looked at all of the faces I'd grown to adore, it dawned on me that besides my family and Jemma, I hadn't known a single one of these people before I fell. The awareness of how very lucky I was to have survived long enough to meet them took the breath out of me. I realised that not only would I have missed out on meeting everyone if I hadn't been lucky enough to survive but I also wouldn't haven't known them if my accident hadn't happened at all.

Without falling, without hurting, without getting everything I didn't want, I would have missed out on the best part of my life. If it wasn't for the turbulent and winding road, I never would have arrived so miraculously, and perfectly, here.

~

When you're going through one of life's more difficult chapters, there's never a clear-cut moment when you finally turn the page and begin writing whatever comes next. Coming out the other side feels a lot like watching the sunrise. You can stare at the sky, unblinking, and see the colours change and light bloom right before your eyes, yet there is never a specific moment when you can point and say, 'Look, *now* it is day.'

I didn't know the precise moment my darkness morphed into light, or if I was even fully there yet, but it didn't matter. I didn't need a magical and pivotal moment to tell me to move on and begin the rest of my life, because I had begun writing it already. On that very day years earlier, I fell from the sky and was certain that my story was ending. As I felt the warm ocean breeze on my face so many seasons and versions of myself later, I was now certain of something else—that day was only the very first page.

I looked down the hill at the world I'd created. The memories that felt like dreams, the picnic blanket big enough to share, the date tattooed on my arm, and I heard a gentle whisper. It was similar to the one that had haunted me all those years ago when I was living a life not meant for me, only this time the voice didn't scare me at all. Instead, it made me beam. I saw my friends smiling over at me and heard the whisper again.

Mine.

48

ENDINGS

On a warm December night, I was lying in bed at home when I heard an email ping on my phone. It was almost midnight and I couldn't sleep, so I decided to check it. It was from my Swiss lawyer. A familiar and automatic sense of dread washed over me as I cautiously clicked it open. I read his words and froze, my breath caught in my throat. My blood was pumping so fast I could hear it in my ears. I was having a full-body, physical response.

'The case has been finalised. I'll call you in ten minutes.'

I was in complete shock, so I read the words again to make sure my eyes weren't deceiving me. It had been almost six years with barely any movement and now suddenly, on an unsuspecting Thursday night a few days before Christmas, without any warning, it was over? I didn't understand.

The ten-minute wait was unbearable. It physically hurt to

stay still so, after pacing the room like my life depended on it, I started cleaning the bathroom. I vigorously scrubbed at the bath and shower screen because I desperately needed somewhere to put my energy. After what felt like an entire era, my lawyer finally called. I answered instantly and, as I clung onto his every word, he confirmed what he had said in the email. The case was over and the result was in my favour. It was over. It didn't have any control over me anymore.

After a long back-and-forth, predominantly made up of my quivering voice whispering 'Are you sure?' after his every word, we hung up and I fell onto my bed in sheer disbelief. I got under the covers, curled myself into the fetal position and hugged my legs to my chest. I was visibly shaking and, despite the midsummer night, my body was freezing cold.

Who was I without this? What would I now do? Where would my future go from here? I had never allowed myself to ask these questions and I realised that meant I had no idea what the answers were. When there was only one door open in front of me, I could walk through it with confidence. But when there were endless? Well, it turned out I didn't have a clue what to do with that.

For the first time in my adult life, I was in complete control of my life narrative. I could do whatever I wanted without anyone telling me not to. I could live without the fear of being watched or criticised or belittled. For the very first time, there was an entire world opening up to me and as I looked towards my open future, it terrified me.

My niece Layla once explained to me how she deals with her nerves.

She told me, with the inherent wisdom and practicality of a child, that you have two choices: You can be nervous-scared, or you can be nervous-excited.

I was going to choose the second option, even if my hands were shaking.

~

A few months later, I went to my lawyer's office in Sydney to sign the papers and finalise everything. I was greeted by one of the female lawyers who had been working on my case and I could see that she was heavily pregnant. Something in me felt startled. In the time I'd known her, she had met her partner, got married, had a baby, gone on maternity leave, come back to work, and was now pregnant again with her second child. I could see the passing of time through her, but all the while my world had been frozen still. I felt like I had lost so many years.

Once we were finished, I asked if I could see the main lawyer I had been dealing with so I could thank him. Although I still didn't agree with his non-personal approach and the claim process in general, I understood he was good at his job. I knew he was an amazing lawyer and he had really helped me. When I saw him, I shook his hand and genuinely thanked him for all of the work and time he had put into my case over the years.

I will never forget his parting words to me. He looked me directly in the eye, tilted his head sideways and said, 'In the forty years I have been a lawyer, I have never encountered anyone as positive as you.'

I was stunned into silence. It was the kindest thing he had ever said to me. Before I could soak up the compliment or find the words to respond, he added, 'What I can't understand, though, is why? What do you possibly have to be happy about?'

I heard it, the soundwaves registered in my brain, but I didn't listen. Instead of feeling infuriated or hurt like I so often had at the things he'd said to me, this time, I didn't feel them. They bounced right off me because suddenly it all made sense.

I smiled politely and turned out of the office for the final time. As I stood in an elevator I would never return to, incredulous that it was finally over, I laughed to myself because I finally understood everything perfectly.

Physically and on paper, I might not have it all, but man was I thankful that I was still soft. That I loved the world. That I could still see so much light. I didn't have everything, but I had so much more than some people. I had something that couldn't be taken away.

I had joy and it was always going to be a part of me.

~

For the first time, life was a blank page in front of me. For the past six years I'd had to be sensible and grown up and cautious, but I didn't want to live that way anymore. I wanted to be young, I wanted to be carefree and I wanted to hold the entire world in my fingertips. So that's exactly what I was going to do.

The court case was over and there was nothing tying me to the accident anymore. I didn't have to talk about it, I didn't have to be assessed, I didn't have to hide my happiness. I didn't have the slightest idea what I was going to do with the rest of my life, but it didn't matter. I was free.

So here I am, sitting at my dining table, eating my breakfast and writing these words. I am filled with gratitude, I am more excited than I have ever been and I am glowing—exactly as I'd hoped I one day would. I no longer have a hole in my foot, I no longer have a hole in my heart and I no longer have anything holding me back.

My sister just turned to me and asked, 'So what do you want to do today?'

I look at her with tears filling my eyes. A smile creeps across my face and I say the words I have been waiting nearly six years to say.

'Absolutely anything I want.'

Acknowledgements

This book is something I have been dreaming up for as long as I can remember. When I was younger, I didn't yet know what story was going to fill these pages or which path life would lead me down. But to write a book—to have it published, to have you holding it in your hands and reading my words—is my greatest dream come true.

There are a lot of people I want to thank for helping bring my dream to life but, before that, I want to thank the people who have helped bring *me* to life. The people who enabled me to become someone who has a story worth telling.

Firstly, Jemma—the person I most certainly would not be here without. Thank you for loving every version of me. For becoming the first uninjured person to talk their way onto a rescue helicopter. For not leaving my side in Switzerland, or since. For being the calm to my chaos. There will never be a moment I am not aware of my luck to have you in my life. We have been by each other's side for twenty-five years now and there is not a doubt in my mind that we will be laughing, leaving a path of destruction and making 'our face' in inappropriate settings evermore.

Tommy—the first person to read every one of these chapters. Thank you for saying they were 'great' well before they were. I have been trying to write this story for so many years and it turns out you were the missing piece to actually making it happen. Cooking for me every night (even though I say I'll definitely do it tomorrow), rubbing my feet so I can sleep, letting me in your nook when I'm stressed, lying beside me at 3 am while I write—you created the time and space and support for me to finally get this down. So, thank you. But more than anything else, thank you for showing me how it feels to be properly loved. Wholly and purely.

Mum—for *everything*. For knowing how long to put food in the microwave, for knowing where any belonging of mine is at any given moment, for knowing how to get the smoothie stain out of the carpet, for never making me question whether or not you would be there. How lucky am I to just know that you always will.

Layla—my light. Right now you are still too young to grasp the effect you've had on my life but I hope that one day when you're old enough this book will help you to understand. All of it is for you, all of it is *because* of you. You're seven now, and when I tell you that I love you, you roll your eyes and tell me that you know. You say I tell you a hundred times a day. I promise to never stop.

Tara—for uprooting your life to be there for me. For offering to postpone your wedding until I could walk down the aisle beside you. For doing so many tiny but monumental things without ever expecting any praise or thanks. For being the person that both little-Emma and current-Emma has looked up to her whole life.

Hayley—for cleaning up my shit (literally and figuratively) more times than I can count. I know you think I only love you for giving me Layla, but that's not true. You were the first person I thought about when I hit the ground.

Vinnie and Billie—they say lightning doesn't strike twice but I'm so thankful that it did. Thank you for showing me how full my heart is capable of feeling. I love you endlessly.

Nanny and Grandpa—not a day goes by that I'm not grateful for getting to spend so many of my years with you in them. Your evergreen adoration for each other is the best example of love I've ever seen. Nanny, thank you for teaching me how to be both light *and* strong. Grandpa, thank you for being the backbone to all of us.

Dad—for showing me the world outside our front door and giving me the opportunity to fall in love with it. For taking me camping enough times that falling asleep in a tent has become my favourite place to be. For making sure you were there even though I know it would have been hard.

My family—to those mentioned in these pages and to everyone else, you know who you are. If I was to write a book about what you all mean to me and what you have done for me throughout this journey, you wouldn't be able to hold the weight of it in your hands. I can't imagine how differently things would have gone for me if I didn't have your unconditional love.

My friends—thank you for helping me to create home in a place unfamiliar, for making me think I'm much funnier than I am, for forgiving me if your name wasn't mentioned in this book. I like to think that those who I love know how much I love them because I tell them often. But in case I don't say it enough, just know that by far my favourite thing about surviving has been having the remarkable opportunity to meet each of you.

Sam—for changing my entire trajectory. I know for sure that without meeting you and seeing your example of what was possible my life and this book would never have turned into something worth reading. I wouldn't change a single thing that happened, because it led me to you.

Elle—for so many things but especially for showing me that I didn't have to do it all on my own. That I could let people in. Thank you for coming to every one of my foot appointments with me, even when I swore I wanted to be alone. I don't know if I've ever thanked you properly for that, but it meant more than you could ever possibly know.

Bec—for seeing me when I wasn't even sure of who I was. For knowing that I want chippies when I'm sad. For belting in the car with me for nine years straight. For showing all of us that even when life doesn't go the way we planned, we are capable of turning it into something better than we ever imagined.

Chloe—for injecting so much fun into my world. If our paths didn't happen to cross in the most unlikely of ways, I would forever be wondering why I felt like something was missing. You are my soul sister.

Liv—for making me laugh more than anyone on the planet. Before you, I didn't know it was possible for my energy to match another's so seamlessly. I didn't know how 'myself' I was capable of feeling. Thank you for constantly turning something as mundane as brushing our teeth, or picking up groceries, or anything else we've ever done, into memories I will never forget.

Sam M—for believing in me and this book well before it existed. The words you wrote for my cover are one of the kindest things anyone has ever done for me, yet it is only a fraction of the things you give me and everyone else in your world, hourly.

Kayla Itsines—something that was only a moment for you, gave a lifetime of purpose to me. There will never be enough words to describe how cataclysmic of a gift that is for someone who couldn't see in the dark.

My medical team—words can't do justice to how grateful I am to have had access to not only your incredible expertise, but your gentle hearts as well. To the nurses, particularly in Prince of Wales, you are hope in human form. There are so many stories—so many small moments that weren't actually small at all—that I will hold with me eternally. When I look back on what could have easily been the scariest time of my life, you are the reason I only ever think of it fondly. To every doctor, specialist and exercise physiologist who has helped me (there are far too many to name), I hope you know how appreciated you are, not only by me, but by everyone whose lives you change on a daily basis.

To those who made my dream come true—my lovely agent Tara, for making this possible. To Kelly, for taking a chance on me and believing my story was something worth telling.

To every single person at Allen & Unwin who played a part in bringing this book to life—thank you, thank you, thank you. If you told me ten years ago that I would one day be typing out book acknowledgments to my publisher and literary agent, I would have fainted in sheer disbelief. Thank you for helping me to create something I am so proud of. Thank you for turning my second chance into this.

To you, reader—most of all, to you. If you have read through all of these pages, my greatest hope is that you have gained something from them. A different perspective, solidarity during one of life's falls, an interesting story or maybe something more. When I had my accident and stumbled upon so many lessons, I changed cosmically. I desperately wished there was a way for others to gain those same lessons for themselves without having to go through all of the hurt to learn them. This book is my attempt to do just that. So, if you have followed me on social media, said hi to me in the supermarket, hung one of my drawings in your home or supported me in any way whatsoever—I will try my best tell you what it means to me here (but I will definitely fall short).

You are the reason I started truly believing in myself. You are the reason I was compelled to keep looking for gold in the moments I swore I was only surrounded by dirt. You are the reason I got to write this. Every high and every low, you have been there for me like a true friend.

Thank you for changing my life.